WHERE WE BURIED THE SUN

One Woman's Gulag Story

Where We Buried the Sun

Alla Tumanov

Translated *by* Gust Olson

NeWest Press

Canadian Cataloguing in Publication Data
Tumanov, Alla, 1931–
    Where we buried the sun : one woman's Gulag story

Translated from Russian.
ISBN 1-896300-05-7

    1. Tumanov, Alla, 1931– 2. Soviet Union—Politics and government—1936–1953. 3. Political prisoners—Soviet Union—Biography. 4. Student protesters—Soviet Union—Biography.
I. Title.

HV9712.5.T84A3 1999   365'.45'092   C99-901338-6

Cover and book design: Brenda Burgess

Front and back cover photographs: From the archives of the author

NeWest Press acknowledges the support of the Canada Council for the Arts for our publishing program. We also acknowledge the financial support of the Government of Canada through the Book Publishing Industry Development Program (BPIDP) for our publishing activities.

Every effort has been made to obtain permission for quoted material and photographs. If there is an omission or error the author and publisher would be grateful to be so informed.

Printed and bound in Canada

NeWest Publishers Limited
Suite 201, 8540-109 Street
Edmonton, Alberta T6G 1E6

Dedicated to the memory of
three remarkable young men

Boris Slutsky,
Vladlen Furman,
Yevgeny Gurevich,

executed at twenty years of age
in the cellars of Lefortovo Prison

"And the stone word
             Came crushing down
       On my living
             And still breathing chest."

ANNA AKHMATOVA,
Requiem

". . .then a woman with blue lips standing behind me in the line. . .
came back from the stupor typical of all of us, and whispered in my
ear (they all whispered there): Would you be able to depict all this?
And I said:—I would. Then something like a smile crossed what
once used to be her face."

ANNA AKHMATOVA,
Requiem

"To understand what is going on and yet do nothing means being
an accomplice to the regime."

BORIS SLUTSKY,
one of the three group leaders
who were executed

Contents

Introduction

It was just another manuscript among dozens submitted to the editorial offices of NeWest Press—a publication in Russian, printed on that peculiar Soviet-era paper that looks old even though it is brand new. I could not understand a word or even the pictures as I leafed through, yet I stopped, arrested by one haunting image. It was a woman's face—or was it a girl's? It looked more a death mask than a living face; you could see how extraordinarily beautiful she might be, if light and laughter ever animated those striking features. What on earth had been done to this girl? The answer lay in one terrifying word: Stalin. For most of us in Western democracies, the name Stalin— the pseudonym of a Georgian revolutionary named

Iosif Dzhugashvilli, who was for thirty years the absolute ruler of the Soviet Union—carries only a historical resonance today. Yet for people who lived through that terrible epoch of Russian history—and for the many thousands imprisoned and persecuted in so many countries today by the Stalinist ideas of totalitarian rule—the name is synonymous with the deepest abyss of the human experience. There were two great evils in the Second World War—the fascism represented by Hitler and Mussolini, and the singular brutality of Stalinist rule. Yet in the context of the war and the alliances it produced, Stalin was the West's ally, even a hero in the Western propaganda of the day.

Hitlerism was comprehensively defeated, yet Stalin survived to continue his reign of terror, free of hindrance from the democratic countries of the world. Jews were the great victims of Hitlerism, yet the Jews who survived the war found no solace or refuge if they happened to live in the post-war Soviet Union. They were the victims of Stalinism's persecution, as were many Soviet citizens. The innocent and the guilty were equally swept up in the terrible tide of totalitarianism: it was a crime to have free thoughts, to speak your mind, to even dare to imagine that life could be better or different. Stalinist rule was a comprehensive violation of the Universal Declaration of Human Rights, which was adopted by a resolution of the United Nations in December 1948. Yet in the picture presented to many in the outside world, Stalin's Soviet Union was a model of democracy and fraternity and progress. The image was a grotesque lie—but the world would not know just how grotesque until the dictator died in 1953. In the climate of Stalinism, it took a rare courage indeed to dare to think freely, to question, to oppose. Yet that is what a small group of young people did, because they knew that the society they lived in was not the one promised by the Bolshevik revolution. They wrote a manifesto that sought to remake Russia as a better and more decent place—and that in itself was an act of treason that came to be known as the Slutsky rebellion.

The Russian book in my hands that day was the memoir of one of the participants in the rebellion; the photograph was taken after she was arrested by the secret police. Yet the book was not just another memoir of the Gulag, the notorious prison camps at the dark heart of a society that was supposed to represent "the radiant future of humankind." It was, as a Russian-speaking friend of mine put it, a deeply moving account of a remarkably brave and foolhardy rebellion against Stalin's absolute dictatorship, and the harrowing consequences thereof. It was not the bewildered story of an innocent victim, not the wide-eyed puzzlement of a casual bystander swept to ruin by circumstances beyond her control. Rather, it was a clear-sighted and clear-hearted account of one who chose to fight against tyranny, to resist a monstrous evil with the limited resources at her command. The young woman in the photo was no random victim, but an actual opponent of Stalinism. In its essence, her story spoke of a quest for decency and dignity in a country that knew only the illogical logic of terror. Above all, it was an account of survival—of how the young woman with the haunting eyes lived through the soul-breaking despair of Stalin's prisons, and learned to remake herself as a person of dignity and worth. That was when I knew that Alla Tumanov's story needed to be told in English. And what a story it is. Today, the Alla of the photograph is a Canadian grandmother living in Edmonton. And Alla is indeed extraordinary, when light and life fill her eyes. Over the months we spent turning her Russian memoir into a Canadian story I saw many expressions in those eyes. I saw them filled with the memory of experiences many of us will never comprehend. Yet those same eyes always conveyed an ardent serenity.

Alla's Canadian life—the luminous coda to this remarkable memoir—is an utter contrast to the turbulence of her youth. Yet it is a very Canadian story; a story of immigrant arrival, a story of Canada as refuge and haven in an arbitrary world. And it is more than that. Alla's story is also a universal story, for there are many Allas in the world today. They might live in Tibet, in Myanmar, in the former Yugoslavia, in Algeria, in Cuba, in any of the many places where evil is done. More than half a century after its adoption, the Universal Declaration of Human Rights is still a dream for many people in the world. Today, as in Alla's youth, people are jailed for daring to speak, for daring to think, for daring to question. Alla's ordeal was not an isolated case; it is the harrowing reality faced by many political prisoners today. We live in a climate where the power of economics often turns a blind eye to human rights violations. The lessons of history are forgotten to such an extent that there is even nostalgia now for the time of Stalin. There are apologists who actually contend that dictatorships provide stability, and that many people fare well under such rule. One hears their voices today, saying that trade and human rights should be separate issues, or that the violation of human rights is an internal affair. In doing so, they seek to trivialize a collective horror.

Alla reminds us that her time, and the continuing travails of human rights advocates today, is not the dry stuff of history. The legacy of Stalin's dictatorship lives on in the survivors and their memories. It lives too in our collective sense of responsibility. It is part of our conscience, not merely as individuals, nations or races—but as human beings. In that sense, Alla's story is our story. It is a story we must never forget, for it serves as a perpetual reminder of the darkness that dwells in the human heart.

Satya Das
Edmonton

1

Arrest

Arrest is like a burn—an unexpected desperate pain
—and a scar for life. They came at night, honest
to God, just like in the rule book. What was the
time? Somewhere around twelve, I don't remember precisely. The doorbell rang. Voices in the
entry. Mother opened the door. There were only
the three of us at home, father had left on a
business trip. My eleven-year-old brother was
sleeping soundly on the sofa opposite my bed in
the room we shared. He was still sleeping when
my mother, perplexed in her long dressing gown,
appeared in the doorway; behind her stood several
men in civilian clothes. Half awake, it seemed to
me that there was a whole crowd of people in the
room. I raised myself up on my elbow—what did

they want? I hadn't the slightest idea that they'd come for me, after all, I'd stopped meeting the boys. They had disappeared from my horizon, for which I was very grateful. I had decided to break with them after realizing the complete futility of our dangerous game. A long month had passed, full of exams, holidays—Zhenya and Vladik hadn't called once. Thank God, all of that was buried and forgotten. There was no need to explain, no need to confess to my own cowardice. They wouldn't understand my thoughts about the hopelessness of our undertaking and would despise me.

This sort of night time incursion by the police on the beat, the usual verification of documents, the raids against residents without the proper registrations, happened often enough in our particular part of the city.

"All members of the family show their documents!" one of the visitors barked. He came right up to my bed. "First name, surname? Get dressed!" He remained standing near the bed, but I didn't move.

"Please, leave her room," my mother said with a hesitant voice.

"No, let her get dressed in my presence. I'll turn around." He turned his back and I quickly put my clothes on.

For some reason it was suddenly terribly cold. Oh, how I wanted to stay in my bed, go back to sleep! What did they need me for?

"I'm ready," I informed the black back.

"Proceed into the next room," he ordered in his axe-like voice. Shivers ran up and down my spine because of that voice. No one had ever spoken like that to me before.

We went into the dining room. Mother had already changed into her usual skirt and blouse. For some reason the janitor Fima was sitting there on a chair. Her wide Tartar face was particularly red, probably from the frost and cold outside. I sat down on a chair at the round dining table. There were a lot of people in the room, I couldn't count how many were crushed into our apartment. Every now and then the front door slammed—someone was going out, someone was coming in. I couldn't make out the faces, they were all the same. The one with the bark was obviously the chief. He was giving orders to everyone else. He handed me a small sheet of paper.

"Read this through and sign your name."

The letters were in dark black ink: "Arrest Warrant." After that was my surname. Mother signed another paper, "Search Warrant." Mother's eyes were focused on me, horrified, and filled with tears.

"Mama, please don't cry! I beg you! Everything will be cleared up, it will all be fine." I tried to embrace her, but a shout stopped me: "Stay away from each other! You are under arrest, sit here!" The evil, colourless eyes fastened on me and I sank down helplessly onto the chair.

Fima the janitor approached the table and also signed some papers. *Ponyataya*—their seldom-used word for witnesses at an arrest flared up in my memory.

No matter how hard I try to recall the order of events of that evening—try to pull out memories, millimetre by millimetre from the still living and painful lump in my brain—I cannot do it! The sounds, the fleeting glimpse of faces, the upside down jumble of my home, my world.

I sat numbly. One thought ran through my mind: now they were going to find the manuscript in my desk, the organization's "Manifesto" that I had written by hand myself, and the two sets of minutes of our "meetings," composed of just the three of us: Zhenya, Vladik, and I. Could I slip into my room unobserved? But what would I do with it all? Tear the pages up, eat them? No one was looking at me, everyone was searching through the corners of our small, three-room apartment. The chief was immersed in searching the books: a whole mountain of books was piled on the floor in front of him. He was standing in front of the shelves and scrupulously inspecting each and every book: leafing through the pages, shaking them out, cutting some of the bindings. Now he was holding a volume of Lenin's. He'd found something! He called his assistant over and poked a finger at the notes in the margin. I had made them, reading the article "The State and Revolution" at Zhenya Gurevich's suggestion. There followed another success: Stalin's "Issues of Leninism," covered all over with my notes. Whole paragraphs were marked, question marks and explanation marks dotted the margins. The article on "Lenin and the Nationalities Question" had received most of my attention: everything in it seemed false to me, and I had marked it up, down, and sideways. The chief's face came alive; he no longer looked as glum as at the beginning. I waited in horror for his next discovery.

The search of my brother's and my room began. They got my sleepy brother out of his bed; he blinked his eyes, looking around from side to side. Mother took him out of the room. They sat me down on the chair between the bed and the sofa. Two of them undertook the search: one, the assistant, rifled through the mattress, bedclothes, shook out my dresses, the things in my closet; the other, the chief, dug through the drawers of my desk.

"Now, now he's going to find it! All this trouble was in these pieces of paper; if they didn't exist, if I'd destroyed them in time, none of this would be happening!" I thought in a fever. My heart was pounding somewhere in my throat.

My school assignments were piled up on the desk: "I love my Motherland with a strange love," "Pushkin, the Sun of Russian poetry," "Stalin—our Glory of Battle, Stalin—our Ecstacy of Youth!" The chief leafed carefully through each of them and put them aside. Sometimes, he glanced over at me. Suddenly a heavy thud thundered behind me with the crash of something breaking. I turned round: my favourite doll lay on the floor, her ceramic legs and arms spread out, her head with natural golden hair cracked in two. This symbol of my life, its broken pieces lying before me, struck me painfully. My long, drawn out childhood had come to an end.

"Did you write this?" Those horrible sheets of paper were there before me. It had come! Somehow it was easier now, no more surprises.

"Yes, I copied the text, I wanted it as a keepsake."

"I'm not interested in why you wanted it. You can talk about that another time, in another place," the chief interrupted. Obviously he was pleased with his find. He was even looking rather happily at me. My little "archives" were studied, selected papers were filed away in a suitcase along with those classics of Marxism, the volumes of Lenin and Stalin. I didn't know then that my diaries, the verses on anti-Semitism that I'd also copied down, and the notebook that I'd filled with jokes I liked were also taken as evidence. All was valuable: the file grew in girth during the search.

When we left the room it turned out that their search had met with other successes, too. They showed the chief some gold coins, pre-revolutionary five-ruble coins, left by one of my mother's relatives and put aside in case we needed crowns for our teeth. This discovery was the occasion of a great outbreak of indignation.

"Why are you hoarding forbidden items? Can you possibly be ignorant of the fact that Tsarist money has to be surrendered? You will answer to the law for this concealment of gold!" the chief thundered, shaking his finger. You could hardly hear Mother explaining about the dentists. No one had ever raised his voice to my mother in my presence. It was humiliating and unbearable. Suddenly I heard myself shouting: "Don't you dare speak like that to my mother! I am the one you've arrested, not her!"

My protest had an effect. The chief spoke to his subordinates in a half-whisper: "Look out for valuables! There have to be more around here."

Time stood still. How long had this search lasted? Mother looked terrible, she had visibly aged by several years. Certainly she knew that none of this was accidental. An old friend of the family and I had recently had a conversation. He had been visiting on business from Leningrad, and when he came by kept dropping critical remarks about the authorities. My parents had never done anything like this in front of me. In response, I had told him about the feelings of two of my friends (I didn't mention anything about the organization, of course). Mother and our guest suddenly changed countenance and, without explanation, made me promise that I would stop meeting these dangerous youths. Mother, of course, remembered this conversation. And now disaster had fallen upon us, and she understood how serious it was. It was so very strange that neither of us, she nor I, dropped a single tear!

It was beginning to get grey outside, the light of the lamps in the room mixed with the light of the winter morning. It seemed that the search would never come to an end. Worn out and dulled I sat in the dining room, looking from one thing to another, from one moving figure to another. I remember hardly anything: what had happened during these last early morning hours? Mother was probably ordered to gather up my things for me. Somehow a small suitcase appeared, which I used to take with me to Pioneer camp (it would continue to have a long, long "camp" life for many years). I remember that they took me "under guard" to the toilet—in my own home! They refused to let the door be closed, keeping it slightly open; they watched to make sure that I didn't do anything to myself.

And now I was in the entryway. I put on my old winter coat, the one that I'd already grown out of, and the felt boots that were even older. How they would serve me well in the cold solitary to come!

"You may say your farewells," my escort said.

I hugged my mother and brother. I recall my mother's farewell words, which she almost said to herself: "Poor dear girl, she's never gone anywhere before without her mother."

My last look was at the home I was leaving: two doors of the three opening out onto the entryway were closed, sealed with large black wax seals. My God, I thought, what a disaster my arrest was for the poor members of my household.

Many long years have passed since that terrible night, yet I will never forget it. Even the words "forget" and "remember" are unsuitable. Everything that happened has stayed with me, in me, like an aching part of my body, constantly reminding me of itself with its dull pain. I often have the same nightmare: the arrest. It doesn't always play out the way it actually was, some things might be transformed. Sometimes it's not me they've come to arrest, but one of my relatives or friends. But I always awake exhausted, wasted, and for the rest of the day I'm tormented by something that has no name.

Why, as a rule, do arrests take place at night? Is it easier to detain and seize unawares? It wouldn't be difficult to take some victim away in the daylight. Is it easier at night to avoid outsiders, not worry neighbours, not evoke sympathy? But that can't be the rea-

    WHERE WE BURIED THE SUN

son: one of the most important aspects of an arrest is to inspire fear. Maybe it is even more horrible when you can't see, and then fears shiver up and down your spine, each new one worse than the one before. I think that the main object of this spectacle, played out millions of times and well rehearsed, was to impose such a psychological trauma during the innocence of night, when you are asleep, half dressed, sheltered in your home from the outside world—that no one could ever recover from it.

The preparation for investigations would begin that night. A shiny black automobile was waiting at the entrance. When was the last time I had ridden in an automobile? I couldn't even remember, it was such a rare treat. And now I was going for a drive along the empty morning streets. My glance slipped from the snow-covered courtyard to the walls of the building, to the windows. Goodbye, but I'll soon be back.

2

There Were Sixteen of Us

There were sixteen of us, ranging in age from sixteen to nineteen. In the last weeks of 1950 and the beginning of 1951 the MGB[1] arrested sixteen high school and university students in Moscow, Leningrad, and Ryazan, all members of an underground organization. But if you counted all our contemporaries who shared our views and simply hadn't joined the newly born youth group yet, then there would have been a significantly larger number. Why were the authorities so eager to tie the noose around our scrawny necks? They didn't have to hurry: after all, we'd been strung along for a long time already. If they had, they would have uncovered a frightening picture of the growing dissatisfaction among the children of the Pioneer and Komsomol organizations.[2] But apparently the authorities didn't need any details about the numbers of what they now call "dissident" youth. They knew very well the mood of all classes of society —the *seksoty* (secret agents) were ever vigilant.

As it customarily happened, there was no unity to this "dissidence." People looked on reality in different ways, according to their age, experience, or simply intelligence. Some could see that the injustice and falsehood were no further away than in their own domestic circle: at work, in the communal apartments, among their neighbours. Others understood the injustice of the present regime, but only the current one: the one before it had been radiant. A few understood the sources of all that had happened. But all people were united in a terrible, oppressive fear. Fear ruled society, established its own laws, created morality, determined lines of behaviour. In order to survive you had to follow the new rules. But even this couldn't save you. The older and wiser ones, who grew insightful or who doubted, tried to get by as inconspicuously as possible. They waited in the eternal hope of something better.

"After all, this structure with clay feet cannot survive forever," these wise ones would whisper or, more often, think to themselves.

It would crumble sooner or later, and then everything would be fine—there had to be something to believe in. How it would become fine, no one quite knew. Some would say that it would be like when Lenin was still around; others that it would be like before the Revolution. The elderly actress Yablochkina, when asked how she imagined life under communism, replied, "Everything will be just as good as when Tsar Nicholas was on the throne."

Whether this was just a joke or what she actually said is difficult to say. But jokes have accurately reflected the truth of life throughout the course of the Soviet regime. There was probably no other state in history where the people suffered so much for these salty jokes, into which they poured so much anger and bitterness over their inability to change their lives. And finally, there was perhaps no other country where such political jokes were created with such passion, where people responded to all the events of their unhappy lives with jokes that might threaten them with punishment or even destruction that was far from a joke. I can say with confidence that the hundreds of jokes I have heard have had an enormous influence on my outlook on the world. From the ridiculous to the great is a single step, and what might start as something to make you burst out laughing could lead straight to serious meditation.

Many families struggled so that the children, God help them, would never suspect the disillusionment or doubts of their elders. Around the children they were silent about the arrests that were going on, about their fears at night when they heard the sound of the elevator. They didn't talk about the lack of goods in the stores or the pervasive poverty of life. Children ought to absorb the propaganda of Soviet life, to love Stalin more than their parents, to hate everything that they were supposed to hate, to join the Pioneer and Komsomol organizations with enthusiasm and, believing in everything that their parents no longer believed in, they could build that ephemeral radiant future. It was a paradox, possible only in such a false society, that parents raised their children not to be friends who shared their views, but as their enemies. The children they raised were deceived and grew up to be alienated from their parents. Some of them dreamed that their children wouldn't have a divided consciousness, a double life, that they wouldn't live in discord with the society around them, from which they couldn't escape. Others, shrugging their shoulders, thought that once the children grew up, they could find out for themselves. Better not to fill with our doubts and disappointments. An irreversible corruption of these children took place before their parents' own eyes. They raised little "Pavlik Morozovs"[3] who would avenge themselves on their thoughtless, cowardly parents who counted on the children to find out for themselves! Some of these children renounced their parents when they were arrested; some sincerely, others just to save themselves, cursing them for all to hear.

Only a small number of children's minds somehow, for reasons they couldn't explain, remained immune to the propaganda. In some rare families parents shared their thoughts with their children. Then another kind of tragedy took place: the dividing of the child's consciousness, the beginning of a double life. There were constant instructions: what you could say to the people around you and what you couldn't. And again everything became lies, you couldn't get away from them! To hide your thoughts when you are a child—is this not abuse of a child's very soul?

There was still one more path to insight for the child, a terrible road of the cross, the unbearable destruction of a life just beginning for a young person—the arrest of a child's parents. If you were lucky and only one parent disappeared, then life wouldn't break down irreparably. Things could go on "just as usual." For the first little while. But very soon the ground beneath your feet would begin to heave. Sidelong glances, whispers behind your back, someone would stop talking to you, stop saying hello. And then the children in the collective, encouraged by the older ones, would set loose upon the unhappy child a pure and noble hate, unsullied by doubt. The child would be given the name of "son or daughter of an enemy of the people." It would be a mark forever. And then there came exclusion from the collective, and the young soul could only look on as if from the outside. The hypnotizing strength of the crowd would eventually disappear and the child would acquire insight through his personal unhappiness.

But often it wasn't like that at all. After the family's devastation, the child would end up in an orphanage, would forget those parents and grow up an "honest Soviet," with all the inferiority complexes that entailed, tormented by vain attempts to be like everyone else. Who knows which of these fates was more common?

But waiting was still one more plague of the totalitarian state. The parents might not be imprisoned and they might—thank God!—live with their children in two rooms and not just one. And they might discuss behind closed doors what their beloved and protected offspring were not supposed to hear, and yet even in this safest of living arrangements they would be helpless to protect those offspring from chauvinistic hatreds. Having experienced anti-Semitism from childhood, I can speak of its influence on my own personality. Nor do I doubt that Russian chauvinism had the same impact in all the republics of the Soviet Union. It is no accident that the camps held prisoners from all the ethnic nationalities that made up the Soviet Union, and they had all been accused of "nationalism."

Anti-Semitism—what a long, ugly word! It is so difficult for a child to utter it. Even more difficult to fathom what it means. But once you know what it means, having experienced in your own flesh the evil link between that word and your life, you become an entirely different person. Your character becomes peculiar, easily wounded, unhealthily sensitive. Like someone with a hump or a limp: eternally aware of your isolation.

People who lived in the 1930s, the 1940s, the 1950s—what was the lot of that generation? The echoes of sombre trials, executions, arrests. Then the troubles and deprivations of the war—death notices, bombings, evacuations, famine. Then the postwar violence against the intelligentsia. This was all one side of the coin. The other was those heroic marches, banners, revolutionary songs around the campfire, the thunder of the five-year plans, the exaltation of patriotism. Our world was woven of all this. We truly believed in the eternal ideals of mankind: in freedom, equality, fraternity. We were willing to fight for them. But there was only one path that we knew, that of our fathers. It wasn't discredited in our eyes, despite the reality that surrounded us, the reality that it had brought us to. We were ready to begin all over again. Thus was our organization formed: "The Union of Struggle for the Cause of the Revolution." There were sixteen of us, each of us naïve and honest, and we thirsted for justice.

ORDER FOR ARREST

<table>
<tr><td>

Affirmed

Deputy Chief

of the Moscow Region MGB

Colonel Salynsky

6th February 1951

Seal: Administration of

MGB of USSR

for the Moscow Region

</td><td>

Arrest Sanctioned

Prosecutor of the City of Moscow

State Councillor of Justice, 2nd Class

Vasilyev

6th February 1951

Seal: Attorney General of USSR

Prosecutor of the City of Moscow

</td></tr>
</table>

RESOLUTION
(for arrest)

City of Moscow, 1951, 1st day of the month of February

I, the deputy chief of the branch of the Administration Department of the MGB of the Moscow Region, Major Muzhesky, having inspected the materials gathered by the DMGB MR[4] in connection with REYF, Alla Yevgenyevna, born 1931, native of the city of Kiev, Jew, citizen of the USSR, non-member of the Party, student of the correspondence division of the Science Faculty of the Lenin State Pedagogical Institute, resident at Kachalov Street, building No. 16, Apt. 140,

DISCOVERED

that REYF, Alla Yevgenyevna is a member of an anti-Soviet group of youth. The criminal activity by REYF is confirmed by depositions of other arrested members of the group, GUREVICH, Y. Z., of 29 January 1951, and MELNIKOV, V. Z., of 30 January 1951.

THEREFORE, I DECREED

that REYF, Alla Yevgenyevna, residing in the city of Moscow on Kachalov Street, building No. 16, Apt. 140, be subject to ARREST and SEARCH.

> Deputy Chief of the branch
>
> the Department of the DMGB MR
>
> Major Muzhesky
>
> Agreed: Deputy Chief of the
>
> DMGB MR
>
> Colonel Baklanov

(see fig 2.1)

3

Our Building

We moved from a communal apartment on Nikitsky Boulevard to our brand new separate apartment in a just-built building on Malaya Nikitskaya. This was a most unusual and joyful occurrence. I don't remember the move itself, I had been sent for a few days to stay with a cousin so as not to get under foot. I was six years old and none of those sentimental feelings in regard to bidding farewell to the old apartment where I had spent my early childhood darkened my happiness. All the more since our new place was not that far from the old one, and I could still walk along my favourite boulevards—Nikitsky and Tverskoy. The apartment was enormous, or at least it seemed so to me. I walked from room to room and counted: one, two, three—and if you added the kitchen—four rooms in all; and after all the kitchen is all ours, no sharing. The walls smelled of fresh paint, the parquet shone, and the empty rooms were very elegant. Now and again they would drag furniture up the stairway into some neighbouring apartment. Shouts rang out and the door of the elevator clanged as it hurried up and down. The new building was bursting with life. It had been built very recently and was being settled by fortunate householders. While the builders were finishing the first two towers, the third was already under construction.

It was 1937. The country was making its heavy way towards communism. Bravura music poured out of the loudspeakers: the patriotic songs of Dunaevsky, Blanter, the Pokrass Brothers. Children and their parents sang along to these songs, everyone from young to old. "Life has grown better, life has grown happier!" the loudspeakers blasted. I knew for sure who I had to thank for all this wonderful life: "Thank you, Comrade Stalin, for a happy childhood!" And though I didn't love Stalin more than I loved my mother and father, I did love him very much! Stalin's kind eyes shone from all the portraits and his face was just as familiar as those of my closest relatives. My father worked at the State Planning Commission and our family belonged to the middle stratum of the bureaucratic elite. My father didn't belong to the Party but, all the same, the position he occupied was quite an important one. On the whole, our family was favoured by "the powers that be" and supported them completely. This time father had had the good fortune to join the building cooperative, "Kremlin Worker." Housing cooperatives were still a rarity at that time. The majority of people lived in communal apartments, and it was considered normal. There were very few who could dream of their own separate apartment. We were among the chosen ones and took it all as our due.

Once I had investigated all the nooks and crannies of our new home, I began to explore the neighbourhood. The courtyard hadn't yet been cleaned up of all the construction trash, but you could already see the places where trees would be planted and lawns laid out. They were even putting out a sandpile for the children. The spring sun shone on the still unpopulated square, the first tiny leaves were beginning to burst on an old tree, and it was all unbelievably happy. I particularly liked the new little guard's booth by the entrance to the courtyard. An old bearded guard, just like the ones I'd seen in the pictures of my fairy-tale books, sat there. He would unlock the gate for automobiles and then lock them again as though he owned the place. He would even ask strangers who they were visiting, and let pass by "his own" who wouldn't even glance at him, though they would occasionally greet him. It was very nice to feel at home, to belong by rights to this special, protected, comfortable world. Our building! Our guard!

After only a few days I knew all the other children in the courtyard. Some of them were in the care of a nanny. I was let out into the courtyard alone, but had to have the housemaid with me when I walked along the boulevards. It was rather pleasant to be alone without supervision. You could run around the building site where adults tried to keep you off, chat with the sweet elevator women who sat at the various entrances and nibbled sunflower seeds. The elevator women, who didn't yet know who everybody was, what "rank" they had, started out ingratiatingly polite to all of us.

"So your daddy still hasn't come home from work yet? Does he go by automobile, or does he go on foot? It's not that far to the Kremlin."

Her conviction that my father worked in the Kremlin was something I didn't bother to disabuse her of. Other children continually boasted about their parents. Having assured her that father worked in the Kremlin and rode in his own automobile and that they were soon going to buy me my own German shepherd, I cupped my hand and stretched it out for some of the deeply impressed woman's sunflower seeds: nibbling seeds in the "classical" manner was particularly tasty, especially since I was forbidden to do it in public.

The children in our building, like the building itself, were out of the ordinary. Everything that my best friend and neighbour had from abroad—including a stylish bicycle and a scooter—filled me with jealousy. I had a scooter too, but Liuka's was better, with brakes and a low saddle. I already knew that the family had brought all these beautiful and unusual things from Germany, where Liuka's father had been working for several years. Liuka was a chubby red-head who ran around the courtyard in a brightly coloured, imported swimming suit which everyone admired. Another girl, Inna Garina, also had an unusual bicycle, and it was foreign as well—from England!

"Let me ride!" the children would beg.

"Get in a line," Inna would instruct them in a business-like way, fluttering her white eyelashes. "And only one turn around the courtyard! Don't use the brakes, either, or you'll spoil them!" She was careful to give the rules to everyone as they got on her bicycle. Her power over the rest of us was like the law and each one of us dreamed of being in her good graces.

"Mama, I have two of the very best best friends, Liuka and Inna. Liuka has come from Germany and she has so many foreign toys! And Inna's father is director of the automobile plant." I was completely overcome by my new friends.

We knew everything that went on in the building, little tattle-tales that we were, and whispered our secrets to each other. The news that Stalin's son was settling into an apartment on the eighth floor of our tower raced through the whole courtyard. Yakov Dzhugashvili, Stalin's eldest son, had kept his father's old surname for some reason. Why wasn't he living in the Kremlin? All the leaders and their children for sure should be living in the Kremlin, behind its high walls, to be guarded not by an old bearded man in a sheepskin coat and felt boots but by Red Army soldiers with bayonets: it was as clear as could be! This one was hiding on the eighth floor, and only had three rooms, just like the rest of us. It was all very strange... Although my best friends and I knew everything, the secret of the relationship between Stalin and his eldest son remained hidden to us.[5]

The family of Kalinin's son moved into the fourth floor of our tower. "Grandpa" Kalinin[6] sometimes visited this son, and then on the landings of the staircase would appear silent, faceless men in hats and identically dressed. By their very presence we knew that an important visitor had graced our home. In another tower, the family of relatives of Molotov[7] settled in. In the first two years our building was filled with VIPs. Almost as celebrated as the relations of the leaders' were the people from the stage. The nationally acclaimed actress Polovikova lived on the first floor of the seventh entryway. Not far away was her daughter, the film star Valentina Serova, whose fame was linked to many adventures, including the tragic death of her first husband Serov, a pilot and hero of the Spanish Civil War, and the verse dedicated to her by the poet Simonov, her second husband, and the famous drinking sprees that sent her so early to the grave.[8] I found out about all this later. During the war, when everything was rationed, we often saw trucks being emptied at her entryway. In the courtyard everyone knew that these were boxes filled with wine and fresh food. The unloading was directed by that famous war correspondent, Simonov. The elevator women kept count of all the boxes while the tenants would pass by, unsurprised. There were a lot of extraordinary people around, and we tried to find out a little more about each one.

In a proletarian state, where everything belongs to the ordinary man, the worker or the *kolkhoznik*,[9] the main thing was not to be an ordinary man, to be outside of this category. It was important to make your way to some higher spot, even if it was only a little hillock, just to feel happy. The chauffeur of any boss was better than a truck driver, while the elevator woman of our building looked down from her hillock on the elevator woman of the building next door. Any puny boss despised his subordinates. All of them were ruled by two emotions: servility and envy. Each one lusted after the place of the one who stood just a step higher in our "egalitarian" society. The good women of our courtyard followed all the important wives with calculating looks, judging their outfits. Sometimes it was difficult to make out just who was more important: Lenin's former housemaid, who lived in the first entryway, or some manager of a maintenance department in the Kremlin. The latter, of course, had more authority, but Sima's granny had actually worked for Lenin!

And she was an honoured guest at all the constituency gatherings in our block where she told tender tales about what Illich[10] was like in his last years, how simple he was with his domestics. It would be very difficult to say who was the more important!

I didn't understand everything that went on in our building. Some apartments stayed empty for a long time. They said that the people who were supposed to have moved in were no longer around. And where were they? "Went away," was what my parents replied. One such apartment on our staircase was finally occupied. We became friendly with the family of the architect Dobrokhotov. I found out that the apartment had been originally designated for a very important executive. They had cut out a further, fourth room from the adjoining apartment, making a special niche in the corridor for a housemaid's bed. When everything was ready, the executive disappeared without a trace. From all that previous luxury the Dobrokhotovs were left with a boarded up door into one room, the entrance covered over by a shamefaced cupboard. Just the presence of this unusable door reminded everyone of some secret. Looking at it, I remembered Perrot's story of Bluebeard, with its hiding place for the murdered wives, and I felt awful.

There were many other strange things in our building. On the first floor a girl named Svetlana lived with her mother in a three-room apartment, but they occupied only one of the rooms. The other two rooms were empty for several months, until another family moved in. Svetlana didn't have a father, they had taken him away. Where? Adult answers didn't explain anything. And so, even in our "elite" building, communal apartments began to appear, something completely unforseen by its designers.

Little Zhenya, nicknamed "Squeaky" since he was always crying at any provocation, was another member of our courtyard crew. We knew that he didn't have a father or a mother and lived with his relatives.

"Squeaky's parents have been arrested. They are enemies!" Liuka told me in secret.

"What did they do wrong?" I asked.

"I don't know for sure, but something enemy-like," she whispered in my ear with conviction.

It was just as mysterious why the niece of Kalinin's son's wife lived with his family. Her parents were also enemies and had been arrested. Natusia, a quiet girl with light-blue eyes and flaxen hair, played in the courtyard by herself and never took part in any of our games. Once a week her older sister visited and they went out together somewhere. I was very sorry for these children who had no parents. The word "orphan" sounded so depressing. But all my attempts to strike up a friendship with these poor children foundered on their aloofness.

For some reason, my best friend Liuka also lived alone with her mother. Her father had gone away to work in the far north, to the city of Magadan. They kept saying that he was about to return. But year followed year and he never showed up. Rozalia Abramovna, Liuka's mother, once went to visit him and returned alone, very sad. Modest Yakovlevich Ryzhov appeared finally only in the middle of the war, around 1943-1944. As we found out later, this wise man had escaped arrest and, perhaps, certain death, by volunteering as a civilian engineer in the far North regions where they sent hundreds of thousands of prisoners off to the camps and hard labour. He knew what was waiting for him, a specialist who had worked for years abroad, an old revolutionary, and a member of the intelligentsia. He had long ago changed his Jewish nationality and surname on all his documents to Russian, but this was not the time when such foresight could save him. My mother knew Modest Yakovlevich from her youth in Kiev. Then he had been Motya Stolyarsky and was active in the revolutionary movement. I heard the adults talking about him and couldn't understand why Liuka's father had to change his surname and nationality. Why didn't he live at home? But I didn't think too much about all this; I lived well enough myself, my world was simple and fair.

No calamity darkened my childhood at all. My mother devoted herself to making a warm and comfortable home for our family. She devoted her whole self to us—my father, me, and my brother, who was born in 1938. Burying all her talents as an artist and poet, she lived only for us in self-sacrifice, patience, and occasionally heroism. I was the spoiled darling of the entire family. My relatives praised me to the skies, went into ecstasy over my many talents (I sang, danced, and recited poetry), overwhelmed me with presents, took me to the theatre, the circus, New Year's parties. Mother sewed my clothes for me, altering her and my aunt's old dresses. I would twirl for hours in front of the mirror, bewitched by my reflection. It is said that childhood forms the adult person: what would grow up from such a little "narcissus"?

In the summer, mother would take us children out to a *dacha* near Moscow. For us, life there was heavenly. For her it meant lugging heavy bags of food, travelling on overcrowded electric suburban trains, and cooking on paraffin stoves, and Primuses. But year after year she took on the burden, despite Father who thought that we could get along quite well without the *dacha*. I mainly saw my father on Sundays. The rest of the week he was at work until late at night; Stalin liked the night-time style of work. All the authorities in all the departments stayed at their desks until midnight out of the fear that he might suddenly call someone at the top and then along the chain going downwards, until even the most junior boss might be needed.

I didn't know what the adults talked about; they kept all the dangers and disillusionments hidden from me. My parents, like the majority of people at the time, feared arrest. Like the others, they listened to sounds on the stairway at night: would the elevator stop on our third floor at an untimely hour? Many of my father's co-workers were arrested. In connection with one of them, a former Tsarist officer, he was questioned in the local branch of the State Security Police. He returned home after the questioning petrified with fright. His co-worker disappeared forever.

By pure happenstance my family never appeared among those who were connected one way or another with the terrible name of People's Commissar Yezhov.[11] Yezhov's wife was a friend. Mother had known Genya Feygenberg in her youth in Kiev. After moving to Moscow, Genya started to "circulate in the higher circles" and mother, following her strict rule to stay far away from the powerful of this world, ceased to have anything to do with her. They did not meet for several years, but kept track of each other through a cousin of Genya's who was an old friend of mother's. From this source we knew that Genya was climbing the hierarchical ladder as she changed her husbands. The last one turned out to be the all-powerful Yezhov. Once, looking for work, Mother betrayed her principles and turned to her old friend for help. Genya, at this time, was employed as the editor of a certain magazine and would be able to pull strings. Mother phoned her and Genya invited her to drop in at her office to decide where Genya should direct her influence. The next day mother firmly resolved not to use such an appealing opportunity and did not go to the assigned meeting. Less than a week later, the whole country discovered that People's Commissar Yezhov, who ruled the country with an iron rod, was an enemy of the people.[12] The fate of our family would have turned out so very differently if we had fallen under the patronage of the wife of an enemy of the people; many such similar situations testified to this. This time we were saved by the intuition of my wise mother.

Genya Feygenberg's life ended tragically. After her husband's arrest they placed her in the Kremlin hospital and poisoned her. Her adopted Spanish daughter learned of this many years later, when she tried during the period of massive rehabilitations to discover the fate of her adoptive parents.

"Your foster father was an enemy of the people and was shot for his crimes. Your mother, on the other hand, was a beautiful, honest person. Cherish her memory."

The KGB inquiries office answered her in these or similar words. This was already in the days of Khrushchev's famous and brief "Thaw."[13] I learned of the story much later. For a long time adults sheltered me from the shadowy sides of life. They wouldn't even tell dangerous jokes when I was around. I would obediently leave the room as soon as they asked me to. "This is not for children!" I would hear them say. A Soviet childhood should be cheerful; this was clear in all the books and posters, and they sang about it in all the songs. "Oh, it is wonderful to live in the Soviet land! Oh, it is wonderful to be beloved of the land! Oh, it is wonderful to be of use, and wear the red tie with pride!" I would sing in kindergarten, already aware of how lucky we were: we lived in the very best country in the world.

In 1939 I entered the first grade. The school was situated in a grand old mansion next to our apartment building. It was a typical stately home of the eighteenth century. We went up to our classrooms, complete with tile stoves, on creaky wooden stairs. During our breaks we walked in pairs along narrow corridors which had not been planned for crowds. The Assembly Hall was particularly interesting: huge, with tall narrow windows, highly polished parquet floors, and a dark moulded ceiling. There were rumours that Pushkin had danced with Natalia Goncharova in this hall at their wedding ball, and that they had been married in the church on our street, then known as Malaya Nikitskaya, and later as Kachalov Street. The Goncharov estate bordered on this street, too. There were few school children who knew these facts, however: the wedding, the church, the ball afterwards in the lordly mansion. It might all be out of a fairy-tale. But, according to Soviet ideology, Pushkin's noble descent and his ties with the gentry intelligentsia were an annoyance and were presented as insignificant; of much greater importance was the poet's connection with his serf nanny. Following the new Soviet tradition, the ancient church was deserted, its walls peeling; it housed a high-voltage electric research laboratory. The mansion-turned-into-a-school also had a sad appearance: the old building hadn't been repaired for many years and was falling down. Several hundred pairs of children's feet, galloping up and down the rickety stairs, hastened the wear and tear.

In these years of Five Year Plans, no one took much care to preserve historic treasures. You should tear down the old, so that its memory will disappear! The explosion that brought down the largest of Moscow's cathedrals, that of Christ the Saviour, rumbled through the city.[14] In only a few Muscovite hearts did this explosion cause any pain. Flooded by new people relocated from the country-side, Moscow could not save its past.

Streets and whole regions of the city were renamed. The old cherished names which bore great significance and reflected the city's history disappeared, replaced by new, revolutionary ones. People obediently grew accustomed to the unfamiliar names and abbreviations. For some time the new name was pronounced together with the old: Gorky-Street-that-was-formerly-Tverskaya, or Kachalov-Street-that-used-to-be-Malaya-Nikitskaya. Some of the stubborn old-timers kept using these long versions: they couldn't take leave of the past. But even they eventually grew used to the new names. The crowds of visitors and people on business trips hastened the process: they never knew that Marx Prospect had once been Okhotny Ryad (Hunters' Rows) or that Sverdlov Square was once Theatre Square.

The city's streets were festooned with all the slogans possible, in order to give the citizens a cheerful and militant spirit. "The Five Year Plan in Four!" or "The Party of Bolsheviks is the Mind, Honour, and Conscience of our Epoch!" Occasionally you would come across the garish posters of that chief poet of the building of communism, Vladimir Mayakovsky: "From the old world let's just keep 'Ira' cigarettes!" Several years had already passed since that "bawler of the Revolution" had committed suicide. We tried not to remember that.

> *And I,*
> *   like the spring of humanity,*
> *Born*
> *   in labour and in battle,*
> *Sing*
> *   my fatherland*
> *This republic of mine!*

These were the verses of my favourite poet. When I read them I was almost overcome by their patriotic fervour.

We may live a hundred years
without growing old.
Growing from year
            to year
in our good spirits.
Praise the land of youth,
    you hammer
        and verse.

The applause was thunderous. The whole school was celebrating the anniversary of the Great October Revolution: children and adults had the holiday in common. The sun illuminated the Assembly Hall with its decorations. I stood on the high stage and Stalin smiled at me from his portrait on the wall. In his arms he held the girl from Uzbekistan, the famous heroine of the cotton fields, Mamlakat. Stalin loved children very much. Proud of myself, I stepped off the stage.

I dreamed of becoming an actress or ballerina. I had every reason to believe that my dreams would come true: first, I was able to recite poetry with great expression and, second, I danced gracefully at the local ballet school and all my relatives were enraptured with my talents. And most importantly, my uncle, Liubimov-Lanskoy, a national artist of the Russian Federation, was director of a Moscow Theatre. I had connections which would open the door to art. "Connections are higher than the Cabinet," was a new saying widely used in private conversations.

In general, I foresaw my future correctly. I would indeed become an actress, for a short period, at any rate. And I was to be very famous, although not over the entire Soviet Union—only in the camps in the Inta region, on one of the numerous islands of the Gulag Archipelago. But connections, in fact, had nothing to do with it, or my famous uncle either. I simply let Fate take over, being spared briefly from heavy common labour thanks to those little abilities of mine which had fed my vanity in childhood.

In the Country

I spent the summer of 1948 in the countryside, near the town of Kashin in the Kalinin region. The grandmother of my friend Galya Cherenkova lived in the country and all of Galya's family had lived there at one time, too. She was a bit embarrassed about her descent from peasants, but there weren't very many of our companions who knew about that. On the other hand, everyone knew that her father was a driver. And Galya was also embarrassed about that. It's true that it was because of extenuating circumstances that her father was a government chauffeur. He was the personal driver of some very important boss. Thus, Galya and I were neighbours in our building, and then neighbours at our school desk. Our friendship was a strange one: I felt sorry for Galya since she was lame, with a congenital dislocation of the hip, and because she had no mother. Her mentally ill mother had thrown herself off their balcony on the fifth floor, right in front of her husband and two small daughters. The newly widowed father was a very nice young man, and it was hard to believe that he was burdened with a family.

I always felt Galya's envy towards everything that surrounded me. She envied our one-family apartment, the intelligentsia atmosphere in which I was raised, my better marks in school: in sum, she envied absolutely everything. She probably didn't particularly like me, either. But, nonetheless, we were friends; we walked to school together, we came home together, sometimes we even did our homework together. My parents weren't happy about our friendship, thinking that I should make friends only with children from "intelligentsia" families. The word intelligentsia was always emphasized and had a particular and profound meaning. But what did my parents understand by this? "I met a woman who must be from the 'intelligentsia'" or "That person is definitely from the 'intelligentsia,' he chats so politely." People who were otherwise stuck in the problems of daily life, who read nothing, had no hint of any kind of spiritual life, were given a honorary membership in the intelligentsia when they dressed neatly, chatted politely, and didn't make their living from physical labour. In all of this there was a certain ingrained sense of superiority, apartness, a feeling of being elite; in other words, a class feeling. In our Soviet society there were only two recognized classes: the workers and the peasants. The intelligentsia was considered to be a "stratum" between these two classes. And how that "stratum" strained when it praised the heroic labour of the masters of the country—the workers and collective farm labourers! But God forbid that the children of the ones singing the praises should join the class of these heroes being praised. Parents did all they could so that it wouldn't happen, and my family was no exception. Still, despite our unfortunate friendship, my parents let me go to the country to visit Galya's relations.

"Countryside" and "collective farm" or *kolkhoz* were concepts I had taken from books. The illustrations in the books were supplemented by colourful pictures from joyful films where the collective farm life was portrayed as a never-ending festival. "The wires played, the wires sang: we've never seen such things before!" the happy *kolkhoz* workers sang about the introduction of electricity. The cows mooed just as joyfully and the brand-new sparkling tractors rumbled. The life of the *kolkhoz* workers was so attractive on the silver screen and in the books that sometimes the urban reality that surrounded us seemed so much less happy and interesting. It was with great curiosity that I looked forward to meeting the genuine countryside.

We went down country roads in a motor car (from the government auto depot) driven by Galya's father, Mikhail Emelyanovich. Clouds of dust raised by the wheels prevented us from inspecting the scenery racing past us. We were so shaken and tossed by the potholes that we might have bitten off our tongues. Sand grated on our teeth, and our eyes filled with tears from the dust. I didn't expect to ever reach our destination. It was dusk when we drove into the village and the houses along the street were dark.

"They can't already be asleep?" I asked in surprise.

"Well, of course not, they wouldn't be sleeping. They're, well, 'dusking'," Galya's father answered. "There isn't any electricity in the village, so they sit in the half-darkness, saving on kerosene. And when it gets completely dark they'll light the kerosene lamps. But not for long: they go to sleep with the chickens and get up with the roosters. Just you wait a bit, you'll see what real country life is all about," he said with meaning.

We stopped in front of a substantial cottage, an *izba*, built, as they say, for the ages out of large rough logs. A bent old woman in a white kerchief and long apron was waiting for us on the porch.

"You took your time getting here. I've been worn out waiting for you," Galya's grandmother said sternly. Then she kissed the traditional three times with her son-in-law and granddaughter. She looked at me questioningly.

"This is my friend, Alla," Galya introduced me, and Grandmother stretched out her dry dark hand towards me. In what capacity I had come along wasn't made clear at the beginning. Mikhail Emelyanovich had to discuss my stay in her home with Grandmother and, of course, work out the payment. Galya's uncle, who lived with his mother, greeted us, too. He was deaf and dumb, but a very cheerful and active person. He talked with everyone using his fingers. If anyone didn't know the language of the deaf and dumb, he could follow their lips.

We were invited into the "hall," a large room with an entrance through the kitchen. In the kitchen my gaze was captured by a dark icon in the corner over the table. A lamp burned under it. The larger part of the kitchen was taken up by a huge Russian oven. The whole life in such an *izba* was connected with that oven. It would feed the family and heat the cottage. The family could bathe in it if necessary and even sleep on the sleeping bench, the *polati*. And such wonderful *pirogi*, meat pies, could it bake, and bread out of this world! Cabbage soup was boiled on it and then stewed in the warm oven's belly. And such *kasha* of cooked grain, made with a brown crust in black sooty cast-iron pots—I never ate anything so delicious. I made all these discoveries later.

For now, we sat decorously in the "hall." It smelled of clean, freshly washed floors, the boards scrubbed white. Homemade rugs covered the floor, making the room seem dressed up, even though it was almost empty. A great number of photographs hung on the walls: some of them under glass and others hung with just a tack. The pictures had yellowed and faded with time and the corners were worn. I went up to the wall to look over the faces there. I knew from Galya's stories that Grandmother had had sixteen children. Some had died in childhood, but she had raised the majority. When the war broke out, ten sons went off to the front. Only one returned home. Young and middle-aged men in soldiers' uniforms looked at me from the photographs. Some of them had left behind wives and children, others hadn't managed to settle down. I stood and thought what grief had come to this woman who had endured nine death notifications. And then her daughter had left life so tragically. And still the mother had endured it all and continued to live on. How much strength she must have needed!

Galya took me out into the vegetable garden. The small lot extended from the house down to the field. It was covered with carefully tended beds. Only in one place was the earth untilled: that was where the beehives stood. Galya's uncle was in charge of them.

It had grown completely dark and the grass was wet from the dew. The bright sickle of the moon hung in the sky above us. Suddenly I grew terribly despondent, and wanted to go home. I even resolved to return to Moscow with Mikhail Emelyanovich in the morning. At that moment he came out into the garden and announced happily: "Granny has agreed to let you stay. She isn't asking for a lot of money, she just wants to have enough groats and flour for emergencies which I'll bring when I come back to get you. I've promised and we've settled on it. So come on in and join the party. The table is already set."

We returned to the *izba*. After the darkness outside, the kitchen seem bright and welcoming. But as my eyes grew used to the light of the kerosene lamp on the table, everything turned strangely dark and gloomy. The corners of the room were hidden in the darkness, only the faces of the people around the table were illuminated, and the sad eyes of the Mother of God gazed at us from the icon. Her eyes seemed alive because of the flickering flame of the icon-lamp, and I couldn't tear my eyes from it—a real icon to which people really prayed, hanging there in the "red corner" of the house, and not on a wall in a museum.

We were seated on benches around a long wooden table. Galya's father had the honorary seat in the "red corner," under the icon. Across from him sat our hostess, Yefrosinya Semyonovna. Grandmother's look was very solemn. It was clear that our visit was quite an occasion for her. In the middle of the table was a glazed bowl with hot *kasha*, steam rising from it. Not one of us had a plate, but there was a large wooden spoon in front of each. The *kasha* smelled delicious, and I was immediately aware of how hungry I was after our journey. But how could you eat *kasha* without a plate? My question was soon answered: Grandmother was the first to stretch out her spoon towards the bowl. She scooped up a spoonful and carried it to her mouth, with her other hand placing a slice of bread under the spoon. Then Mikhail Emelyanovich did the same, and Uncle Shura after him. Galya looked at me a bit guiltily, but followed the example of the adults. I was very hungry but a feeling of fastidiousness that had been instilled in me from childhood kept me from eating out of the common bowl.

"What's the matter with you? Aren't you hungry, or don't you like *kasha*? We don't have your city niceties here in the country," Grandmother said sternly.

"Give us some plates, please," Galya said, coming to my help.

Our hostess was obviously displeased with such a request: it broke with family tradition. Nonetheless, two plates appeared in front of us. The *kasha* was particularly tasty, made from millet and crumbly with a brown baked crust. I had trouble dealing with the big spoon; I couldn't manage it in my mouth. The adults didn't have any problems, they simply licked the spoon clean inside and out, taking the *kasha* with dark homemade bread. And then we had carrot tea with honey, which was especially aromatic from the bits of honeycomb. Even though it was from their own hives, the honey appeared only rarely on the table. It was meant for sale and was a major part of the family's income. That I found out the next day, when I carelessly asked for some honey with my tea.

Dreamy after dinner, tired from the hot tea, Galya and I sat at the table listening to the grownups' conversation. Grandmother kept complaining: she was having difficulty with the housework and there was no help to be had. Her son didn't want to dig in the dirt and had started fooling around with photography. He kept going off to weddings and funerals in neighbouring villages and, as soon as he was gone, that was it; he might be away for a week.

"I have to do it all by myself: feed the cow, take care of the piglets, and work in the garden. I just don't have the strength anymore! Oh, that God would take me soon," she wiped her eyes with

the corner of her kerchief, but she didn't have any tears in her eyes
at all. Her lament was more for show, to catch her son-in-law's
sympathy in the hope that he might be able to help somehow. After
all, he'd become so important, a city man! Driving around in a pas-
senger car, dressed like city folk. Of course, it wasn't sweet for him,
either, being all alone with the two girls. And he was still so young
and already a widower.

From time to time the voices fell silent, but then the conversation would pick up: Uncle Shura began to explain things with his
fingers. They answered him with theirs, but that quickly got tiresome, and talk began again, and Uncle Shura tried to catch the sense
of it by the movement of their lips.

I found out to my surprise that life in the village was a hard one.
For each "work day," the unit of payment on a *kolkhoz*, they received
very little, but were able to feed themselves from their tiny personal
plots. It was not profitable to keep farm animals, the taxes were so
high.

"I would've sold our Beauty long ago," Grandmother said. "But I
feel so for her, she grew up from a calf with us. And we don't see
any milk hardly, and then have to haul it to the collection point. I
only keep the very littlest bit for myself. There's no place to mow
the hay. Even the poorest plots belong to the *kolkhoz*. They've just
sentenced Vanka Yeremin, and he'd only mowed the tiniest bit."

It was obvious that Mikhail Emelyanovich was getting tired of
the old woman's complaining. He twisted about on the bench and
kept trying to calm her down with the same words:

"Just wait, Mama, have a little patience. It's only three years
since the war. You've got to understand that! It will get better soon,
real soon." But she hurried on to tell all her burdens, paying no
attention to his encouraging words.

Finally Galya's father got up, and we understood that this boring
conversation had come to a close and we could go to bed. Grandmother
took us into a small room off the "hall." It had an iron bed with an
ornate headboard painted white. A heap of embroidered white pil-
lows rose in strict order: the biggest on the bottom, then the middle-

sized one, and then the smallest, the *dumka*, completing the picture. The bed was skirted with lace fringe which fell to the floor. All in all, the bed made quite an impression. It was meant for guests, but of course it was obvious that Galya would be sleeping there. They put out an ordinary country cot for me, on the floor right up next to the finer guest bed. Exhausted from all our thoughts, we fell asleep immediately.

When a knock on the door awoke me in the morning, I couldn't remember where I was for several moments. Galya was sleeping soundly beside me and I began to shake her awake.

"Hey, Moscow sleepy-heads, get up now. You've already slept through half the day," Grandmother said good-naturedly on the other side of the door. And in fact it was already ten o'clock and Grandmother, as Galya had told me, got up at five. I was a bit embarrassed that she had already been hard at work while we were just lolling about, like gentry. After we quickly washed up in a basin outside, we went into the kitchen. The table was set for the two of us. This time she had put plates out. Breakfast was strange, but it was tasty: the whey from sour milk with diced green onion floating in it. We ate this dish with aromatic black bread.

While we were having our breakfast, Grandmother kneaded the dough for bread. The work was very hard for her: little droplets of sweat shone on her forehead, and she sighed in time with her movements, sometimes stopping and taking a breath. I had never seen the birth of bread before; it always appeared fully baked on the shelves of the bakeries. When she was finished kneading, she covered the tub with a white towel and started rearranging the pots in the warm oven to make room for the dough. She moved it all around with a heavy oven fork on a long handle. In her experienced hands the heavy fork looked like a light stick. I admired the old woman's lithe and precise movements. She was so agile, and she still possessed great strength. It seemed as though I was watching a genre painting from the nineteenth century come alive, or a scene from a play about the olden days, where everything was recreated down to the minutest detail. It was all so distant from present-day life.

Grandmother informed us that tomorrow was to be the patron saint's day for the village. Each village in the region had its own saint, and its day was always celebrated with great ceremony.

"So tomorrow you mustn't sleep so late; the merrymaking begins early, with songs and accordions. They'll come from all the villages around to help us celebrate." Grandmother had to explain the local customs to me, of course. Galya was among her own here. I wondered if Grandmother would be going to church. Her answer surprised me. Looking at me with anger, she said, "Hasn't Galya told you how those wicked Komsomol chatterboxes like you burned down our church before the war? Now we have to pray to a stump or else trudge twenty-five *versts* to the nearest church. Damn them! Damn you all!"

She muttered those last words, then turned to the oven and began clattering about with the oven fork. The conversation had obviously taken a bad turn. We felt awkward now and, thanking her for the breakfast, hurried outside.

The village looked completely deserted. We walked past old cottages with rickety porches and raised mounds of dirt around them, called *zavalinki*, where people used to sit and watch the world go by. Little front gardens with a few flowers—hollyhocks and yellow balls—framed the cottages from the street. These untended gardens were quite pitiful and didn't do anything to improve the view. The street looked grey and beggarly. The village wasn't large, with only about thirty houses on both sides of the road. An enormous field of ripening oats began right after the last of the dwellings.

Galya and I walked as far as the edge of the village and clambered up on thin logs that were stacked within big wooden forks beaten into the ground. This was the boundary marking the end of the village.

"Where are all the people, then?" I wondered.

Galya was silent for a moment and then hesitantly began to speak.

"Everything is so strange to you here, but I'm used to it. We come here each year and it's always the same old thing. You ask where the people are: why, you could count them on the fingers of one hand! Some of them never came home from the war. There were a lot from the village who were killed. Some are still serving in the army, others have run off to the city, most of them in fact. Who would want to live here? No electricity, no radio, they show movies in a barn, the village store is empty. You feel like puking when you go in. You could die from boredom here! And the things they eat in the country! My Granny isn't doing that bad. There are only the two of them, and Uncle Shura earns a little extra with his bees and his photography. The family was well off, once upon a time, but they were declared *kulaks* and suffered for it.[15] You know what *kulak* meant in their case? Just that they could manage the farm well, working from dawn to dusk. As if it's easy to feed sixteen children! When the children grow up, then they're supposed to help their parents. All in all, their farm was successful. Even when they took the land away and forced them to join the collective farm, Granny's family lived better than most: they had had a good start. You'll see in what poverty the others live. It was like that before the war, too. You can understand why my parents set off for Moscow as soon as they got married. You people from the city don't know anything about the countryside or the village," Galya concluded her story.

I listened with surprise and distrust. My friend had never said anything like this before. For the first time I realized that she felt for the village and was not ashamed of her close connection with it. Where were those happy *kolkhoz* workers we were always hearing about in Moscow? Maybe Galya was exaggerating and it wasn't all that gloomy. Anyhow, her grandmother had been a *kulak* and punished for it: she'd have a grudge against the Soviet authorities. Our conversation had ended. We went silently through the field towards the river.

The next day we awoke before dawn in anticipation of the festivities. I associated holidays with decorated streets, coloured lights, flags, posters, and portraits of the country's leaders. Even my beloved New Year could not get along without red banners proclaiming: "New success in labour for the New Year!" or "Fulfill the Five Year Plan in the coming New Year!" The purpose of every holiday was clear, and I rejoiced along with all the rest.

Now something new awaited me, a holiday in the countryside. It was all strange and mysterious, a holiday in honour of a saint. Why did each village have its own saint? Why were the other villages coming to celebrate with this one? I could understand the old people who were ignorant, out of date, and illiterate. They were the only ones remaining who believed in God in our atheist country. I had absolutely no doubts concerning religion. Ignorant people had dreamed up God. "Religion is the opium of the people," every school child knew that. We were taught to despise everything that was connected with "faith": the church, the people who ministered there, church rituals, and religious books. It never entered our heads to read the Bible or the Gospels: they were all fairy-tales, made up stories, and bad besides. We were made fools of in this way, so that we couldn't even understand biblical subjects in art. We would walk by paintings in the galleries with indifference and knew nothing of religious music. The world's Christian culture, like the other religious cultures, was hidden from us. We didn't realize our loss and so we weren't bothered by it. It was all quite clear in our picturebook, emasculated world: things were either white or black, good or bad, as simple as two times two is four.

Galya and I kept running impatiently out to the porch, so as not to miss the beginning of the festivities. But just like the night before the street was empty and there were no decorations to be seen. Speckled hens and a brown rooster wandered about the road and the rest of the village was just as unpopulated and quiet as before. When would the holiday start? Something had meanwhile changed inside the house: the freshly whitewashed oven was sparkling clean, newly starched curtains hung in the windows, and the wooden table was covered by a white embroidered tablecloth. Grandmother looked different today: her long dark dress and braided hair were special. Even her face, usually so gloomy, was clear and satisfied. Uncle Shura had dressed up in fresh clothes too. A tray sat in the middle of the table with freshly baked cottage cheesecake. We were invited to enjoy the holiday fare. After she crossed herself, Grandmother began cutting the cake. We drank fresh milk, still warm, out of large enameled mugs and ate the dark cake.

After breakfast some other trays appeared on the table with more of Grandmother's baked cakes. In the middle stood a large bottle of homebrew vodka, *samogon*, plugged with a rag and surrounded by cut-glass tumblers. Everything was ready for the guests.

Suddenly the sound of an accordion reached us from the street and we ran out onto the porch. People were coming out of their houses and many of them were sitting on the earthen *zavalinki* in front. In the middle of the road came a small pack of young men, their shirts outside their trousers in the Russian fashion and wearing creased boots, and girls with bright kerchiefs tossed over their shoulders. The accordionist, in a red shirt and black cap, flung wide the bellows of his instrument, filling the village with his music. The girls, running in front and turning around toward him, beat out the steps of a *chechotka*, a tapping kind of dance, and shouted out provocative rhyming songs, *chastushki*, which were sometimes quite sharp.

> *"A sweet young man sits on the porch with an expression*
> *on his face,*
> *And his face expresses what he's sitting on on that porch!"*

One dancer shouted, and another joined in:

> *"Another sweet young man sits at the gate his mouth*
> *stretched out wide,*
> *And no one can figure out where the gate is, and where*
> *the mouth!"*

After such a warm up, the girls flew into a dance around the musician. Taking their place, some young men tried to outdo the girls. The street-side audience laughed loudly, throwing out jokes and trying to provoke the young people.

Having enjoyed themselves for awhile, the hosts of the village began to invite the visitors into their homes. Everyone went every which way and at that moment the guests from the neighbouring villages arrived. They also went down the roadway, singing out *chastushki*, and being welcomed into various houses to be treated. Then the new arrivals from other villages gathered into groups to perform for their hosts. At first it looked like a competition between the different villages, but then everyone got all mixed together and began to sing and dance with each other. They danced a formal quadrille, a dance I had never seen before. Everything was very gay and it was nothing like our school parties, where in recent years we had gone all out to recreate the conditions of a pre-revolutionary ball. In ill-suited footwear and dresses we solemnly performed the steps of the mazurka, tarantella, *pas-de-grâce*, and other dances of the "ancien régime." School uniforms had been reintroduced, and schools divided into those for boys and for girls. The simplicity of the post-revolutionary secondary and workers' schools had disappeared. The outburst of patriotism during the war years had given birth to a sentimental longing for the past. Stalin introduced the uniform of the Tsarist officers with its gold-braided epaulettes and cockades. He himself shone in his portraits in the uniform of a Field Marshal, its threads woven with gold.

A persistent inferiority complex ruled all the feelings of that small, pock-marked, red-headed man. He belonged to a national minority and thought to encourage Russian chauvinism so that others would forget his origins. He rose from the depths of society and his whole soul was repulsed by that environment. His ambitious nature surged towards those doors that had been closed to him. He had wanted to be educated in a private school and wear its fancy uniform, but instead he had gone to a religious school and worn the hated cassock of a seminarian. He had wanted to dance at aristocratic balls, to mingle in high society, to attain rank, honour, and power. He had dreamed of living in the Winter Palace. All of the impossible dreams of that little Georgian had come true: power, the Kremlin, the rank of Field Marshal. And his happy subjects, those who were still alive after the destruction of purges, famine, and war, danced to his tune at those balls and in their lives. The poor and hungry villagers, however, danced differently. And I must say that the village which I now saw before me had come right out of another time.

The village grannies recalled the stories of their grannies, about the time of serfdom, and said that life had been better and fuller then: "See, my kin had a much bigger allotment of land and even twelve children! And now you can barely feed two or three." I heard such conversations more than once. I couldn't believe my ears. Unlike the rest of us, the collective farm workers had no internal passports, which meant that they were indeed serfs of the state! They couldn't leave the *kolkhoz* of their own free will and move to the city. The work on the farms was hateful, and the people's hearts weren't in it. Fields were overgrown with weeds and potatoes rotted in the ground or in storage. The difference between *kolkhoz* cows and privately owned ones was striking—like children in families compared to those abandoned to an orphanage. Their way of life differed in no way from that of the pre-revolutionary period. Animals and people, as a rule, lived together under the same roof, so that the heavy scent of the cowshed made its way into the living quarters. You could hear the cattle mooing and the pigs squealing on the other side of the wall. Wooden cradles, *lyulki*, hung from the ceilings, just like in the paintings of the old masters. The mother would rock her baby with her foot by a rope tied to the *lyulka*. I watched how at the same time she would spin a stone grinder with her hand, crushing the grain: there was only one mill for several villages and that was far away. In the *izba* it was usually dark and unwashed children dressed in rags played on the floor.

All these impressions weighed down upon me. I was oppressed by what I saw and heard, but couldn't analyze it then. I was simply horrified by what I saw in the village. Galya and I agreed to leave, gathered up provisions for the road, and early one morning ran off, leaving a note for Grandmother. And even though we were unprepared for survival on our own, our flight was crowned with success:

we got as far as the town of Kashin and caught a train that got us home that evening.

Thus ended my acquaintance with the "rich and happy" Soviet village. This seemingly insignificant episode in my life left a lasting mark: I had begun to discover that many-faced, many-layered falsehood of the society that we proclaimed the best in the world.

5

"The Time of Troubles"[16]

The senior class of school dragged on through an endless and boring year, although it would culminate in a most solemn moment—graduation. Without the slightest feeling of regret, I was preparing to bid school farewell forever. I had not had such a boring time in all the ten years I had attended school. Literature had always been my favourite subject, the only one to give me genuine pleasure. But in this last year, even literature filled me with boredom. Behind us were the eighteenth and nineteenth centuries: we moved on now to the twentieth. The most significant works of this century that appeared in our curriculum were those of post-revolutionary Soviet writers. So we dwelt on them for the entire year. Previously we had studied wonderful Russian literature and it wasn't so very important who our teacher was. I believe that they had taught us badly, and of course everything was subservient to the Party line, to ideology. One's own opinion was not tolerated, everyone was to think as the teacher did, and he was to think as the curruculum prescribed. Teacher succeeded teacher and they were on the whole grey and ordinary. I can remember only one inspirational lesson, one with an original approach, that reflected the personality of the instructor.

The only brilliant lecture I ever heard was on the twelfth-century *Tale of Prince Igor's Campaign*.[17] A strange, peasant-like man in felt boots, *valenki*, paced from corner to corner of the classroom and told us about that distant time, as though he himself had served in the army of the Russian prince. This unusual teacher was with us for a very short time, as a substitute. He had taught somewhere in a technical school and so was considered second-rate. But it is that "second-rater" that I remember.

Our literature teacher in the final year was Natalya Alekseevna, a tall, grey-haired, delicately faced woman, with what they call the traces of a former beauty. She had extraordinarily beautiful hands with long fingers and always manicured finger-nails. From child-hood I had paid particular attention to a person's hands and often, without justification, took a dislike to people with ugly hands. I liked Natalya Alekseevna. She was quiet, majestic, and never raised her voice. She never scolded us, never appealed to our conscience or patriotism as the other teachers did. But her lessons were depressing and monotonous. It seemed that she herself found it boring to tell us about Gorky's heroes or Mayakovsky's epic poems. She didn't even hide very well the fact that she was indifferent to the poetry of the national minorities, such as Dzhambul or Suleyman Stalsky. She would spend a single class on the theme of *The Iron Flood* by Serafimovich when the study plan allotted it three.[18]

On the other hand, when the plan moved on to "The Poetry of the Beginning of the Twentieth Century," Natalya Alekseevna came alive. The poet Alexander Blok awoke both the instructor and her students. But I especially remember one lesson. That was a day when no one was called up to the blackboard. It was a lecture on the various poetic movements of the beginning of the century. Natalya Alekseevna was transfigured, suddenly looking about ten years younger. Flushing red, she recited from memory in an entirely different voice the poetry of Balmont, Severyanin, Briussov, and Nadson. They were her youth! It was clear now why she had become a teacher, in order to instruct her students by entirely different standards. She would have probably preferred, if permitted, first to read us the poetry of Akhmatova, Gumilev, Tsvetaeva, and Mandelshtam, but that would have been impossible as, at that period, such poets simply did not officially exist. She was permitted to discuss the second ranking stars of the time, and of course at the end had to consign them to anathema—they had broken with the people, they didn't reflect reality—and "reward" them with the label of "Decadents." The topic was optional; that is, it wasn't required by the plan. Listen and forget, is what they expected, and what most of the students did. For some reason, I did not forget this single interesting lesson which had revealed the secret life of my old teacher.[19]

As a rule, my teachers didn't elicit any particular emotion from me, neither love nor hatred. They were handed out to us for the year, just like the City Department of Education textbooks were. New ones—teachers and textbooks—appeared the next year and the old ones were forgotten. But there were exceptions. In our next-to-last year clever, black-haired Sarra Borisovna Bass was our history instructor. She was simultaneously our homeroom teacher and responsible for all the classes at the same level. So we had to deal with her often. I couldn't stand her piercing voice, her sparkling enthusiastic eyes, and the passion with which she gave her lessons. She demanded the same passion from us, those same phrases crackling with pomposity. And the girls vied with each other to please her, damning the Tsar and praising the Decembrists[20] to the heights. There was a sacred halo attached to the exploits of the terrorist Populists and the whole collection of clichés were shouted out at the blackboard by ardent school girls. And at the end, the marks of those who performed like that were the highest possible—a five.

Then, of course, I couldn't understand the real essence of the subject they taught us, claiming that it was "history." It never occurred to me that they were simply giving us ideological propaganda, supposed facts which were distorted often to the point of being unrecognizable. It was the style of the history lessons that I found disgusting. I intuitively felt the falsity of it all. All instructors were responsible for the ideological education of their charges, and all did what they could according to their abilities. Sarra Borisovna climbed out of her skin in the process: her hypocrisy was striking.

Her daughter, Galya Tsfassman, was in my class. She was a mild, quiet girl, with braids and perfect curls that framed her face. She was never favoured in any way by her mother, our instructor. I think that Sarra Borisovna herself was proud of her impartiality and objectivity. But thanks to her daughter we learned a small detail about this woman's life. Galya's uncle, her father's brother, was the famous jazz pianist Vladimir Tsfassman, who had been harshly denounced as one of the "rootless cosmopolitans" at the height of the stormy campaign of 1948-1949.[21] It was probably because of that experience that we could detect some anxiety in our teacher's behaviour. As I realized later, Sarra Borisovna's reasons to be worried were most understandable.

The condemnation of "rootless cosmopolitans" took on a universal character at this time, as did all such campaigns. On the radio, in the newspapers, at concerts, cultural figures were subjected to libel and ridicule in all possible ways. And in the rage of the bacchanalia that was being played out, it was Jewish names that were spoken of most of all. Writers, actors, musicians—all were accused of "bowing to the West," "smuggling in Western ideas," or "obeisance" to the West. For most of us, these clichés stuck in our teeth. No one doubted the anti-Semitic nature of what was happening.

Rumours spread around Moscow of the arrest of members of the Jewish Anti-Fascist Committee. The poets Markish and Kvitko were accused of something or other. I had known Kvitko's work since childhood as all Soviet children had read his simple verse, "I wrote a letter to Klim Voroshilov. Comrade Voroshilov, People's Commissar." In January 1948 the newspapers reported that the director of the Moscow State Jewish Theatre, Solomon Mikhoels, had died in a car crash. He too had been a member of the Anti-Fascist Committee. And soon the rumours made the rounds that Mikhoels had been deliberately killed.[22]

The Jewish Theatre was located next to my school, on the Malaya Bronnaya. I had never been in it as Jewish culture held no interest for me. I recall that we took my grandmother there once, and did it just for her sake as no one else in the family knew Yiddish. It's embarrassing to remember now, but although I walked past the theatre every day, I had never taken the trouble to see what was playing. On that January day in 1948 I ran into an obstacle on the way to school—the roadway was blocked by an enormous crowd and it was impossible to get through. I asked someone what had happened.

"The great Jewish actor Mikhoels has died!" a man answered with great emotion. "We are bidding him farewell today."

This information made no great impact on me. I stood for awhile in the crowd and then went on to school by another route. Soon a terrible refutation of the official version of Mikhoels' death began to circulate by word of mouth. It was difficult to believe those rumours, but the climate of the period only seemed to confirm the reality of what sounded so unreal.

The fact that I was Jewish began to take on a new meaning. I felt in communion with those who were being persecuted. I sympathized, seeing that they were innocent. At the same time, I began to sense my own estrangement and alienation. My surname was also "foreign" and sounded somewhat German. During the war I hated that name. When they would call me to the board in school by that name, the very tone of those words, "Reyf, to the front!" was oppressive. I envied the children with simple, ordinary Russian surnames. This envy had passed by the time I reached the senior classes, but my dislike of my own name remained. Jewish first names and surnames always figured in the multitude of jokes about the Jews. In time the names began to sound horrid and dissonant. Those bearing such names were so uncomfortable that they would often change them. I recall one instance when my family was discussing the "awful sufferings" of a friend. When he came to defend his doctoral dissertation, he had to be addressed by the name that appeared on his birth certificate. "In the world" he had long been known as Pavel Mikhailovich, but now he suddenly had to face the shame of having the whole auditorium hear him addressed by his Hebrew name of Peisach Mordukhovich. The humiliation was a double one: first, he had to acknowledge that he had hidden his original name, which must mean that he was ashamed of it; and second, the name itself was an antagonizingly dissonant one, both for him and for those who heard it. Pavel Mikhailovich was ready to abandon his defence, but somehow overcame his shameful weakness and became a doctor of medical science.

Many people attempted by all possible means to change their Jewish first names and surnames for Russian ones. It was well known and no one was surprised; after all, your career and your life often depended on how your name sounded. And it wasn't just Jewish names that were unpleasant to the Soviet ear: any foreign-sounding name put others on guard. My brother could not forgive our parents for having followed an aunt's suggestion and given him the name Edgar, after Edgar Allan Poe. Everyone teased him about it as a child and later he became "Igor." Many Jewish artists and writers were known by their pseudonyms, which were always Russian. During the campaign against the "cosmopolitans" these pseudonyms were as a rule exposed, to relieve any doubt as to whom we were dealing with.

One of the performances of the popular puppet concerts at the Obraztsov Theatre made a horrible impression on me. The show was called "An Ordinary Concert" and featured satirical characters which appeared one after another in a whirling kaleidoscope of action. Eventually, four puppets appeared on stage. They had exaggerated, stereotypically Jewish features and wore outrageous checked clothes (obviously foreign). To a parody of jazz music, which was particularly taboo at the time, the puppets began to tap out a *chechotka* against a background of English-sounding speech. It was called "Cosmopolitan Chorus." The audience received it with the same delight as the rest of the show. I left depressed.

Once, at a cousin's party, two hand-written verses were passed around. One was attributed to Margarita Aliger and the other was entitled *Ehrenburg's Reply*.[23] Both authors were well known, but no one knew whether the poems were actually theirs or not. Both were Jews so it was perfectly reasonable to assume they were the authors of these verses. The poems made a great impression on me. I copied them down right there, mixing up some of the stanzas in my haste. Later these verses figured in my case, confirming the "nationalistic" tendency of our organization. I saw nothing seditious in the content of the poems. They simply represented that timeless, bitter, Jewish sense of grievance at the unjust hatred directed towards the Jews, both in our country and throughout the world.

> *I'll ask Marx and Einstein,*
> *Who are full of great wisdom,*
> *If they can reveal the secret*
> *Of our guilt before eternity.*

It seemed that these poets were expressing my own personal thoughts. My school was a perfect mirror of the country at that time. We listened to the condemnation of "rootless cosmopolitans" and unthinkingly repeated all the clichés and epithets. Sarra Borisovna was in a frenzy! In history class and school assemblies she repeated everything that was blared out daily on the radio and printed in the newspapers. I always sensed the falsity of her words and it was terrible to hear her speak.

It was against the background of this atmosphere that the preparations for a great national rejoicing took place: the celebration of Stalin's seventieth birthday. It never occurred to me to suspect Stalin himself was encouraging this bacchanal. I had absolutely no doubt that all of the people revered our leader. Where else could that ceaseless torrent of congratulatory telegrams printed in the national papers have come from? And the grandiose halls, full of gifts for Stalin—what miracles of art the people gave him as expressions of his love and gratitude. Our whole class went on an excursion to the Museum of the Revolution to inspect—we used a magnifying glass— the miniature drawings in which some virtuosi had written letters full of devotion to their leader and teacher. People from around the world sent gifts to Stalin. I remember the present of a French woman—a child's knitted cap, the only thing left after the death of her daughter during the Fascist occupation. It was about this woman that I wrote in my graduation essay. I picked the "free" topic of "Stalin: Our Fighting Glory, Stalin: Our Youth's Ecstasy!" I received a mark of only four instead of the five which I had expected. I had made a single mistake, writing Stalin's patronymic, Vissarionovich, with a single "s"! As Natalya Nikolayevna said, "It was an unforgivable mistake and, despite the brilliance of the essay and with great regret, the committee had to award a four."

"What on earth made you do it?" my teacher lamented. What on earth indeed? I had seen that word day after day, for almost two decades! Was this, perhaps, the first sign of the sedition that would lead me so far astray?

On 20 December 1949, the entire nation celebrated the birthday of Stalin, the wise and great leader of all the peoples. The encomia knew no bounds. In congratulatory telegrams he was called the best friend of miners, of railway workers, of collective farm workers, of corn producers, and so on and so forth, *ad infinitum*. For several days before the anniversary, our school prepared for the celebration. Our history teacher was hysterical! In class we practiced the slogans we were to shout out at the school's evening assembly. As ill luck would have it, I had a loud voice and excellent diction, and this is what my declamatory skills would be used for—for once I was not happy about them. Sarra Zinovyevna wrote out a number of slogans on the blackboard and I repeated them for the whole class, loudly and with passion.

"Your voice should express complete joy. It should be filled with the sound of love for our Leader," my teacher kept trying to persuade me, making me repeat the slogans over and over again. I was embarrassed. It was unpleasant, but I could not refuse to take part.

Finally the solemn day arrived. After our lessons, the whole school assembled in the auditorium. Standing, we listened to the radio broadcast of the solemn session at the Hall of Columns in the House of Unions. Stalin was greeted with an endless ovation. At a sign from our history teacher we too applauded our invisible leader. Then the speeches of greeting began. I can't recall who spoke or about what but it was an unbroken torrent of words, filled with adulation and eulogy. After each speech in Stalin's honour, the hall erupted in loud applause, interspersed with the new slogans: "Long Live Our Leader and Teacher, the Great Stalin!" or "Under the Banner of Lenin, Under the Leadership of Stalin: Forward to the Victory of Communism Throughout the World!" It was all shouted out by shrill, strained voices; you could hear no joy, only hysteria. And again a squall of ovations. Against the background of this "wave," we, practiced shouters, at a sign from Sarra Borisovna, screeched out as loud as we could the slogans we had memorized: "May Our Beloved Stalin Live For Eternity!," "Stalin is Our Banner," "Stalin is Our Pride!" and so forth.

It was a strange sight. It seemed to me that from the distant decorated hall which we could only hear on the radio, some little round teacher must be directing the whole proceedings with her index finger and a wave of her hand. I remember that I was not the only one not myself that night: several of the girls were too embarrassed to smile and kept looking at each other. We all wanted it to end as soon as possible.

I don't remember when I reached the firm conclusion that this reverence for Stalin had an ugly character. At that time I thought that it was only certain stupid people and toadies, like our history teacher, who went so far overboard. It must be unpleasant for Stalin, I said to myself, but he didn't have the power to dampen their ardour.

Graduation is always an important milestone. In my case, the milestone turned out to be a critical moment which changed my entire life. I was not prepared for what awaited me and indeed, how could I be prepared? But everything that I saw around me inexorably led me to what was about to happen. I would meet those people who thought as I did but were more mature than I, people who were willing not only to discuss but to even take action. Everything that was ahead was the logical continuation of each step I had taken up til now. It was my fate.

6

A Day in the Life of Lefortovo Solitary

Translator's note: The reader will see that in this Record of Interrogation, Alla Reyf "acknowledges" her "guilt" of being "of an anti-Soviet disposition," a member of a "Trotskyite organization," and "undertaking active hostile work against the Soviet state," among other crimes. The narrative of this book completely refutes such an "acknowledgement." In other similar documents her co-accused also "acknowledge" their guilt in these terms. It should be understood that such "acknowledgements" of such "crimes" represent the standard practice of the time, when the interrogator who "transcribed" the session also carefully chose what words would be recorded. Sometimes these words were actually uttered by the accused, but were obtained by force— not only physical force, but the force of long interrogations late at night.

Record of the Interrogation of Prisoner

REYF, Alla Yevgenyevna

dated 20 February 1951

> REYF, A. Y., date of birth: 1931; place of birth: Kiev; nationality: Jewish; citizenship: USSR; member of the Komsomol. Until arrest, student of the extension division of the Lenin State Pedagogical Institute. Residence: Moscow.
>
> Interrogation began at 23:00.

QUESTION: *You stand accused under articles 58-1 "a," 19-58-8, 58-10, pt. 1 and 58-11 of the Criminal Code of the RSFSR, i.e., that you are a member of a Trotskyite terrorist organization and on orders from that organization took active part in hostile work against the Soviet state. Do you understand the accusation?*

ANSWER: Yes, I do. I am accused of being a member of a youth Trotskyite organization and in carrying out anti-Soviet activities.

QUESTION: *Do you acknowledge your guilt?*

ANSWER: Yes, I do. I am guilty of being of an anti-Soviet disposition, being a member until the day of my arrest of a youth Trotskyite organization, named the Union of Struggle for the Cause of the Revolution and on that organization's behalf undertaking active hostile work against the Soviet state.

QUESTION: *What criminal activity did you undertake in the Trotskyite organization?*

ANSWER: As a member of the Trotskyite organization USCR I transcribed the manifesto of the organization, in which hateful slander was levelled against the Soviet state and methods were proposed for the struggle against the current state structure. I did not undertake any other work in the USCR.

QUESTION: *When did you join the Trotskyite organization?*

ANSWER: In September 1950.

QUESTION: *Under whose influence?*

ANSWER: GUREVICH introduced me to the Trotskyite organization.

QUESTION: *Be more specific as to the identity of GUREVICH.*

ANSWER: GUREVICH, Yevgeny Zinovyevich, was a student of the Moscow Institute of Food Economics, with whom I became acquainted in the autumn of 1949 through a girlfriend named Mila. I do not know her surname. From my conversations with GUREVICH I discovered that he too was interested in the humanities, and that brought us together. As a consequence we struck up friendly relations. He visited me at our apartment, where we often talked about literature, art, and natural science. Besides that, GUREVICH was particularly interested in philosophy and spoke with me a great deal about the topic and what it taught. Later, I noticed a sharp change in GUREVICH's views on life.

QUESTION: *What were these views exactly?*

ANSWER: In our conversations he began to touch mainly on the internal and external politics of the Soviet Union and expressed opinions of an anti-Soviet, Trotskyite nature. At first I was indifferent, but then I asked him why he had changed his views so quickly. He answered that I knew him very little and told me that his anti-Soviet views had already been formed in 1947-1948, when he was in the senior year of high school, but at that time these unhealthy opinions had no opportunity to develop. Lately, GUREVICH continued, after he became acquainted with a certain Boris (whose surname, I discovered later, is SLUTSKY), these anti-Soviet opinions were revived again.

QUESTION: *Were you acquainted with Boris SLUTSKY?*

ANSWER: I was not acquainted personally with SLUTSKY and only knew about him through GUREVICH.

QUESTION: *What did GUREVICH tell you about him?*

ANSWER: In the summer of 1950, GUREVICH and I went to the movies. In the foyer of the theatre GUREVICH told me that he had met Boris SLUTSKY at a consultation before the entrance exams at the university they both wished to attend. He characterized SLUTSKY as having an anti-Soviet disposition and reported that his father had been a confirmed Trotskyite in the past and had allegedly perished at the front during the war.

Later, GUREVICH telephoned me at home and we agreed to meet outside. On our walk around the city GUREVICH informed me that he was continuing to meet SLUTSKY and as a result of numerous conversations on the anti-Soviet theme, GUREVICH had finally come under the influence of SLUTSKY and completely shared his anti-Soviet opinions.

According to GUREVICH, SLUTSKY supposedly "proved" to him Trotsky had apparently been an outstanding historical figure and had done much of great value for the triumph of the Revolution in *Russia*. In successive conversations GUREVICH spewed out foul slanders against Soviet life and the leadership of the Bolshevik Party, announcing with conviction that he was now devoting his life to the struggle against the present Soviet state system and for the resurrection of the historical truth about Trotsky, who had allegedly suffered in the cause of "world revolution."

In conclusion, GUREVICH told me, "You should either join me or we should never meet again."

QUESTION: *And did you agree with the proposal by GUREVICH to undertake hostile work?*

ANSWER: Although I shared GUREVICH's anti-Soviet views, his proposal to undertake organized anti-Soviet activity greatly shocked me and I completely fell apart. Therefore, I was unable to give him a positive reply and told him that at first I had to study the question and then I could give him my opinion. GUREVICH praised me for that answer and said that I was behaving properly in not giving him a positive reply at once, as such a question was extremely serious and could not be decided on the spot. After that GUREVICH advised me to consider his offer properly and then give him my decision.

In a short while I again met with GUREVICH and told him that I agreed to undertake the struggle against Soviet power. GUREVICH approved of my decision and told me that the anti-Soviet organization was already in existence and that I was to consider myself a member from that moment.

QUESTION: *What did GUREVICH tell you exactly about the anti-Soviet organization which you were joining?*

ANSWER: I asked if there were many members in the organization and GUREVICH answered that he had no right to speak of the membership of the anti-Soviet organization, but that, in his words, it consisted of several dozens of people and that they had already constituted a "organizational committee" (OC) including SLUTSKY, GUREVICH, and MELNIKOV.

Later the anti-Soviet organization was named the Union of Struggle for the Cause of the Revolution (USCR).

QUESTION: *What criminal activity did you undertake in the Trotskyite organization?*

   WHERE WE BURIED THE SUN

ANSWER: As a member of the Trotskyite organization USCR I transcribed the manifesto of the organization in which hateful slander was levelled against Soviet power and methods were described for the struggle against the current state structure. I did not undertake any other work in the USCR.

QUESTION: *You are not being frank here. Tell the entire truth!*

ANSWER: I have told the truth about my participation in the Trotskyite organization USCR. In November 1950, dissension erupted in our organization and I left it together with GUREVICH and MELNIKOV.

QUESTION: *Why?*

ANSWER: Disagreement arose between the members of the OC, SLUTSKY, and GUREVICH. In particular, SLUTSKY proposed hostile activity by the organization by means of *anti-Soviet agitation*, while GUREVICH *defended the method of propaganda*. As a result a schism took place in the USCR.

In November 1950 at an illegal meeting at my apartment, in the presence of GUREVICH, MELNIKOV, and myself, a new youth Trotskyite organization was formed, named the Group for the Liberation of the Working Class, to which I belonged up to the day of my arrest.

The interrogation concluded at 3:30.

I have read the minutes of the interrogation.

It correctly records my words.

(Reyf)

INTERROGATION WAS CONCLUDED BY INTERROGATOR OF THE DEPARTMENT ON PARTICULARLY IMPORTANT INVESTIGATIONS OF THE MGB OF THE USSR,

Colonel (YEVDOKIMOV)

(see fig 6.1)

In prison, morning begins at night. A clang of the *kormushka*—that small square cut into the door that folds back into the cell like a tray—the sharp cries of "Up!"

Oh, no! It must be a dream that I haven't been able to get to sleep at all. It feels as though I have just arrived back from the interrogation.

Consciousness again begins to dissolve into sleep, but not completely. Somewhere in the distance the *kormushki* are clanging in other cells. The repetitious, monotonous "Up!" resounds dully: "Up!" "Up!" I don't move but am engulfed by the fear that the hateful shriek will strike its blow again. Better to get up before the order comes. It's remarkable how soon you get accustomed to submitting to someone else's will: your own is broken. Not a shadow of protest, at least not visibly. It was so with me, as it was with most. Only a few individuals snapped. I was reminded of this over and over again during my five years of incarceration, both in prison and later in the camp.

The window, illuminated by the prison searchlights, shows that it is night. At this moment it is particularly oppressive and cold in the cell. My movements are slow. I am weighed down by the sleep that will not depart. I have to wash and straighten up my cot and do my exercises. I submit mechanically to these "have to's." But a few half-hearted exercises cannot free me from my sleepiness. It is a useless struggle. I am worn out by the many night-time interrogations. Mornings like this are just another form of torture. Wrapped up in my coat I sit down on the cot and drowse sitting up. But you can only get away with this if you keep your eyes open and your face has to be turned just right so that the woman keeping surveillance, the *nadzorka*, can always see your eyes, and your eyes have to be open. Any turn of the head to the side, away from the peephole, and immediately you hear a shout through the *kormushka*: "Turn your head! No sleeping!" But it is possible to sleep with your eyes open. You can sleep sitting up too, even standing. You can sleep marching in a column of prisoners, moving your feet mechanically. There are lots of ways of fooling the guards, but I didn't master this art right away. For now I have learned to sleep in the tiny intervals between the *nadzorka*'s regular inspections through the peephole. A plodding lethargy spreads throughout my body, but my sense of hearing is on guard to catch the sound of the light steps approaching down the corridor. The *nadzorka* stops at the neighbouring cell and, in a moment, I will hear the weak scratch at my door. By a strength of will I open my eyes and simultaneously hear the sound of the screen falling down over the hole. The steps go away and again I can sleep for four or five minutes, until the next rustle and scratch at the door. Tormenting yet sweet! These two alternating sensations are incredibly intensified in the routine.

But now I catch a new sound, the cart with breakfast is coming down the corridor. The *kormushka* opens again: "Breakfast!" I can't see the person distributing the food. Hands place breakfast on the *kormushka*'s counter: a ration of black bread with a little mound of granulated sugar on top. I stretch out and offer my green metallic mug. The hands take the mug and return it full a of dirty brown strong smelling liquid. It's coffee, smelling of everything except coffee. The drink is welcome simply because it's hot. Sleep has left for good now. Sipping at the coffee, I chew with satisfaction on the flabby bread sprinkled with sugar. Life has returned! It's no longer so gloomy around me, the window shows grey now and through its dull glass you can almost make out the reflection of the rising winter sun. The tormenting electric light that burns in the cell all night is turned off. In a way, the half-darkness of the cell and the approaching daylight in the window bring with them a certain comfort. It is the most difficult thing, to begin the day, to acknowledge again each morning what has taken place. But then the day takes over and crawls along on its own, without any help or effort from me.

Can you come to love your place of incarceration, your solitary, stone cold cell? Coming back from the interrogation, from that terrifying world of accusations, threats, and humiliations, where fear, exhaustion, and sleepiness made me sign anything written by the interrogator, I almost feel protected by the walls of my cell. This is my refuge, if only briefly, for a few hours a day. Later I heard from many prisoners that they too experienced the same strange contradiction, of that feeling of attraction to their place of imprisonment, the place of their suffering.

The colour of the walls of my solitary cell was remarkable! I never imagined that a colour could be so oppressive! It's difficult to describe the colour: dark green with an admixture of brown. Everything was painted in this repulsive colour: the sink, the pan in the corner on the floor, the dish, and mug. There was a small window high above the floor, metallic screen soldered onto its dull glass. It would be hard to smash glass protected like that, and it hardly let in any daylight. I can see a narrow slice of sky when the dayguard opens the casement with his long pole that has a hook attached at the end. Some nights the moon looks in at this casement.

Six endless months had passed from the moment of my arrival in this solitary cell. For the first few days I hardly got up from the cot, sitting in a motionless pose from reveille to lights out. Any movement brought on a tormenting ache. A sick organ needs calm. I need to be rigid; one must not move or think. The latter was impossible. But I taught myself to direct my thoughts where I wanted. Exciting journeys alternated with visits to friends, gay parties. I played my favourite sport, volleyball. I skated, dressed up in beautiful clothing. I even had love affairs and argued with anyone I wished. The seasons changed as I desired them to. The bright pictures of normal life, full of colour, smells, and sounds, passed through my consciousness. I deliberately kept myself from thinking about the present.

So the hours passed. The rumble of the opening *kormushka* and the gritty noise of the lock in the door passed through my body like a current, returning me to reality. This life in dreams was perhaps a defensive reaction which kept me from going out of my mind, helping me survive. At first I would have nothing to do with food and returned it uneaten. I wouldn't undress to sleep. I even tried to lie down in my felt boots until the *nadzorka* noticed and made me take them off. Day and night the damp cold was oppressive. I wore my old winter coat, which I had outgrown, and the felt-lined boots from my childhood. But they couldn't warm me up and the coarse military blanket hardly helped at all. The torture of the cold was my first prison torment. Hunger had not yet arrived. It sneaked up unexpectedly. Suddenly the ration of bread wasn't enough. Four hundred grams of flabby black bread could hardly be stretched over half the day. The tastiest food was saved for the evening: a crust of bread, which I sucked on as long as possible. But even my hunger was not enough to help me overcome the revulsion I felt for the fish soup, the smell of which spread throughout the whole prison announcing supper time. Eyeless fish heads floated in a grey swill. The very sight and smell of the food brought on nausea and destroyed my feeling of hunger. You can probably get used to anything, and I would have got used to this horrid soup. But apparently it wasn't yet genuine hunger, which would have turned even this soup into a delicacy.

So the most difficult first days of my incarceration passed as in a dream. I could feel the position of my heart for the first time, clenched up into a lump, but it gradually relaxed. Later I could breathe in and out more easily. Time, the wisest of doctors, had come to heal my spirit. Once in the baths I noticed with surprise that my legs were swollen and realized that I had to get some exercise. At first I made myself walk in the cell. I counted the steps, making myself walk one hundred paces from the door to the window and back again. This soon became a habit and I didn't notice how long I paced from one corner to the other, until my head began to swim and my legs gave way with fatigue. In the mornings I did exercises and stopped refusing to take the twenty-minute walk outside. A defined daily rhythm appeared: my life had begun to pass in a new routine. The horror of solitary, which had failed to crush me, began to fade away, to dissolve into the details of daily prison life.

+ + + + +

I have no sense of what the actual time is: I keep track of the hours by "guesstimate." Up at six, breakfast at eight. Between twelve and two we are let out on a fifteen or twenty-minute walk. You can refuse to go, as I did in the beginning. But now I am impatient for my walk, to see the sky over my head, if only for a few minutes! I listen to them taking my neighbours out, and then it is my turn. The *nadzorka* looks in through the *kormushka,* one of the few whose face I like.

"Are you going on your walk?" It seems to me that there is a glimmer of compassion in the depths of her eyes. Hers is the kind face of the ordinary Russian woman, and this expression of kindness distinguishes her from the others, who are gloomy, malicious, and faceless.

One night I had a dream, or—strictly speaking—a hallucination. My father came up to my iron cot and I felt his warm hand on my head. The sensation was so real that I jumped up and broke into sobs when I realized that it had been just a dream. Suddenly my *kormushka* opened. I waited for the usual shout, but this *nadzorka*, her face right in the opening, said quietly, "Don't cry, what do you have to grieve for? You're not the only one here. You know how big the place is, this prison! And it's chock-full, too!" She emphasized the word "full" and her voice expressed such a calming submissiveness: you're not alone, there are many others like you. I'll never forget what balm her words were to me! It was extraordinary, the very fact that she had spoken like another human being to me, for the first time over those many months when I had heard so many rough commands. Later, when I would meet her in the corridor after an interrogation, it would seem that her eyes were smiling. Even the touch of her hands during a search were not so unpleasant. I rejoiced whenever she was the guard on my ward.

"Yes, yes, I'm going on the walk!" I don't have to put anything special on: I even sit in the cell in my overcoat. For a moment the daylight is blinding and the frosty air takes my breath away. I am in a small square courtyard, surrounded by a tall wooden fence. The boards are joined together so that there isn't the slightest crack through which to see the light from the adjoining courtyard. Sometimes you can hear the footsteps of your neighbour. It is strictly forbidden to stop, listen, or admire the sky overhead. To do so calls forth a shout: "Keep moving!" The vigilant eye of the soldier with his automatic rules over the whole complex. He marches along the planking high above us. Impossible to exchange a word or a note —it is just like the other solitary cell, except outside. In the summer I admired the bits of grass that had forced their way through the cracks in the asphalt. But when I attempted to take a "bouquet" of three yellow dandelions back to my cell, a *nadzorka* snatched them away. "Don't violate the rules!" she said, viciously. Not violating the rules was not easy in prison, as everything was forbidden.

Many of the rules seemed strange at first. Before going to bed your socks and towel had to be hung on the foot of the cot, the mug placed on the bedside table with its handle facing the door, and the aluminium spoon had to be lying next to it, so that it was all visible to the guard through the peephole. Over the course of time you begin to work out the mechanics, extremely refined ones: everything is predicated on planting the idea of suicide in your mind and everything is directed toward its prevention. The towel and socks, it turns out, can be used to strangle yourself; the mug handle can be used for cutting your throat (if it were possible to tear it off the mug!). But what can you do with such a soft aluminium spoon? I would never have guessed if one day a guard on the floor, the "boss" as the *nadzorki* called him, hadn't reprimanded me rudely for sharpening the handle. I categorically denied his accusation; he then pointed with his finger to the fine scratches on the metal and threatened to inform the interrogator of my crime. It was only when he left that I guessed how the scratches had appeared: I had been using this unlucky handle to cut my bread. Now it was clear that, if you were clever and ground the handle sharp, you might cut your veins with this "terrible weapon." The prison stairwell, with its curtain of netting, also reminded you of yet another method of suicide if the netting wasn't there.

Once I overheard the sound of breaking glass from one of the neighbouring cells. A great to-do followed in the corridor, voices crying out and the sharp words, "Doctor, quick!" The noise continued for some time, quick running steps, agitated voices, and then it quieted down. I sat in my cell, all ears, my heart clenching with pain, my imagination drawing the picture of what had happened in the next cell. A mug had been thrown at the window and, although I imagined that the windows, soldered over with wire, were unbreakable, this poor unfortunate had obviously attempted to do so and then made an attempt with a shard of the broken glass. I couldn't calm down the whole night, remembering the shouts and moaning. My cell was particularly gloomy, and my fate, particularly hopeless.

Another tragedy was played out in prison (I wanted to say, "before my own eyes," but it was really "before my own ears."). Over the course of a long time, perhaps several weeks, I heard a man gradually go out of his mind. From one particular cell a man's voice began calmly, but loudly and insistently, to demand something. At first I couldn't make out the words. They called in the "boss" to deal with him, and things quieted down. But after several days that voice again began to insist that they take him to the interrogator. Then I heard the voice as it sobbed and cried out, "Why have you given no reasons for my arrest? Why do you hold me here without charge?" For several days the cell emitted that subdued sobbing. And then, after some time, the voice called out as though in a fit. They went into the cell and you could hear them stopping up his mouth and, apparently, tying him up as well. Then he was dragged mumbling past my door. I never again heard the sound of that man's voice.

From that moment more than thirty years have passed, but my memory preserves a heavy load: all the sounds, all the smells, all the colours, all the horrors of prison.

Occasionally I heard the sound of more happy news: a tasty dinner was coming. The word "tasty" could be used for the invariable borscht: beet soup with vegetables and even cranberries (the only thing that protected us from scurvy). Or the heavy sound of the cart-shop: this diversion came by once every two weeks. They allowed me to use this unheard-of prison luxury only six months after my arrest. The sensation of unceasing hunger had finally passed. Incredible things appeared on my bedside table: white bread, sugar cubes, cookies, and even fruit drops! But the most remarkable thing was that you could borrow books from the prison library off that cart. Every eleven days from early morning I was all ears, trying to catch every sound outside my door. The book cart approached with its own special sound, unlike any other. Clutching my three books, that I had read several times now, I raced to the open *kormushka*. "Books!" I had heard the word when the cart was at my neighbour's door. I give back my three old books and in exchange they put three books on the *kormushka* counter. I can only see the hands and I wonder what are

 WHERE WE BURIED THE SUN

these hands going to pick out for me this time? My heart stops: will the books be good ones? After all, my life for the next eleven days depends on the answer to that question. At first I value the thickness of a book: as a rule the thicker ones are better because you can read them for longer. But poetry is even better. From childhood I loved to memorize and recite poetry. Here in prison my memory has become particularly acute and I can fit anything into my head without difficulty. I already know *Eugene Onegin* almost by heart.

Sometimes you would happen to get books that were at first glance completely inappropriate. For some reason the prison library held a number of issues of the journal *Mountaineering*. I had never been interested in mountaineering but, as there was no choice in the matter, I began reading and soon was captivated by the interesting adventures, ascents and descents, the conquering of large and small peaks. I clambered up with the mountain climbers, all of us tethered together by a single rope, depending on each other. I hung over an abyss, clutching onto barely visible ledges in the mountainside. I would hold my breath, the adventure around me seeming more real than my cell. Several times I got my hands on copies of literary almanacs and loved such reading; I particularly remember these books. In general, the library was limited and pitiful. Later I was "lucky enough" to compare this library of the Lefortovo Military Prison with that of the "most refined" prison, the Lubyanka. *They* had things to read! But more about that later. For the time being any books brought a certain indescribable happiness to this, my first solitary cell.

There is never enough light in the cell for reading: in the daytime there is the feeble sunlight; at night, the electric light. But this is no hindrance for young eyes. Just as I had learned to stretch my ration of bread across the entire day, now I savour my books, stopping in the middle, going back to the beginning, reciting sections by heart—anything to keep from reaching the last page. But even when I do reach that point, all is not lost; sometimes there is a commentary (I had never noticed these sections before), which I now think most respectable and informative, and the book is not finished yet. When this final boundary is crossed, you can open the book once more. Usually there would be five or six days left before they brought the new books around, and I would begin reading a second time, and even occasionally a third.

I amused myself with games. For instance, I made as many words as possible from the letters of a single word. I created intricate designs out of folded candy wrappers. In the summer, flies would sometimes make their way in through the open window. That was a joyful adventure! I became an inquisitive naturalist and investigated every movement of the insect before I watched my prisoner fly free. Indeed, I think I would have even welcomed a bed bug into my solitary cell.

For several months one of the distractions that helped me get by was "correspondence by knocking" on the wall with the neighbouring cell. Unfortunately, I was ill-prepared for prison life having never learned the Morse code. How I regretted that omission! My neighbour, though, didn't seem to have learned it either. So she and I had to invent our own personal code. At first I wanted her simply to answer my knock with one of her own. Huddled far back on my cot, so that my back was up against the wall and masked by my coat, I softly knocked with my knuckles, holding my hand behind my back. Breathless, I waited for her reply, but it didn't come. Over the course of that first week I repeated my plea several times, but in vain. I was about to accept my failure when I suddenly heard a knock on the opposite wall. Waiting until the *nadzorka* let the peephole cover back down and the sound of her steps faded down the corridor, I went over to the wall and gave an answering knock. A knock came back in reply.

I confess this was my first genuine feeling of joy for a long time: someone on the other side of the wall wanted to be friends! But how to do it? I couldn't just move the cot against the wall, I needed a plausible reason. I thought and thought and finally came up with an idea. I called for the "boss" and complained that I couldn't sleep properly on my right side, that I was used to sleeping on my left. (In actual fact, it was the other way around and it was most uncomfortable retraining myself. I began to have palpitations and would wake up from nightmares.) But, strangely enough, he agreed to my request and transferred the cot to the opposite wall. I did not immediately begin a systematic "correspondence by knocking." So as not to arouse suspicion, for several days I simply knocked in answer to my neighbour. I walked and walked around the cell, thinking up some sort of method for transmitting my words. But no matter how much I tried, I could only come up with the simplest cipher. Its essence was that each letter in the alphabet corresponded to an increasingly larger number of knocks: a = 1, b = 2, c = 3 and so on, until finally z = 26. It was a clumsy system and easy to lose count. But, surprisingly, my neighbour caught on right away and we very quickly became proficient in relaying our little dialogues. If one of us made a mistake, we would knock twice and begin again. Of course you can't say very much by means of such a system and, as you waited for the noise of an approaching *nadzorka*, the knocking was often interrupted. All the same, it was absorbing occupation: to conduct a conversation with an invisible person just like yourself, not an enemy like the other, "visible" ones.

I liked my invisible neighbour from the start, and from the beginning of the day was impatient for each "meeting." I found out her first name and surname (for some reason I can't now recall her first name). Her surname was Nelidova. She had a little child "outside" and was terribly worried about him. We described our appearance to each other. After I knocked about myself—tall, dark wavy hair in braids, straight nose, grey eyes, black eyebrows—she replied "Oh, but you are a beauty!" It was quite funny, but I was flattered. Once I felt extremely depressed and I knocked a single word, "Anguish." In reply, Nelidova attempted to calm me and while I "listened" to her kind, tender words I felt a bit better.

But our contact was brief. One day the door unexpectedly opened and a furious sergeant, the one who was senior on the floor came in. He was the only one who had the right of entry.

"Why are you knocking on the wall? Don't you know that it is forbidden in prison?"

I mumbled something in reply and he departed with the words, "The interrogator will be informed of this."

That very night I was summoned to the interrogator, at that time Colonel Shilovsky.

"So, you've decided to break the rules. Trying to make contact with your people?" His tone was unthreatening and I tried to justify myself by speaking of to the oppressive loneliness.

"We should put you in the punishment cell for this. However, since it's the first time, I've forgiven you. I think that it had better not happen again. I have another prisoner and she's fresher fruit than you. A regular Fanny Kaplan.[24] Her last name is Ulanovskaya. She's been in the punishment cell several times already and we've had to put her in a strait-jacket."

He was clearly warning me about what would happen if I disobeyed. Later I found out that many insults fell to the lot of this Maya Ulanovskaya, but then, she would never be a dutiful sheep, as I was. I don't know what would have happened later. Perhaps the thirst to communicate would have been stronger than the fear of punishment and I might have begun to knock once more. But the next morning they moved my cot back to the other side of the cell. Nelidova banged out a desperate farewell with two blows of her fist against the wall. Obviously she had had some "troubles" too, as she never knocked on the wall again. And no path through the camps ever led me to her in the future. I would never forget the sound of her weak knock on the wall, that illusion of conversation. For those precious minutes my endless, oppressive solitude disappeared; there was someone close and dear with the same troubles. I would often remember the saying, "Company in distress makes trouble less." I dreamed of the labour camps as a sort of salvation. At least there would be other people there, no matter what else! Later I discovered that the members of our group weren't all in solitary. There were various reasons: in some cases stool-pigeons were placed with prisoners they wanted to find out more from; others had hallucinations and were given companions to protect their sanity; and in still other cases it was simply compassion on the part of the interrogators. It was difficult to determine what impelled our warders to behave as they did. Did they experience any feelings of compassion towards us? After all, most of us were still youngsters, between sixteen and nineteen years of age. They certainly couldn't not understand the purity of our motives. The machine which had trapped us held them in its iron grasp too, demanding its norms of behaviour.

Of the entire five years of my incarceration, the most terrible months were the fifteen I spent in solitary. Time passes most slowly and oppressively in the evening. The window begins to darken and turn into a black square. The dim electric light and the brown-green walls give the small space an oppressive atmosphere. That familiar sensation of fear creeps back: if they don't call me to the interrogator during the day, then for sure it will be at night. I attempt to read, but the book cannot distract me from my heavy thoughts. Now and then I catch my eyes roaming in vain across the lines on the page, even turning the pages, but I recall nothing of what I have just read. That feeling of absurdity returns: how could I have possibly ended up in here?! Another, entirely different fate had been waiting for me! The life that surrounded me had seemed safe and solid. This is an impossible accident, a delusion. Now I will just shake my head, cry out, jump up, and the whole terrible dream will be over!

Not for the first time during these months I overcome by a storm of fury. I can barely restrain a shriek, I bite my fingers. A single thought pounds painfully in my brain: accident, mistake, foolish coincidence. Had I turned at the next corner, refused to meet him, not said just that one word, then it would all have been fine, as it had been before. I would be with others, simple Soviet citizens, and be just like them, like all of them, in their millions! Was I already so different from the rest? In complete desperation I rush about the cell, six paces to the door, six to the window. Like a pendulum, from corner to corner, until my head begins to spin. How much time has passed? Soon it will be "lights out" and time to forget for awhile in sleep. Perhaps there will be no night-time interrogation, and they will let me sleep straight through. I listen carefully to the prison silence.

At that time of night, life has shut down in the prison. You hear no slam of a door, or squeak of a lock, no one is taken to interrogation. The guards shuffle evenly along the corridor. Sometimes I can tell that it's a man, and not one of the usual *nadzorki* (and that breaks their own rules). In this case, using the pan in the corner is pure torture: the corner where I squat is as clearly visible as anything else in the cell.

But now the light switch on the other side of the door turns on and off twice; the bulb on the ceiling goes out and then lights up again. This is the long awaited "lights out": now I can lie down and sleep. I force myself to wash up. I mechanically repeat the customary ritual: turn the mug handle towards the door, check that the spoon is visible, hang up socks and towel on the end of the bed. It would be better to give up this existence completely, even to die would be easier. But the notion arises simply because it must, it is allowed for in the rules. I, however, desperately want to live and hope never deserts me. Somehow, all will turn out.

I curl up under the cold, prickly blanket, my feet almost at my chin, arms hugging my shoulders. But nothing helps and I grow numb from the cold. A final trick: I suck in the air from outside the blanket and exhale under it. At that moment the *nadzorka* catches sight of me breaking the rules. Her voice roars out through the *kormushka*, "Hands on top of the blanket!" I hate her dull voice, I hate her! I flush with a wave of offence and hate. I work my hands free from the blanket and lie staring at the ceiling. If only there were some respite from that light! The naked, dull bulb in its wire enclosure now seems unbearably bright. My gaze skitters across the ceiling; each irregularity, each crack is loathsomely familiar. I could construct a topographical map of the cell, its walls, ceiling, and doors. Many years later I was astounded at the description of the prison cell in Nabokov's novel *Invitation to a Beheading*. Although he had never seen the inside of a prison cell, he saw every detail with my eyes. Even the bulb in its wire casing, just like Nabokov's, was off-kilter and called forth my irritation simply because of its asymmetry which the eye could never avoid seeing.

A strange mask always watched me out of the corner of the room above the covered radiator. One day, out of a bulge in the wall, it formed itself. And now I only have to glance at the spot and I lock eyes with it. Thanks to the deep shadows, the face seems alive. The corner of the mouth is twisted in a mean grimace. It is frightening to see this face, and I shut my eyes. And so another day is behind me, an endless prison day. But I am one day closer to freedom.

7

I Meet Abakumov

The day began normally. I had slept the previous two nights during the hours allotted by the prison regime: from lights out to wake-up. My interrogator had forgotten about me, calling me neither by day nor by night. I hope that I can pass this day, too, without any tribulations. How pleasant it is to know for at least one day in advance what is waiting for you. I'm not even in command of my very next minute. My desire is quite modest: to pass this day within the strict framework of the rules, alone with myself, with my thoughts, and my books. I would even call such a day a happy one. Happy for the prisoner. Instead of that general knowledge a person has of what he will be doing for at least one day, I feel like a pitiful puppet on a string: tug, and they've pulled me out of my home; tug, and they lead me away somewhere; and yet another tug on the string and I'll turn up somewhere far far away from Moscow. Now, nothing depends on my own volition, my own exertions, or my own desire. I am completely deprived of choice and it is very difficult to come to terms with this! In my thoughts I return again and again to these catastrophic changes in my life and my thoughts torture me, exhaust me. I have to dream about something, somehow run away from the cell. Who could keep me from it?

But today my journey "beyond the prison walls" has not come about; an uncertain disquiet disturbs my peace. For some reason they have cancelled my walk. Probably it's due to the severe cold; it rushes in when they briefly open the window. The day seems particularly long without this distraction. Now and then from outside the door I hear the flapping of the little flags they use to control prison traffic. The little flags flap like distant shots. Added to the sound is the clanking of locks as cells are opened and closed, someone being led out, someone being led back in. Ordinary prison business. Now and again it seems that the heavy steps of the guard hesitate at my door. I listen, tense, but no, this time they pass by. They haven't come for me, they've come for someone else.

Finally the long-awaited sound of the cart carrying lunch. Noon has passed and the next twelve hours will pass as well. The beet soup —borscht—is tasty and cheers me up. The disquiet that had been eating at me disappears and I immerse myself in a familiar activity: "sorting" through the *kasha*. It is difficult to make up a full spoon of clean millet. Half of the portion is inedible rubbish. My work over the *kasha* had distracted me so much that the sound of the key turning in the lock came completely out of the blue: I had heard neither footsteps nor the quiet conversation on the other side of the door. Lunch interrupted, I had missed my chance to have a quiet day. Now I was even glad that the sword of Damocles had fallen: it is better so, rather than waiting for it to descend.

According to the rules, I had to stand up in front of the soldier coming into my cell. "Your surname, first name, patronymic?" is the usual question the convoy asks. The young fellow, a corporal, looks at me with indifference. I try to remember if he had taken me to my interrogator before. It is difficult to say. All the men on the convoy look alike: piglet-pink country faces showing not a shadow of a thought. Each one a choice, A-1 cut, thickset and short.

"Get ready with your coat!"

That is something new. They are going to take me somewhere outside the prison. I would prefer to go to my interrogator; unpleasant but at least familiar. Again there is that uncertainty that foretells nothing good. I put on my coat and walk out of the cell. Our trip down the stairs and corridors ends at a door that is exactly like the door of my cell. The lock rattles and I step into a tiny cell no bigger than a wardrobe. It is a "waiting box"; I had been in one just after I was arrested. I sit down on the bench right in front of the door. Fear has already begun its familiar work: somewhere in the vicinity of my stomach, or maybe in my heart, everything cramps up and my knees shake. I clench my teeth to stop them from chattering. Take me quickly, quickly, anywhere you like, just don't keep me waiting here! An hour passes like this, or maybe it just seems that time has stopped. An eye stares at me, blinks, inspects me for a long time; I lower my head.

Finally the door opens. "Surname, first name, patronymic? Move on!" I am taken into the courtyard. A vehicle is waiting in front of the door: a black van. Because of the winter dusk, I can make out nothing around me nor is there any time. The rear door of the van is open. I scramble up the steps and find myself in a tiny cage. A metal bench, metal walls, and instead of the eye-hole, a grill. The cage door slams shut. I hear them putting other people into neighbouring cages. Sharp commands on the other side of the wall: "Forward! Keep moving! No talking!" The outside door bangs as they lock it, and the van sets off.

I have never been in such a tight, pitch-dark place before! The thin walls of the van lets in all the sounds of the street: horns, the ringing of the trams, the noise of the wheels, even people's voices are audible. We drive along Moscow's streets, normal life all around us, people passing by with no suspicion of who is inside the van. At that point I didn't know that I was in one of the infamous "black ravens." The "raven" wasn't always black; sometimes it was painted in cheerful colours with the inscription "Bread" or "Meat." With such camouflage it would drive around and through the city, distributing its unusual cargo.

The street noise irritated an old wound in my soul—it was all I could do to keep back the tears. Then the vehicle turned suddenly and stopped. The passengers are led out in turn. It is already dark outside. Again I end up in a box, no different from the earlier one. And again there is a long wait. When they finally released me from the box, my legs gave way from exhaustion.

This time two convoys lead me, one in front, one behind. We go up in an elevator. We get out and a bright electric light hits my eyes. Everything here is unusually smart: the wide corridor is laid with a carpet and there are tall doors on either side. Well-dressed women appear and then disappear behind these doors. For the first time in a long while I see people out of military uniform. Where am I? In some special prison?

"Stand with your face to the wall!" one of the convoys commands. We have stopped near a door covered in a particular style. I stand with my nose to the wall, neither dead nor alive! At just such a moment, a friend of mine had made an interesting discovery, which she later told me about in the camps. Having been commanded to put her face to the wall, she suddenly saw before her the "wall newspaper"[24] of the Ministry of State Security (at which point she worked out where she was). There in the lower section of the paper was the usual "Corner of Satire and Humour." Pictured at a table was an interrogator who was gazing up at the ceiling in supplication. His thoughts hovered overhead: "Dear Lord, send me a horrible crime!! If you don't send me one, I'll make one up myself!" Like all normal people, even the workers at this office had a sense of humour. My friend was shaken by this joke: her own case had been completely fabricated. I did not get to see such a newspaper.

I was at a loss: where had they brought me? The convoy went

through the door, obviously to announce my arrival. The door swung open and I was ordered to enter. I walked into a large reception room. There were chairs along the walls and behind desks, two women at typewriters. The next door opened in front of me. I stopped on the threshold in surprise: I had never before seen such an enormous office. In the middle was a long meeting table polished to a high shine. In the far away distance stood a massive desk, toward which I was led and then made to sit down at a little table beside it. Right in front of me over the desk hung an enormous portrait of Stalin in the uniform of a generalissimo. It had been such a long time since I had seen that wise and kind face. Consumed with inspecting the portrait, I did not at first notice the appearance of two men. One was in a military tunic. He was heavy and large with a fair head of hair. The other was tall, well-proportioned, with silver-grey hair. For some reason, it was the latter man who attracted my attention. His suit sat elegantly on him, and his face was that of a member of the intelligentsia, something I had not seen for such a long time. But he was not the chief figure in the room. Behind the desk a corpulent military man made himself at home. There were three large stars on his epaulets: a general, then. For some time he shuffled papers on the desk, moved objects around, in just the same way as my interrogator had. Then he raised his eyes and carefully inspected me for several seconds. Finally, breaking the oppressive silence, he asked:

"Your surname is Reyf? Who are your parents?" His voice was soft and sounded tired.

"Yes," I answered. "My father works in the Ministry of Special Construction and Installation Works and my mother is a housewife."

"Did your parents know about the existence of this anti-Soviet organization?"

"No, I never spoke to them about it." I had repeated that phrase many a time at all my interrogations.

The important general was obviously just asking questions *pro forma*, and wasn't interested in my answers. After all, my interrogators had asked the very same questions and everything was written down in the records of my interrogations. There was a pause, after which the general asked the following question in quite a different, almost playful tone:

"And who was making out with whom in your organization?"

As it turned out in the investigation, romantic relations were not an insignificant factor in the decision of several of the girls to join the organization. The interrogators relished this theme with a particular satisfaction, attempting to portray us as amoral people. No little taunting fell to my lot.

Is this to begin all over again? I knew none of the members of the organization except for Gurevich and Melnikov. I liked Zhenya Gurevich. And the investigators knew all about this "important fact," I thought. Why is he asking me again? There was another pause, and I fearfully awaited his next question. Unexpectedly, the general stood up and the convoy appeared at the door.

"You may leave," the general said indifferently. The audience was finished.

On the way back to prison my thoughts were busy with the mysterious grey-haired observer of my conversation with the general. He hadn't spoken a single word. Who was he then? The general held no interest for me: he was from the same lot as all my other interrogators, convoys, and guards. But who was he, this one with the face of a member of the intelligentsia?

At my next interrogation, I was told that I had been paid the honour of having a conversation with Abakumov himself, the Minister of State Security.[26] This information didn't have any particular effect on me: I already had figured out that we were of interest to those at the very top!

I couldn't imagine, as I left the office of that omnipotent minister, his hands neatly crossed behind his back, that in just a few months, in July of 1951, he would come to share my fate—the hangman and his victims would be sitting in the same prison. Abakumov would endure the punishment cell and beatings, and be shot together with his assistants.

Never, either before or after this strange incident, did I have the opportunity to meet with the Soviet rulers. From the time of my childhood my mother had cautioned me to steer clear of those in power. The experience of many years had shown that, once they had reached the heights and exercised the longed-for authority of power, they themselves would slide down into the abyss, where all such people ended up sooner or later. This scenario was played out so often it became a rule.

8

Beria and I[27]

My interrogator was in a rage, running around the large office and pumping himself full of anger. His puffy face, covered in ginger freckles, had turned red and a blue vein stood out on his forehead. I was afraid he might have a stroke right there. But appearances did not reflect the internal reality of Colonel Shilovsky. This was just one of his tricks, well rehearsed and acted out many a time. Once he'd heated himself up to such a degree, he ran up to my little desk and banged his fist on it.

"Get up! Stop denying it! It is all well known to us, anyway," he shouted. In the corners of his twisted mouth saliva glistened. Though repulsed, I don't have the strength to turn away: his angry reddened eyes are glued to my face. I stand obediently in anticipation of the conclusion of this familiar scene.

I'm no longer interested in what he is shouting about: the interrogation has lasted over a year, and one and the questions are repeated night after night. The interrogations are more often than not held at night. At first I was surprised at this, but then I understood that this was itself a form of torture and had a long history. Things were more terrifying at night, more inescapable—at night it was easier to break a person's will. Psychologists had learned at what time it was necessary to wake someone up in order to more severely traumatize him. Around twelve at night a sharp voice through the *kormushka* brought the consciousness that had just fallen into a deep sleep back to life: "Get ready for the interrogator!"

For several seconds I can't work out where I am. I am sitting stunned on my cot. All my strength is consumed by an unsuccessful attempt to check the shivering of my body. Sometimes, waiting for the convoy, I sit so long that I begin to fall asleep. The noise begins again but this time the door opens and the convoy comes in.

"Glasses?" he asks. They routinely took glasses away from the prisoners during the night. Half-awake, I answer automatically, "Yes" and he goes out after them. He returned swearing, "Why are you trying to fool me?" I don't have the slightest idea what he is going on about.

"Get out of the cell! Hands in back!"

I don't really need the orders: I do it all automatically by now, I am used to it, and in fact it makes it easier to walk. We walk along narrow metallic corridors. The endless rows of crude iron doors with inset peepholes stretch along the walls. Someone's life is rotting behind each door. A *nadzorka* moves unhurriedly along the soft carpet from one door to the next. She wears boots, a tunic, a beret on her head, and a grey pancake instead of a face. One door after another, she goes up to the peephole and for a few seconds inspects her ward. What is she thinking during those seconds, what does she feel? The satisfaction of a job well done, probably, displaces all her other feelings. But perhaps even this is going too far. Simply put, they are paid well for working in the prisons, more than in other places. There are special rations, privileges—*that* is the secret of their psychology.

But now I am of no interest to the *nadzorka*, it is the convoy who has responsibility for me. Her indifferent gaze slides over me and passes on. I move past her. My cell is on the fifth floor. Far below, at the bottom of the stairwell, the traffic regulator waves the little flags sharply—the way is clear.

"Keep moving!" my convoy commands. "To the right! Stop! Turn your face to the wall!" Again the little flags crack and fingers snap: someone is being led this way. Traffic regulations work wonderfully: in fifteen months in the Lefortovo Prison I have never met another prisoner. At first I looked forward to such a meeting, if only for a moment to see someone familiar to me. Then I ceased hoping: the machine worked flawlessly.

We take another turn and descend further and further. Which interrogator am I going to meet tonight? They hadn't called for me for a whole month. Perhaps something has happened, maybe the investigation is finished and now I am to sign the indictment. Then only the trial will be left and the most terrifying part will be behind me. They will send me to a camp for three years or so, five at the most. For some reason I imagined that these were the most appropriate terms for a just punishment, for me in particular. But something horrible and unexpected was awaiting me.

We are in the interrogation section of the prison: soft carpets, doors covered in black leatherette. Silence. Behind each door a file, large or small, is being fabricated. No one will leave these walls without a pile of violations, each more terrible than the next. Everything is arranged beforehand: they arrest you, therefore you are guilty. "If there's a defendant, we'll find a crime," Soviet guardians of the law joke gaily.

With growing anxiety I notice that my "snapper" (that's what I called the convoys who always announced their approach with the snapping of fingers) and I have wandered into an unfamiliar corridor. Everything here is more solid: the carpets, the doors, and their coverings. I recall my journey to Abakumov; it was all very smart there too. Has someone else high up got it into his mind to become acquainted with me?

"Stand with your face to the wall!" the convoy shouts, interrupting my thoughts. He opens the door and announces my arrival, then orders me to enter. The door silently closes behind me. I look around the large office; the others had all been narrow and long. Even the desk here is different, on two pedestals, not at all like the "school desk" at which Lieutenant-Colonel Yevdokimov scribbled down the minutes of our interrogation.

A stout man in military uniform speaks, not bothering to look at me: "Come here and sit down." I sit down at my accustomed place (it is the same in all the offices, from that of a minister right down to the petty interrogator), a rickety little table with a hard chair beside it. We sit across from each other, silent. Each of us is occupied with our own affairs. I am busy trying to stop shaking and bring my breathing under control; the military man is writing something, head down, shuffling through the papers on his desk. I have become quite used to being ignored at first during an interrogation. The interrogator is immersed in complicated work; he really doesn't have any time for you, you aren't at all important to him. The case is clear anyway. Interrogation, the compilation of records: a tiresome *pro forma*. In time I could see more clearly the line of action all these people followed. They are related not only by their uniform—the language they use for communication, the demagoguery that passes for profound thought, the expression of the eyes—but even the features of their faces, even their heights are alike; about average, not too tall, not too short. My previous interrogator would say nothing during our night-time meetings except something like, "Come here and sit down" or "Take the prisoner away." It was torture by sleep deprivation. There are no explanations, all is submission to instructions. There wasn't the slightest necessity to carry on our interrogations. We had already revealed everything, even that which we had only seen in our dreams. Night after night there were interrogations or wordless meetings. We would return to our cells at dawn. Worn out, I would collapse on my cot, and three hours later the *kormushka* would rattle, a voice shouting "Up!" As I had no other person to talk to except my drunken interrogator, I strangely came to connect with my interrogator. And now we were severed forever—I would never again meet with Lieutenant-Colonel Yevdokimov.

There is a new interrogator sitting in front of me now. I have time to look him over: red-haired, an inexpressive face with washed out features. And then I notice his epaulets: three big stars, so he must be a colonel. All the others I had met before had been lower ranking. What does it mean for me, that this one has a higher rank? I try to figure it out and think that maybe he is a prosecutor or lawyer. Then I notice that those reddish eyes are carefully inspecting me. The military man gets up and slowly comes over to my desk.

"My name is Shilovsky and I am your new interrogator." His manner of fixing his eyes on mine is unpleasant and I squirm under his gaze. "Up to now you have behaved badly, lying at every point, trying to hide the most important details of your crime. When will you come to your senses? After all, we know everything about you, and a lot more than any member of your group knows. Therefore, your stubbornness is useless." The words flow, one after another, the same accusations made by all the other interrogators. I am no longer listening to his tedious voice. I am inspecting him more closely now. He is old, with dandruff, repulsive yellow eyes, tiger-like, and the hands of a butcher, with short fat fingers.

But suddenly I catch new words: "Your terrorist organization... Bandits!... Murderers!" No one had said anything like this before. I pricked up my ears to hear a new melody in this old, and, it seemed, already finished symphony. The interrogator's voice grew louder, he was obviously winding himself up tighter and tighter, and ended with the shout: "Enough playing at sheep! Confess: when and how did you intend to murder a member of the government?"

At first I didn't understand what he was talking about. It is probably just another manoeuvre to break my morale. But the interrogator continued shouting. He rushed headlong towards the desk, grabbed a sheet of paper and rushed back, demanding that I sketch out the floor plan of Beria's house.

Only now did I begin to understand that they were going to indict us under a new article of law. The previous ones I had understood: anti-Soviet agitation and organization. Now they were going to add something horrible, and I didn't know what it was called. On that piece of paper I sketched out Kachalov Street, where I had lived my entire life. Formerly Malaya Nikitskaya, Kachalov Street leads from the Nikitskie Vorota to Uprising Square, formerly Kudrinsky Square. This peaceful, quiet street in old Moscow, where practically every building is connected in some way to history, to some famous name. Near the Nikitskie Vorota stands that dilapidated church where Pushkin was married, always behind a scaffold. Along the streets there are a number of beautiful old mansions, some of which are now embassies. At the very end of the street, near the Garden Ring Road, stands a mysterious mansion, perpetually under guard by sombre men in civilian clothes. This is Beria's house. It would be pointed out to acquaintances as one of the "sights" on the street. Many residents of neighbouring buildings would see the minister leaving his automobile at the door of the house. My father, home for dinner, would often announce: "Today we are eating along with Lavrentii Pavlovich. I just caught sight of him driving up to his house." This was his joke, suggesting we were having lunch at the same time as God!

Beria always drove in a convoy of three automobiles ("God travelled in five automobiles," the poet Boris Slutsky later wrote of Stalin [no relation to Boris Slutsky, the member of our group—A. T.]). Sometimes he changed from one to another, so that it would be more difficult to work out which car he was riding in, or the first and the last cars guarded the middle one in which Beria rode. People feared this house, and a shiver would run up your spine when you passed the faceless plainclothes agents who stared coldly at passers-by.

I remember the story of what happened to the famous pianist Arnold Kaplan. One day he was walking home from kindergarten with his son. Just as they reached Beria's house a heavy rain began to fall. Taking shelter, they pressed close to the walls of the house under an awning. Suddenly a window opened overhead and out of it appeared the head of Beria himself. In a soft voice he proposed to Kaplan that he bring his son into the entryway to wait out the rain. At this point the five-year-old ruffian shouted at the all-powerful minister, using a phrase common to a child in kindergarten, "Go away, or I'll pound you in the muzzle!" The horrified father took his son in his arms and ran off down the street to the Nikitskie Vorota, all the while expecting to be followed. This tragi-comic incident is characteristic. Everyone feared the chastizing hands of the "organs," no matter what they were called—Cheka, NKVD, MGB, KGB. You are guilty of nothing, but it makes no difference—someone there will decide whether you are to be free or behind bars, return home or disappear forever. There was practically no family where someone had not yet suffered or was awaiting his turn. My own family was no exception: my uncle, my mother's sister's husband, had already been incarcerated for three years. By some miracle he got off so easy. He was lucky—they put him in during the "soft years." His imprisonment was carefully hidden from me. And indeed I knew very little about what was going on around me. But fear was carried in the air and, passing by Beria's house, I would unconsciously turn aside, not wishing to look at that terrible place, trying to get past it as quickly as possible.

And now the order: "Draw the floor plan of Beria's house!" I draw the street, a little square for the house—more than that I did not know. The interrogator stood over me. Again the shriek: "Get up! You are a terrorist! Don't pretend. Draw the entrance, the exit, all the details! When were you planning to kill the minister?" His blaring mouth is down at the level of my face: "You are all dirty terrorists! Your accomplices have already confessed!"

Tears flow from my eyes. His shouting terrifies me. Perhaps someone did want to kill Beria but I had no such thoughts. The interrogator turned away and slowly walked to his desk the scene has been performed and is over. He pressed a knob and spoke, "Convoy, take the prisoner away!"

It is a long route back from the interrogation section to the prison. As I approach my cell the convoy passes me on from hand to hand, literally. It is a procedure to which it is impossible to become accustomed, even though it is repeated day after day. Before allowing me into the cell, the *nadzorka* gropes me from head to toe. Those repulsive hands slide over my body, rooting in my braids, stroking my breasts, thighs, legs.

"Hands up!" My underarms are next. "Take off your shoes!" My felt boots are shaken out. Nothing is omitted. It is strange that they don't strip me naked. And what can I have taken from the interrogator's? It is primarily another degradation, rather than a precaution. How many degradations have I suffered so far? The whole of prison life is an unbroken degradation. They have cut all the buttons off my clothes and there is nothing to clip my stockings to. My own underclothes have been taken away and I have to wear the coarse soldier's ones, including the longjohns.

The inspection is finished and I am finally in my cell. I can't get to sleep for a long time. I have never been through such an interrogation. So, our organization turns out to be a terrorist group. I believed it immediately, after all I knew nothing about the organization's activities. I had buried one passing conversation with Zhenya at the bottom of my memory, in the hope that he wouldn't remember it either. What had my accomplices managed to do, then? One thing was clear: the investigation was not yet over and, apparently, had passed on to an entirely new stage. I was fearful of the coming interrogations. The mere fact that we were "neighbours" to Beria had brought me misfortune. What on earth had made us move to a building on the same street with him?! It was true that we had moved into our building long before Beria had settled in his residence. Could this shrieking colonel honestly believe that I had any terrorist intentions?

But my fears were unfounded—Beria's name was never mentioned again in any of the succeeding interrogations. Skipping forward a bit, I can add that when I returned home five years later, I saw no trace of our former wicked neighbour. His house stood deserted and decrepit, the windows covered over with shades. To our delight, there was one less "sight" on historic Kachalov Street, formerly Malaya Nikitskaya. Not long after the old house was renovated and we waited with curiousity to see who would occupy this "honourable" residence. But it seemed that no one was eager to move in. Soon there appeared on the door a sign with the words: "Shelter for Vietnamese Orphans." Passers-by laughed—the house was repenting for the sins of its previous master.

+ + + + +

I will conclude this chapter with a story which doesn't, strictly speaking, have any direct connection with my incarceration in prison. It unfolded not far from that ill-starred house, and was an echo of my arrest. The details I found out, of course, much later.

In my prison cell I often thought of the black seals left on the doors of two of the three rooms of our apartment, and imagined that each member of the family must constantly stumble at the sight of those dark circles, left as if on purpose by the State Security to remind them they were being watched.

What happens to the freedom of the family of someone arrested? Ostracism, the loss of the social circle, being conscious of the fear of those who had recently been friends, of neighbours who are afraid to cast a glance at you or exchange pleasantries. To that could be added the constant fear for one's job: they might not get rid of you right away, but they'll get rid of you later or exile you to some god-forsaken place. The thought of the situation in which my family found themselves never left my mind for a moment. Knowing that my family had to huddle together in what looked like a furniture storage room, poisoned my spirit even further. But fate turned out to be kind to my relatives, and that was a rarity in those days. And what happened in regard to the apartment could even be labelled as one of those "ordinary miracles." It all began this way:

One ordinary November day, when the investigation was in full swing, two men in civilian clothes appeared at our apartment, along with the superindendent of the building. They went up to the doors of the sealed rooms, tugged at the door handles, and convinced that everything was in order, tore off the waxen seals. They opened the doors and briefly glanced into the rooms, then locked them anew and left, explaining nothing but passing the key to the superintendent.

Mother, who during all the years of my absence had taken the task of petitions and inquiries with government officials onto her own shoulders, tried to make her way into the offices on Kuznetsky Most, but received no rational explanation of what was going on. It was only gradually, in crumbs of information, that she finally pieced together the true state of affairs of what had happened at the apartment. It was a "deal" that was unusual even for those years: a deal between two exalted organizations—the MGB and the housing division of the Supreme Soviet of the USSR, who had the management responsibility for our building.

It turned out that the housing division, not bothering to wait for the end of the investigation, had petitioned the MGB to transfer back to the Supreme Soviet those two rooms which had been taken away upon my arrest. Apparently, they were going to offer our family a vacant one-room apartment while our three-room apartment (at that time three rooms was beyond the dreams of most people) would go to one of their employees.

Of course, this threatened change in residence was not so terrible in comparison with the sudden tragedy of my arrest. But, nonetheless, you mustn't forget that the "housing question" was one of the most painful subjects for Muscovites, as the unforgettable Woland mentions in Mikhail Bulgakov's novel *The Master and Margarita*.[28]

One of our acquaintances advised my mother to find a "common language" with the manager of our building and, as a way to his heart, take him a roasted goose. Inexperienced and helpless in such matters, my mother took this wise advice, but in the process grew so stressful that afterwards she had to take Valerian in order to calm herself. The manager, of course, accepted the goose and, in a most neighbourly way, expressed his sympathy for our grief. But, as he told my mother, more responsible agents were already involved in the case and very little, alas, depended on him.

And then a daring idea came from one of our closest friends: go to court. To court? Against whom? The Supreme Soviet? A suit brought by the family of an enemy of the people, albeit one not yet convicted? (At that time, that last detail really didn't carry any practical weight.) The very thought of bringing a suit made a person's blood run cold. But it was decided that the risk was worth taking, all the more so because an experienced jurist who specialized in housing questions, a well-known Moscow lawyer, agreed to take on the case.

The first round of this astounding confrontation in the people's court of Moscow's Sovietsky region went to my parents! I do not know, nor will I ever discover, the feelings that struggled in the soul of Judge Flyagin, who brought down the decision in favour of this disgraced and dangerous family. What hesitations and doubts he must have passed through—and certainly he knew, he could not but know, how fraught such a verdict would be for him—but in our family memory the name of this man remains as a symbol of personal courage, and indeed of simple human decency, which can be preserved in even the darkest hours of lawlessness and arbitrary actions. That Flyagin was no exception was proved to my family shortly thereafter, as the epic of the apartment rooms was not, alas, yet finished.

Not willing to accept its defeat, the all-powerful agency made an appeal in the Moscow municipal court. There was no doubt as to the agency's ultimate success: in the municipal court sat its own reliable people who were always ready to hand down an appropriate verdict.

And so, in the third week or so of December (it was 1951) the new judicial sitting took place, called to decide the fate of our unfortunate apartment. From the very first moments the judge behaved so aggressively that it was clear that he was working hard to earn his bread. After he had once again rudely interrupted our lawyer, the latter whispered desperately to my mother: "I'm afraid that they won't even allow the case to be looked at again, but will immediately bring down the verdict they want."

Everything was moving in that direction. The pushy plaintiffs were to learn a practical lesson they deserved: who was who in our socialist state and who had been granted rights therein. No one, apparently, noticed the young woman in uniform sitting behind the low wooden barrier off to the side, by the wall, who had so far done nothing to call attention to herself. Only when the presiding judge, having finished his speech, was about to go off into the conference room with the assessors, did the woman rise.

I have no idea what happy wind had sent her day into that particular sitting of the Moscow municipal court. Avilova turned out to be the supervisor of public prosecutions. Her job was to follow the procedural norms in judicial proceedings and, on her own responsibility, visit selected sessions. Thus, the woman rose. The presiding judge glanced around in astonishment and looked at his watch with annoyance. It was as obvious as God's green earth that the case needed no commentary by any procurator, as far as he was concerned. Even less did he expect a rebuff from her side. So her brief angry speech resounded all the more unexpectedly in the otherwise silent room.

Yes, indeed, the case was clear, she announced. But what was clear was that legality had been crudely subverted. The arrested woman had not had her own separate living space but had lived in the apartment with her family and, therefore, there was no judicial basis for depriving the family of the rooms. Having said this, she quietly returned to her seat and the court was adjourned for a recess.

The recess lasted a very long this time. Through the tightly closed doors the high-toned voices spilled into the hall. It was clear that the judge was applying desperate measures to break the uncooperative members of the jury.[29]

Taking advantage of the pause, my mother went up to thank her unexpected defender. "Don't worry," Avilova comforted her. "Everything will be in order now. Only, it's so pitiful about that poor young girl."

Many years have passed since then, but even now a lump catches in my throat when I think of those words, so casually dropped in the courtroom. But it was not only the procurator who showed herself to be an irreproachably decent human being. The jury members, whom we knew nothing about, demonstrated no less courage. This became clear when finally the doors swung open and the members of the municipal court sat down. The judge was red in the face and angry. He wouldn't take his eyes from the sheet of paper before him, and read out the text of the agreed statement with what seemed to be great difficulty. Both Mother and our lawyer sat breathless, unable to believe their unexpected good fortune.

In a week our large building, with its one hundred and fifty apartments, was preparing to meet the New Year. That evening bright lights suddenly shone out of the two tightly curtained windows of our apartment that faced into the courtyard. The building gasped.

"What, has Alla returned?" neighbours asked my parents in a whisper. But they only received a sad shake of the head in reply. "So what's happened?" But it wasn't appropriate then to share such news. Poor Mother and Father could only answer with enigmatic smiles.

9

The Investigation Ends

The second winter of my incarceration passed slowly. Less and less often did the interrogator send for me and I became used to being alone. The routine of the day was as regular as a clock, its uniformity and monotony comforting but made one dull. The emotional ache which had tormented my first months of imprisonment moved somewhere deep inside and hid itself away. I understood that the threads of my fate were being woven somewhere up there, in enormous offices behind tightly closed doors. As I expected nothing good, I didn't particular wish for the time to hurry.

On my walks, when it grew dark, I inspected the illuminated windows of the prison with interest. They all shone out differently, some with a dull yellowish light, others bright and white. In several cells I imagined additional lamps were shining, maybe even desk lamps. What sort of people were sitting behind those barred windows? Why were they here? I had heard, before I came here, that many prisoners in the Soviet prisons were innocent. Of course, there are guilty ones here, I thought, but no one could have committed such a heinous crime as we did. The sensation of guilt bore down on me constantly. It was the same, I discovered later, with almost all of the members of our group. The sense of guilt began immediately upon arrest and remained during the entire investigation period, right up to the passing of the sentence. I don't think that our interrogators had any intention to re-educate us, but during the hours of our interrogations—day in and day out communicating only with them—we eventually fell under their spell. If I had been free, their dogmatic, clichéd pronouncements would have had no effect on me whatsoever, probably. But here, oppressed by solitude, tormented by feelings of guilt towards those closest to me, I was pliant as clay. My confidence in the rightness of our thoughts and intentions quickly disappeared.

"How could you lift your hand against the Motherland, who raised and educated you?" my first interrogator, Yevdokimov, exclaimed emotionally.

"Where did you see injustice? The fact that people live badly? But this is after such a terrible, terrible war! The country has yet to recover. I'm sick of you snotty revolutionaries!" he concluded. Yevdokimov undertook such conversations only after he'd had something to drink. At times like these he looked sad. His owl-like eyes gazed at me with pity. Once, in an excess of emotion, he caressed my head and said, fervently, "If it were my decision, I'd give a yank to your braids and send you home!" Apparently this escaped inadvertently, because he was under the influence. He never again expressed himself in such a dangerous and embarrassing way. In the summer Yevdokimov sometimes opened the window wide for me and I could see in the distance green streets, trams, people in summer clothing. My heart stood still at the sight of that life which was carrying on without me outside the prison walls. I believe that he did this not to entertain me, but to further torment my soul.

Actually, he's right, I thought to myself. How could I have committed such a crime? It was all gibberish: there were no desecrations of Lenin's legacy that my friends talked about, not a one. And Stalin has well earned the adoration of the nation; in fact it is only due to his wisdom that we defeated the Fascists and that I am alive on this earth—Hitler would have destroyed me, too, along with all the Jews. How could I dare to doubt! Repentance burned within me. It was completely sincere, but I never attempted to demonstrate it before the interrogator. In the cell I would cry as I read Fadeev's novel *The Young Guard*: these were genuine heroes who had given their lives for the Motherland, and I had betrayed her![30] Even more I was tormented by the idea of my guilt towards my family: what would happen with them?

Many of us found ourselves in just such a state of penitence, and so it was not surprising that the interrogators extracted all the information they needed out of us. With deep sincerity we told our most secret thoughts, the ones which no one knew about. We spoke of intimate conversations with various persons, disclosed family secrets, and so on and so forth. Silence in solitary was exchanged in the interrogator's office for a torrent of words. It was like confession. The interrogators were delighted: they could have only dreamed of such an easy and successful case! It was unimportant that these "terrible" criminals, these "anti-Soviet degenerates" were only sixteen to nineteen years old. Nothing looked as naïve on paper as it sounded coming out of our mouths. The wording in our statements sounded sinister! Under the pen of the interrogator our hesitations, doubts, the idealistic motivations that explained our actions, were all transformed into a cold recitation of evil crimes. In the notes that the interrogators made I often could not recognize my answers to his questions. It is difficult to believe now, but once I jibbed a bit at signing the transcription of our interrogation, so badly did it reflect what I had said. I signed it anyway, out of pity for the drunken man.

I watched him run to his superiors for approval with each piece of paper; he would often redo it all and show them again. It didn't seem that important to me, whether the transcript reflected my exact words or the formula of their bureaucratic language (which indeed changed the sense of the words).

Once I refused for a long time to sign the day's record of interrogation. We had spoken of my attitude towards the glorification of Stalin. My objections were simplistic ones: Lenin didn't approve of the glorification of anyone, no matter whom; glorification looked like toadying; genuine communists were ascetics and modest, and so forth. Of course, I didn't believe for a minute that Stalin himself found such behaviour pleasant. It was encouraged against his will by careerists and sycophants. I spoke heatedly, my indignation about the glorification of even a great leader like Stalin was absolutely genuine. These thoughts were my own, inspired by no other person. Yevdokimov listened to me for a long time and didn't interrupt. Then he sat down at his desk and began to write. When he put the finished transcript, written in a large, childish script, in front of me, I saw with surprise that not one of my words was there on the page. In the place of my long monologue was the short phrase: "I slandered a member of the government." I rebelled and asked him to note what my "slander" had been, how hard it had been expressed. But Yevdokimov declared that he could not possibly repeat such criminal words. No matter how I tried to demonstrate that there was absolutely no slander in anything that I had said, he wouldn't budge. Worn down by this hopeless argument, I signed this transcript as well.

Judging by how good-naturedly Yevdokimov behaved towards me, he was, in the ordinary sense of the word, a good man. Simple, not highly educated, he carried out his duty with ardour. He would have been a conscientious accounts clerk on a collective farm, but fate had made him a screw in a diabolical machine: a human mincing machine. Yevdokimov bore his cross humbly, downing a couple of slugs of vodka a day for inspiration. His work was difficult, day in day out, night after night extracting the necessary evidence, rewriting transcripts ten or more times, trying to satisfy his superiors. He was only one of tens of thousands like him, of average height, with an unmemorable face. This picture of the only person with whom I spoke, with whom I spent such long hours both day and night should be deeply engraved in my memory! Nonetheless, not only now but very soon after the investigation was concluded I could barely recall his face. He was a typical representative of that circle— I would almost say of that class which was regarded with such honour in the romantic years of the Revolution. The Chekist with a clean conscience! But honour and glory (mostly invented) had long been exchanged for gloomy mystery. Only one element remained unchanged: danger! A terrible, deadly fate hung over all those who belonged to that class of tormentors. With rare exceptions, sooner or later a higher justice would rule against all of them.

Meanwhile, the daily routine continued and there was a great deal of work in it. It was not without reason that my sympathetic guard had said, "See what a large prison it is? And every little bit of it is full!" My next visit to Yevdokimov turned out to be my last, but I hadn't the least suspicion. It had seemed to me for a long time that he had already extracted from me all that was possible to extract and we had nothing more to talk about. He had found out absolutely everything about my relatives and friends—that each and every one was an honest Soviet citizen, a fiery patriot, and that I had never heard anyone drop the slightest critical word. I don't think that the investigator believed me, but he wrote it all down as I told him. He performed his huge "research" work in connection with the personal address books belonging to my parents and myself. He was interested in every name we'd jotted down, and not just as they were related to my case, but in connection with their own affairs.

"Why have you hidden the fact that your family friend Olender was abroad?" the investigator asked. I hadn't hidden the fact at all —I simply didn't know it. Many of his questions were curious: "Which of you works at the circus? Who works at *gastronom* number one?"

"None of us, of course! We wrote down the numbers so we could find out about tickets, or order groceries."

My answers satisfied him: he was interested in every telephone number only out of duty. Our address books were thick ones, the numbers accumulated over many years, and the poor investigator spent a huge amount of time checking them out. But a job is a job, and he performed his thoroughly.

However, I've found some truth in the saying "Even a wise man stumbles." In this police state, where a detailed dossier has been compiled on every citizen, a secret can still somehow be kept. Our family had a terrible secret—my father's sister lived abroad. At the beginning of the revolution she and her husband crossed over the border at the Dniester River and settled in Romania. There was practically no contact with her. But we had kept up a sporadic correspondence before the war and Auntie Vera had come to visit us in Moscow once as a tourist. I remember her only vaguely. But she brought with her such a mass of remarkable things, presenting them to all her relatives, that we were forever after surrounded by things like table cloths, coats, and hats that we called "Vera's": "I'm going to wear Vera's blouse," we'd say, or "Take Vera's suitcase" or "Put Vera's salt cellar on the table."

Every honest Soviet citizen is obliged to report "to the appropriate place" any meeting with a foreigner, and Father's cousin did so after meeting Auntie Vera. For his exercise of civic duty he was punished and many unpleasant things happened to him. My father said nothing to anyone—and what a miracle!—he was never asked about the visit. In all those official forms where he had to answer the question, "Are there any relatives abroad?" he would write the word "No" with a slightly trembling hand and he would get away with it. And of course they investigated him for security clearance many times: in his post as a manager of the planning division of the central directorate he had access to some classified material.

At my interrogation I panicked, thinking that this family secret might be discovered. If they didn't incarcerate my father because of me then they would certainly imprison him for concealing links with abroad. During those first interrogations I waited with horror for them to ask me about my aunt. But time passed and no one asked me anything about her. Over time I relaxed and realized that sometimes something will slip past that "all-seeing eye." On the other hand, I was greviously tormented by the investigator who let me know that my father had confessed that he had raised his daughter in an anti-Soviet environment. I didn't give in to the provocation and dully repeated one and the same thing: my parents were genuine Soviet people. To be simply "Soviet people" wasn't enough; they had to be "genuine Soviet people." What was meant by this? Loyalty to the system, submissiveness, consent? Everyone interpreted it their own way. When our organization began it seemed to us that we were "the most genuine"—indeed, it had to be that way! To struggle against the existing regime was to be true to communist ideas. The investigation wasn't interested in our sincere views or aspirations; interrogators had to picture us as enemies and everything was subordinate to that.

When the question of terror arose, I cannot say. At any rate, I never mentioned my conversations with Zhenya Gurevich on that subject. I had always considered those conversations to be silly and childish. It was only after I met the new "boss," Colonel Shilovsky, that I understood that the terrorist inclinations of Zhenya and others were known to the investigation. After several difficult interrogations in which he learned nothing of benefit from me, Shilovsky backed off.

From the KGB Archives:

Record of the Interrogation
with the prisoner Reyf, Alla Yevgenyevna
held on 2 November 1951
Reyf, A. Y., born 1931, native of the city of Kiev, Jewess, citizen of the USSR, member of the Young Communist League. Until arrest student at the correspondence division of the Lenin State Pedagogical Institute
Interrogation began at 22:30

QUESTION: *At your arrest, a handwritten document was confiscated which begin with the words "Minutes No. 1 of the OC" and, as has been established by experts, was written by you personally. Do you recall the contents of those "minutes"?*

ANSWER: "Minutes No. 1" were written by me at an anti-Soviet meeting which took place at my apartment on Kachalov Street in the second half of November in 1950. Participants at the meeting, besides myself, were GUREVICH and MELNIKOV.

I cannot guarantee that I can reproduce the exact contents of the "Minutes" but I will tell you what I do remember.

The "Minutes" established the basic questions that had been discussed at the meeting and which had received unanimous approval: the naming of our organization, the affirmation of the so-called "theses," the allocation of responsibilities which we were each to take on in the newly founded organization, the approval of the motion to make a hectograph and compose an anti-Soviet pamphlet with the title "State Capitalism."

Our surnames were replaced in the "Minutes" by pseudonyms: mine was KIRSANOVA, GUREVICH was VOINOV, MELNIKOV was TULIN.

QUESTION: *What was the ultimate objective of your organization?*

ANSWER: GUREVICH did not tell me directly about this. However, even before my membership in the organization he had expressed the thought to me that a war loomed of the capitalist countries against the USSR, in which the Soviet Union allegedly ought to suffer defeat.

Besides that, GUREVICH, slandering Soviet reality, announced as well that in the future there would occur, as he put it, an uprising against the Soviet government.

All these fragmentary, hostile expressions by GUREVICH pointed to the idea that as a result, the existing government structure of the USSR will be changed and that we ought to assist that change with our subversive activities.

QUESTION: *You have not been fully forthcoming about your own subversive activities and have been silent about your methods of struggle, such as the use of terror against the leaders of the Party and the Soviet government.*

Will you now, finally, be open with this investigation?

ANSWER: I have always spoken openly and truthfully to the investigation about our crimes. I know nothing about the terrorist methods of our struggle.

QUESTION: *You are a member of a Jewish nationalistic organization. Why have you said nothing about this?*

ANSWER: I did not know that the USCR organization, or that SORK were Jewish nationalistic organizations.

QUESTION: *What is the ethnic origin of your accomplices?*

ANSWER: MELNIKOV, GUREVICH, and SLUTSKY, whom I knew as members of the anti-Soviet organization, are Jewish in ethnic origin. What the ethnic origins of other members of the organization were, I do not know.

QUESTION: *Did you and your accomplices have any nationalistic views?*

ANSWER: GUREVICH never mentioned any concrete facts to support that. I personally have no nationalistic views at all.

QUESTION: *At your arrest a verse of a nationalistic tendency was confiscated. Who was the author of this verse?*

ANSWER: The verse that was confiscated indeed had a nationalistic content. I copied this verse from a manuscript which passed from hand to hand in school. To whom the verse belonged I don't remember as three or four years have passed since then, and I do not know who the author was.

QUESTION: *Thus, you preserved this nationalistic poem for three to four years?*

ANSWER: Yes.

QUESTION: *And distributed it among your acquaintances?*

ANSWER: No, I never gave the verse in question to anyone else to read.

QUESTION: *But you preserved this screed because it corresponded to your own views?*

ANSWER: I kept the verse only because I considered its contents an expression of protest against anti-Semitism. I only understood that it in fact is nationalistic at the investigation.

The interrogation finished at 2:00 on 3.XI.51

Interrogator: Senior Investigator of the

Special Branch on Important Affairs of the

MGB of the USSR, Colonel (Shilovsky)

A little while later Shilovsky set up face-to-face confrontations between myself, Vladik Melnikov, and Zhenya Gurevich. They both seemed to have changed terribly. I was so agitated during those brief meetings that I could hardly remember anything. Usually during interrogations there was no one present except for the interrogator. Sometimes, one of his colleagues would pop in to make idle conversation. This day, however, a young woman was sitting in his office, not far from him. She didn't raise her head when I was led in. I sat at my usual rickety little table in the corner of the office.

"Now you will have a face-to-face confrontation with your accomplice Gurevich. The procedure is that you are to say nothing extraneous—answer only my questions. Do you understand?"

I nodded and froze. They would be leading Zhenya in. We hadn't seen each other for many months. Our last meeting had been in another life. What would he look like? Shaven, of course. And how did I look? I thought that I had aged horribly, and had lost all my attractiveness. The convoy entered and announced the arrival of the prisoner.

"Bring him in!" Shilovsky said.

They brought Zhenya into the room. He seemed even smaller than before; to look at him, you might only give him sixteen years, no more. He was short and puny by nature, now he looked like a child. Only his eyes remained familiar in his yellowish, pinched face. We greeted each other with a nod of the head and he sat down in a chair which was placed in the middle of the room. What happened after than I can't recall. What questions were asked, what we answered—my mind is an absolute blank. Probably nothing serious happened during the confrontation; the investigation was coming to an end and all the questions had already been asked. This was simply a *pro forma* exercise. Face-to-face confrontations were in the regulations, and they had to be carried out for the sake of the file. I exchanged a few glances with Zhenya. A guilty smile was frozen on his face. We said nothing extra to each other, and in fact there was nothing for us to say. After a few minutes they took him away.

The face-to-face confrontation with Vladik Melnikov was also uneventful. Only one detail struck me. Many of us had been convinced that it was a matter of honour to only speak the truth. In this regard it was irrelevant how many dozens of people might suffer for this "truth" or that it might load a further burden on our already heavy transgression. "Cleanse oneself from filth," mow down others and yourself at the knees. I, of course, cannot answer for the motives behind each person's behaviour, but the majority behaved in this manner, in accord with our "Young Communist League" consciences. The Soviet leaven was too deeply kneaded into us, we had been too well brainwashed to hold out for long with our critical doubts of the justice of the regime. At any rate, prison had stupified us in a horrible way.

I well remember my surprise and offence at our confrontation when Vladik Melnikov categorically denied my assertion that I had copied out on my own initiative the "manifesto" which Zhenya had composed (but it had happened that way, I wanted it as a keepsake). Vladik, in a metallic-sounding voice, asserted that I had copied it by authority of the organization. It turned out that our fate did not hinge on such details—they were of no significance. But at that moment I was terribly upset as he had made me look like a liar. My comrade had unthinkingly aggravated my guilt. In the name of what? Such behaviour was quite typical of many of us.

Almost all the members of our group somehow or other implicated their families, as well as many friends and acquaintances. Thus a list of some two hundred implicated people was added to the already many volumes of our case. I remember the number well as it had struck me so forcefully. Some of these people were arrested and convicted, while others were exiled; most continued their lives, unsuspecting that a file with their name had been opened and was being filled with surveillance reports.

Just before New Year 1952, my visits to the investigator ceased entirely. For some time I would wait each day and night for the next interrogation. But time passed and the *kormushka* would open only to announce the daily walk or bath, or that it was meal time. Once they brought me the decision of indictment to sign. It sounds strange, but I cannot remember what it looked like. Then, from day to day, I was taken to the office to familiarize myself with the material from the investigation. It was remarkable reading. Of course I had no idea of the grand scale of the case put together by the investigation. Over those days I leafed through thirty-two thick, dark-blue volumes. I didn't read all the records in order, passing over many of them, but gradually came to form a comprehensive picture of the case against us. (see fig 9.1)

Much later I understood what joy we had brought to the organs of State Security. Our organization wasn't much, but it was genuine! It had all the attributes of a secret society, with conspiracies, a "manifesto" and "programme," with a hectograph, and even a small, somewhat defective, but nonetheless genuine pistol. Leafing through the volumes, I read it like a detective novel: the tale of a revolutionary underground movement as told by each of the sixteen participants and copied down (albeit not quite accurately) by the interrogators. My fate turned out to be intimately linked with those of young men and women who were totally unknown to me, whose photographs at the beginning of each volume I looked at with curiousity. They all looked scared, unhappy, and completely child-like. We were snapped with numbers at our chests, *en face*, and in profile, according to all the regulations of the prison administration. Only the three "ringleaders," as the investigators called them, were afforded large-size photographs and they looked quite seemly. I immediately realized that they had wanted Stalin himself to know of the affair and, therefore, had photographed Boris Slutsky, Vladlen Furman, and Yevgeny Gurevich with such care. Perhaps it was really so; after all I had had my meeting with Minister Abakumov, and who else would want to see such "veteran" criminals—maybe only Beria? All in all it was rather unimportant; the main thing was that thanks to someone's efforts, portraits remain of these three brave men who gave their lives so young. The photographs were given to their unhappy parents after their cases were reconsidered in 1956.

I no longer remember how many days it took to read through all the volumes. Shilovsky paid me no attention. Usually he sat at his enormous desk and wrote. Sometimes he would go out, leaving the convoy in his place. The young fellow, about my own age, would remain alone with me. Not bothering to hide his curiosity, he would inspect me for a long time. His staring made me very uncomfortable. In the fifties, of course, almost all the supervisors and convoys believed that they were in the presence of actual enemies of the state and that they were performing a honourable duty in protecting the Motherland from us. I came across this naïve belief in the honesty of the regime later, in the camps where prisoners had much greater contact with the guards. Sometimes you could strike up a spirited conversation with a supervisor or convoy and they would find out, to their astonishment, that they were guarding innocent people. Then they would tell us how they had been taught to hate the prisoners, to imagine them as blood-thirsty villains. But such conversations seldom occurred; as a rule the convoy feared us and carried out all the details of their duty with care. These details were harsh and sometimes inhuman—one of them was a phrase heard by prisoners daily: "Step to the right, or step to the left, and you will be considered to be trying to escape. The convoy will shoot without warning." And they did.

My acquaintance with the file was coming to an end. I had already completed almost all of the volumes with the interrogation records of the members of our organization. All that was left, Shilovsky informed me, were the opinions of the experts on the documents they had confiscated, our handwriting, and so on. In the long evening hours before "lights out" I would walk from corner to corner in my cell, recollecting what I had read that day.

So this is what our organization was all about. I hadn't known a tenth of what had gone on in and around it.

✛   ✛   ✛   ✛   ✛

Everything began for me with an insignificant episode: my friend Galya Cherenkova introduced me to two young men. Girls and boys were then separated in different schools so that friendships with boys were rather unusual and surrounded by a romantic halo. As a result, girls seldom just struck up a friendship with boys of the same age. Such friendships soon turned into "romances." Those who had no "romances" looked on those who did with envy, awaiting their own impatiently. At first Galya kept her new friends a secret from me, until one day it turned out that they were rather bored with her and insisted that she introduce them to some of her girlfriends. It was in the fall of 1949 that I had my fateful meeting with these two tenth-graders, Vladimir Melnikov and Yevgeny Gurevich.

These short and thin boys had nothing in common with the heroes in novels that we all dreamed about. They had no idea how to court, they couldn't dance, and I—an "aristocrat" from a building where members of the Supreme Soviet lived—couldn't help thinking how provincial they seemed. I was then particularly sensitive to the fact that I was a member of the elite. It wasn't enough just to live in Moscow, you had to live in the centre of the city, in a special building, go to a school where all the students were members of intelligentsia families, and—it goes without saying—your father had to have a position no lower than in a ministry. Some standard!

My new acquaintances hardly fit these criteria so at first our friendship developed very slowly. But the boys displayed great interest, phoning almost every day and showing up at my building in the evenings. They were inseparable and acted like brothers. Soon enough, however, I noticed that their friendship was not one of equals: it was obvious that Zhenya was the leader. Bright, spirited, he was a great amateur philosopher and dreamed of going on to the Faculty of Philosophy at Moscow State University. I had only a hazy idea of what a philosopher did, besides repeating the theories of Marxism. Indeed, I had no direct knowledge of these theories myself, so that much of what my new friend talked about meant nothing to me and, therefore, was not very interesting. But Zhenya's superiority in this area was clear and, strangely, it did not drive me away but rather attracted me to him. I was especially affected by the passion with which he spoke about social problems. His radiant brown eyes would light up and his face would become inspired and masculine. He actually grew up in front of me, both literally and metaphorically. I began to await our meetings impatiently.

We roamed around the evening city, along noisy Gorky Street, and talked and talked. I noticed that our favourite themes were more and more connected to criticism of Soviet life. Everything that Zhenya told me was interesting and some of it I was hearing for the first time. It turned out, for instance, that Lenin had left a will in which he warned his associates about Stalin, whose character was already becoming clear to him. I learned about the conflict between Stalin and Lenin's widow, Krupskaya, about the staging of the trials of 1937, about the numberless camps scattered all across the nation and holding millions of inmates. Somehow I had already heard hints of these things. They were there in the air and there was a certain intangible dissatisfaction, a secret fear. But this was the first time, I think, that I heard an ordered account of accusations against the authorities and regime. We had no socialism but simply state capitalism, where all the powers rested with the party bureaucracy. The bureaucracy was constantly flouting Lenin's legacy and the interests of the people. Lenin's name never left Zhenya's lips. His faith in Lenin's greatness and justice was unshakeable.

It was impossible not to agree with Zhenya. You couldn't argue against the fact of beggars in trains, old-age pensioners who were half starving (and I knew such people), the festival-like fictions of the collective farms in books and on the screen, and even in my own building there was the worship of rank and hierarchy among its inhabitants; finally, the anti-Semitism which I had already felt both in school and outside. But what could you do? How could you support the truth amidst all those lies, those cheerful newspaper headlines, the songs, the glorification of the great Stalin? Zhenya, however, had a ready answer for this question too. You had to fight! How? He didn't want to talk about that yet. Bit by bit I was prepared to take a most important decision, although I didn't notice the process at all. I was won over by Zhenya's audacity and erudition. He had read Lenin, Plekhanov, Marx, and Hegel. For a start, he recommended that I read Lenin's *The State and Revolution* and Stalin's *Issues of Leninism*, in order to convince myself of what our state had been transformed into and how Stalin had distorted Lenin's ideas. I read the books and marked the pages with question marks and exclamation points (fortunately, the books were from our family library) and I experienced a certain joy when I came across segments and phrases that supported our conversations and my own meditations. Life suddenly became very exciting!

Now school work seemed to drag along. I waited anxiously to meet Zhenya and it was only when I was with him that life was interesting. It already seemed to me that I was not without feelings for him and when he asked for my photograph I had no doubt that our relationship was moving on to a new stage. Although we hardly ever met without his eternal shadow, Vladik, this didn't keep us from discussing political questions—it was just as interesting as a threesome. We would walk down the street unaware of the other pedestrians and talk with raised voices about things that it was dangerous to even think about. It never entered my mind that anyone could be listening to us. Yet for a long time already we had been under surveillance.

For some reason the boys hadn't introduced me to any of their friends, although they were very interested in my acquaintances, questioning me about their attitudes and asking who shared what opinions. I had a friend, Igor Smelyansky, who had just entered the Engineering Faculty of the university. One day he told me how he and a couple of his friends had been called by the MGB people into the Dean's office and asked to act as informants. The prospect of being a informer plunged him into despair, but it was made clear that to refuse would mean the end of his university studies. Then he came to me one day in an unusually joyful state and told me that his medical examination, thank God, had liberated him from service to the MGB, since they had discovered he had poor vision in one eye. I told Zhenya about Smelyansky and he began to press me for an introduction.

The winter passed, we graduated, and it was time to think about university entrance exams. Both Zhenya and I were aiming to continue our studies, despite the fact that it was getting more and more difficult for Jews to enter even ordinary institutes. Besides that, the competition for admission to university was about twenty for each place. Chances under those conditions, then, were quite slim, but I still decided to try my luck in the Faculty of Biology at Moscow State University, and Zhenya in the Philosophy Faculty.

Our meetings broke off for awhile and it was only at the end of August that we three began to meet again, just like old times. I hadn't made it into university, of course, and ended up in the evening division of the pedagogical institute. Zhenya hadn't made the cut either, and to his sorrow went where his marks were accepted: the Food Science Institute. Only Vladik had been victorious—he was a student at the Mendeleev Institute, which was what he had been aiming for.

Each of us began our student life and saw each other only rarely, talking mostly by telephone.

But one rainy autumn day Zhenya phoned and proposed a rendezvous. He was agitated about something. We wandered about under his umbrella and, with a chill in my heart, I heard him tell about a recently formed underground organization. Its purpose was to prepare cadres for the coming world revolution. But the revolution was a matter for the future. Now it was necessary to open people's eyes to the injustice of the present system, to undertake propaganda and agitation among the various strata of the population. I was so shocked by what he said that I didn't ask him a single question.

"And of course you will be one of us," Zhenya stated with conviction, and I didn't dare object.

The business had taken an unexpected and dangerous turn, for which I was not at all prepared. But, absorbed in the telling, Zhenya didn't notice my distraction and kept talking and talking. The outline of the organization took shape in front of me as in a fog: it was divided into groups cells which were led by contacts.

These contacts knew the leaders of the organization, but the members of the groups only communicated among themselves. Our cell was led by Zhenya, and Vladik and I were to be ordinary members. That is all, in fact, that remained in my memory from that evening.

I returned home with a heavy heart. Who could I talk to about this, to whom could I open my soul? My parents were out of the question. I had no close friends whom I could trust. I think that the person closest to me was my aunt, my mother's sister. After several days' hesitation, I decided to ask her advice. Now I am aware that I was more mature than my friends and, therefore, more cowardly. I looked at them like children who had been carried away with a game of underground revolution. I had no desire to be part of such a dangerous game. I can still recall Aunt Nadya's livid face, her pursed lips, as she repeated over and over one and the same thing: "Break immediately with these lunatics!"

I was inclined to agree with her. My conversation with my aunt strengthened my conviction. But how to do it? How could I explain my sudden change? After all, I agreed with all their opinions. So, I would have to confess to being a coward and it was oh so difficult to do that. Our meetings continued, and more and more my doubts were confirmed. For a time, I was struck by Zhenya's frenzy, his desperate readiness to take the wildest steps and all contrary to common sense. Some way or another he had to convince the world that not all was well in the state of Denmark and to do so required that he do something out of the ordinary. Blowing up the subway, for instance.

"Do it at five in the morning, when the working class is leaving home, before the subway trains have begun to run, with an explosion in one of the downtown stations. There will be a panic, they'll find out about the blast, rumours will circulate, they'll find out abroad." Zhenya drew the picture so vividly that I felt a chill run down my spine.

"And what about victims?" I asked in despair.

"There should hardly be any; after all, the explosion would take place in an empty station. But if anyone should suffer, then, well, you know that no struggle is without its victims!" Zhenya concluded, so categorically that it was impossible to argue with him.

Another time Zhenya let Vladik and me in on the secret of another of his catastrophic plans.

"It would be a good thing to assassinate one of the government leaders, Malenkov, for instance. You couldn't make it all the way to Stalin. And the people worship him so that no one would approve of the act."

I recollect that Vladik and I tried to argue with him, but it seemed to me that Zhenya himself wasn't being completely serious but was simply playing with his imagination. Much of what he had to say prompted objections from me. For instance, in order to punish a villain one should be prepared—in the interest of one's goal—to make any sacrifice. Another idea was that in order to create fully fledged members of the communist society, children should be taken away from their parents and raised in special boarding schools. Something familiar and ominous resonated in these opinions, but I didn't try to argue with him, feeling that I didn't have the energy to change his mind. Once, at my place, Zhenya announced that he was intending to call a meeting. Every position would be filled—chair, secretary, the masses—and all by just the three of us. He acquainted us with the "program" of the organization and its "manifesto." I got the impression at that point that he had composed both documents himself. I don't remember much of what they said, but both the "program" and the "manifesto," in rather strange ways, reminded me of the stages in the Bolshevik Party that we had studied as history in school. The organization was to be called the Union of Struggle for the Cause of the Revolution or USCR. I obediently took the minutes of the meeting, although in my heart I protested against this formality which Zhenya was so insistent about. It was all like a game, a dangerous game and I assured myself that this would be our last time together.

Once, not long before this meeting, walking with him through the city, I asked Zhenya if he didn't think that he might pay for his activities with his life. His answer astounded me: "I know that I will perish. But if this brings about something of value, I have no quarrel with death." The words were pronounced with such conviction and simultaneously with such a feeling of being doomed that my heart almost broke.

Did Zhenya foresee his fate, or were these just the words a genuine underground revolutionary was expected to utter? Now, when we know the tragic end to his short life, which was indeed sacrificed for these lofty ideals, the question is irrelevant. Paradoxically, it was the state that gave him these ideals—the same soulless monster against which he thirsted to fight. Heroes like Zhenya knew of no other struggle and were prepared to repeat the same path that so many others had taken to its only possible conclusion—a totalitarian state. The same ideas, the same methods, and the same tragic result. But like blind horses these children went round and round within the limits of that enchanted circle which their fathers had drawn for them long before.

In the fifties, when the country was suffering from a new wave of repression—when there was no chink in the wall to link them to the free world through which other notions, other ideas might filter through—perhaps only this form of resistance was possible. Later, in the camps, I met a number of young people who had been members of underground groups and organizations. And almost all of them were supporters of the ideas upon which the Soviet state had once been formed. It was only within these limits that they thirsted for justice, and Marx and Lenin remained their indestructible gods.

I prayed to such gods, too! And still I had yet to bring myself to explain my feelings and make a break with these young conspirators. Paying due honour to their bravery, I decided to keep copies of the "program" and "manifesto" as a souvenir of our friendship. I would give Zhenya the originals back at our farewell. I carefully copied them into a notebook and hid it in my "archives" which already held the verses about anti-Semitism I had copied down, a couple of political jokes, and so forth. But our final meeting never took place.

It was examination time at the institute. I was very busy and had little time to think about my friends. If they don't show any signs of life, all the better! Everything that was connected with them had somehow disappeared, as though it had never been. Each day I went to the institute, returned home, and never noticed that I was being followed and that in the next doorway someone was always on observation duty. In January, Zhenya and Vladik were arrested, but they let me "walk out" my student holidays. On the seventh of February 1951, they came for me at last.

+— +— +— +— +—

The fascinating reading was coming to an end. There were more than thirty volumes of these dark-blue document cases for our file. Now I was acquainted, if only by reading, with all the members of the organization. The membership was all of a kind: quite young, from families of the intelligentsia, almost all them Jews except for two girls. I saw distinguishing characteristics only in one area: the parents of several of the young men had been "repressed." This surprised me greatly as Zhenya had said time and again that the organization should not enlist any people with a personal animus against the Soviet regime. It turned out that of sixteen of them, five had parents who had been arrested.

The last several volumes of the investigative material held all the physical evidence regarding the criminal activity of the organization, including photographs from the expert examination of the small pistol which Melnikov (I believe) had kept from the war—what young kid would not be thrilled to possess a real weapon? The judicial experts declared that if the pistol had been fixed it could have inflicted a fatal shot at three paces. I remember this statement quite well.

I finally reached the end of the last volume, number thirty-two, I think. I signed the paper affirming that I was familiar with all the material of the case. One more stage behind me. I believed that the worst that was behind me. Again I settled into my cell without being called to the investigator. How long would we have to wait for the trial? It was already my second winter spent in solitary. You would think that you wouldn't notice the passing of the seasons in prison, but that isn't so: winter is both colder and darker, and therefore, more depressing. Again and again I went over through all that I had read: I had the feeling that I had learned the story of something that had nothing to do with me. These young people were strangers, the events unknown to me. The name they assigned the organization during the investigation sounded cumbersome, unlikely, and terrifying: "The Jewish Anti-Soviet Youth Terrorist Organization." It fell under the following sections of the fifty-eighth article of the Criminal Code: 1-a, 11, 10, and 8—treason against the Motherland, organization, anti-Soviet agitation, and terror. Moreover, the eighth article referred to terrorist acts that had been carried out. I hadn't the slightest idea what sort of punishment awaited us under such a terrible indictment. There was no question that they would give us varying lengths for our sentences—each of us was guilty in a different way. I thought that they would probably sentence me for a shorter time, since I had done nothing and had spoken little, mostly just listened. Not like the others, who had recruited new members or indoctrinated their friends, and even printed documents on the homemade hectograph (a description of the machine was appended to the evidence). In general, I figured that I would receive from three to five years in the camps. What the maximum period of punishment might be, I didn't know. Now the only thing to do was to wait for the finale of our epic, the trial.

10

The Trial

Not expecting them to warn me beforehand (a year's experience in the prison had taught me something!), I awaited the trial daily. I would fall asleep in both fear and hope that it would take place the next day, and awake in the certainty that it would be today! Up to noon I would listen in fearful anticipation to all the steps approaching my cell outside the door. After the mid-day meal I would relax—it wasn't to be today. Only in the second half of the day could I read, distracting myself from the constant worry that had worn me out completely. I noticed that there were slight changes in the daily rations, as they began to feed us somewhat better. A tiny piece of meat might appear in the dinner meal. In general, however, in the slow course of time nothing else changed. Practically no daylight entered the cell: the grey morning square of the window began to darken early and soon turned black. Walks provided no enjoyment: I couldn't warm up even in my cell so I often had to decline going out into the cold (the single exercise of the prisoner's will that the prison allowed). I began to mix up not only the days of the week but the months as well: was it still January, or already February?

But you can't avoid what is destined to be and the tortured waiting finally came to an end.

"Get ready for the trial!" a voice bellowed and the *kormushka* snapped shut with a crash. My heart stopped and my legs turned to mush.

What "get ready" meant wasn't at all clear. I didn't have any things to collect, nor papers to gather up. Obviously, I was supposed to "gather up" myself, which I nervously got down to. The main thing was to look presentable—after all, I was going to see my "stranger-friends" as well as Zhenya and Vladik. With a damp palm I carefully straightened my dress. How it had not fallen apart right on my body over the past year I couldn't work out. One explanation was that the dress had come from my grandmother's pre-revolutionary wardrobe. I waxed my shoes with butter and polished them till they shone. Then I brushed out my hair and braided it. I could only use the tin mug with its coffee slops to see myself. Everything was ready. The door opened and the convoy stood on the threshold. "Last name, first name, patronymic? Forward!" I walked out of the cell. Where would they take me? As we were going without our coats the trial would apparently be held in the same building. The usual route along the prison corridors. Not a soul about, the only sound to be heard was the finger-snapping of the convoy and the whisk of the little communication flags.

The convoy stopped me in front of a wide door and swung it open. I entered an enormous room furnished with rows of chairs. There were no people in the room except for two girls sitting against the back wall. The convoy led me to the last row and showed me a seat next to the girls. We greeted each other, but the convoy immediately warned us that it was forbidden to speak to each other. The girls turned out to be Tamara Rabinovich and Galya Smirnova. We inspected each other with interest until they led in the next girl, Ida Vinnikova. She sat down next to me, the fourth one in our row. One after another arrived and were seated. These were my "criminal case-companions" or *odnodeltsy* (the term was one that I had learned during the investigation and forever after described in my mind the connection I had with the members of our group). I recognized each of them by the photographs I had seen, but they all looked much better than I had expected in comparison with the horrible prison pictures. They seemed rather nice to me, my comrades in misfortune who hardly looked like underground fighters.

Despite being forbidden to speak, we exchanged a few words: there was a low rumble in the room from all the muffled voices. The shouting of the officer didn't help, as he tried to maintain some order. The convoys arranged themselves along the walls and stared with curiosity at the strange gathering. We were overcome with a nervous excitement, a kind of euphoria. We had almost all been in solitary and our meeting now seemed like the end of the incarceration. The large room, the rows of chairs, the young faces of our contemporaries—it was all just like a Komsomol meeting. They would now elect a presidium, announce the meeting's agenda, and you didn't have to listen any further, just play a game of "battleship." For some reason we kept wanting to laugh, and could hardly hold it in, but laughter indeed broke out now and then. What were we laughing at? I can no longer remember. Unfortunately, my memory has not retained the details of the trial, only some separate bright impressions remain. I vaguely recall the appearance of the three military judges in the court: a general and two colonels. I can't recall their faces, and it seems that I didn't hear their voices during the course of the trial. I was not surprised that there was neither counsel nor prosecutor; I didn't even think about it. We were guilty, therefore everything that was going on regarding us was legal. The three military men resembled the three fat men from Yuri Olesha's tale of the same name: rather fat, rather pink, and—it seemed—peaceable. Their role these days was secondary: the primary role belonged to us. But in actual fact, in this sinister play—where the roles had been carefully doled out—everyone except us were performers who knew the ending of the play.

As for us, we did not act—we were existing in the midst of a well-rehearsed spectacle. We had come to this room for confession, and we did confess to each other. The main thing, I think, was that we had to come to an understanding ourselves, out loud. Everything had been mulled over already, whether in solitary thought in our cells or even shared with our interrogators. But that wasn't it. Now each one of us had the opportunity to explain—and thus understand—how we had turned up in the prisoner's dock. I cannot speak for the others, but then (as now) I was convinced that the majority of us spoke with absolute sincerity. They did not interrupt us, and each of us spoke as long as he or she wished. Sometimes the story was short and forgettable. Sometimes it was tortuously long, with convoluted explanations that the speaker couldn't fight his way out of. There were many funny details connected with our youthfulness, with the desire to equate our group's activities with the romantic, by now almost canonical revolutionary process.

In her story, Susanna Pechuro recounted how she told her friends about secret caches of arms which turned out to be nothing more than a hidden drawer in a desk where a letter opener lay. She fantasized that the group had hundreds of members and, in corroboration of her words, recited Mayakovsky's verse, *There are Millions of Us*. And now, blushing and particularly attractive, she read this poem to us all, half turning towards the judges. Purity of intention was obvious in every story. Practically no one spoke of terror. It was clear that not one of us had thought about anything that serious, except for Zhenya, and he was supported by no one.

Feliks Voin was a tragic case. You could tell by the way he was so grumpy and refused to speak to anyone. He wore felt boots— *valenki*—and grey-coloured clothing and sat bent over with his head down. And although we were familiar with his story from the records of the investigation, it still was not easy to listen to this young man's confession.

His parents had been repressed and he had experienced all the bitterness of alienation. Feliks became acquainted with Furman in the provincial city of Ryazan, where they were both studying in the medical institute. Vladlen Furman suggested that Feliks become a member of the organization and Voin agreed joyfully. He told his girlfriend, whom he trusted, that he had joined the organization. Another student had listened in on their conversations, and she had then threatened to denounce them if Voin didn't do it himself. He was in complete despair but there was no other way out, he had to go to the KGB. There they proposed that he remain in the organization and report about whatever went on there. Tormented by his conscience, Feliks continued to associate with Furman, said nothing to the KGB, but still felt himself to be a traitor. When they arrested the whole group they brought in Voin as well, indicting him along with the others. The enforced role of informer oppressed him and he obviously felt that all the rest were now judging him. It wasn't like that, of course. Everyone rather felt compassion towards him, but it was impossible in the circumstances to express it openly.

Maya Ulanovskaya's story made a particular impression on me. The investigator we had in common had told me of her obstinacy, and I imagined her quite differently. Now before me stood a sweet, large-eyed girl with a kind, white smile on a swarthy face. We sat near each other and managed to exchange a few words. Maya seemed to be just like the rest of us. But this impression evaporated as soon as it was her turn to tell her story.

Maya Ulanovskaya is the only one of us so far to have published her memoirs (unfortunately, only in Russian), telling about herself and our activities. Maya was one of five members of our group who were fated from earliest childhood to be marked out, numbered among the "lepers" from whom friends turned away, neighbours avoided, and schoolmates whispered about. There were many like her and they were special: children of "enemies of the people," children of the repressed. When I listened to Maya at the trial I was filled with horror and pain. What was she saying? Didn't she realize she was worsening her guilt? Even now I can hear the words she threw in the faces of the omnipotent judges: "I hate you! I have never believed that my parents were enemies of the people. Even if they had done something, they did it honestly. There is no place for me outside these walls. You can send me out from here only with a muzzle!"

I seem to remember that we all held our breath, listening to those final words of hers. We were terrified for Maya. I kept imagining how much pain and insult she had had to overcome in order to think and feel that way. I wanted to comfort her, draw her near, so that she would understand that she was wrong and would repent, as we all had repented. I dreamed of ending up with Maya in the same camp. I would become like her sister, her comforter. But our paths in the camps were fated never to cross.

The stories of all the others were similar to each other in some way, all reflecting the optimistic enthusiasm of youth. We were fine students of the Soviet regime—all the demagoguery, all the ideals had been taken seriously, as they were supposed to be. But life was so unlike these ideals and that meant that the reality had to be changed, reconfigured so that everyone would be happy. Day after day we came to this large room and in turn told the stories of our short lives. But, as a result of these sixteen confessions, the picture drawn of each one's activity (and of us all together) turned out to be entirely different from what the investigators had presented. In actual fact, everything we had done pointed to the same goal— to find others who shared the same vision. And in this we were apparently most successful.

We couldn't analyze then why all of those people, with whom we carried on these so-called anti-Soviet conversations, agreed so easily with us and with apparent ardour continued to talk about the injustice that was going on, about the whole system which so poorly reflected the society that was to build communism. Unaware of the danger or, rather, understanding it only theoretically, almost all of us cast our seditious thoughts in all directions.

Irena Arginskaya went with Boris Slutsky to Leningrad to recruit new members for the organization. A mysterious young man, whom almost no one knew, travelled with them. He was older than any of us. In the course of the investigation it became clear that he had been dispatched as a provocateur: his name was not to be seen in the files, but was mentioned a number of times at the trial—Berkenblit. Irena became acquainted with him in Leningrad. She and Boris were trying to enlist a certain Ariadna Zhukova who, it seemed, had agreed to join the organization, but had changed her mind and informed the "organs." (Later she became well known as a successful literary critic.) But such a situation seldom happened: most of our contemporaries were willing, if not to fight the system, at least to criticize it. Susanna Pechuro explained why she had named so many names at her interrogations without thinking how much harm it would bring to those people: she wanted to show how widespread our opinions were among the youth. And it was indeed true that many criticized the existing order. Our organization did not rise in an empty field: a number of such groups appeared at the time. But we didn't know about that then. Against that background, our repentance appears rather strange—everyone around us agreed with us, our contemporaries and many adults for that matter thought as we did. What then were we guilty of? Of being less rational and more courageous than the others? But we didn't see any of these contradictions and continued to believe that we were criminals, even if only because the regulations of the Komsomol forbade members to establish or even join any other sort of organization. (see fig 10.1)

The last to speak were the organizers of our group—Boris Slutsky, Vladlen Furman, and Yevgeny Gurevich. I vaguely remember their speeches; their thoughts, probably, were more mature than those of the others. I well remember, however, that Boris, speaking last, turned to the rest of us sitting behind him and said in a fallen voice: "Only now do I understand what a kindergarten I have brought with me."

I recall that he told how, feeling helpless, he tried to find some support among adults. But everyone he spoke with shied away from him as if he was a leper. No one tried to dissuade him but would change the topic and turn their eyes away. Boris got the idea of making some sort of connection with a foreign embassy, but did nothing about it.

Boris Slutsky looked more mature than anyone else. He was tall, thick-set, and wore a navy-blue trench coat of military cut, and boots. For some reason I can't remember Vladlen Furman. And Zhenya looked like a little boy, like always; short, thin, wearing an unbelted *gimnastyorka*, the typical soldier's shirt. How can it be that I can recall none of the stories of these three members of the group, the last ones to speak and the brightest? Probably, we were all very tired after the long duration of the trial. I can only recall a few details from Boris' story (and it may be that I only remember them from reading the files). He recognized earlier than the rest of us the lies that surrounded him. As a child, he visited some poor village, and wrote a letter to Stalin about it, telling his beloved leader how badly the *kolkhozniki* lived. That was when they put him under surveillance. Later, his disloyalty was noted in the Palace of Pioneers[31] where he participated in a literary circle and wrote unsuitable poetry. I know nothing about his family, but apparently his father had in his youth been a fervent follower of Trotsky. His parents told him how his father's only possessions before marriage consisted of an old pair of pants and a portrait of Trotsky. This detail was considered by Boris in only one way: his father was a Trotskyite and had hidden his views. It's possible that it wasn't that way at all—Boris had known his father only slightly before he went to the front as a volunteer and was killed.

Unfortunately, I was not personally acquainted with either Boris or Vladlen, so I did not know what they were like in reality. How sincere were they when they repented at their investigations and at their trial? Later we found out that stool pigeons had been assigned to the cells where each of our three leaders were incarcerated. How this fact affected the whole course of the investigation and what methods were used to implicate these three, I do not know. During the trial I came to the conclusion that they were only different from us in their maturity.

(One can understand the following speech by Zhenya Gurevich at the trial, the way it appears in the minutes from the archives of the KGB, only by recognizing that over the course of the entire investigation, which lasted more than a year, we came to know that not a single word or criticism of the Soviet regime would be put into the minutes with the actual words which were used. Instead of our own words on the violation of laws, on state-sponsored anti-Semitism, on the deviation from Leninist principles, on the Stalin personality cult, on the violation of human rights, etc., the minutes would record such phrases as "demonstrated anti-Soviet attitude," "expressed nationalistic views," "slandered the party and the government," "took Trotskyite positions," "expressed a hostile attitude," "blackened Soviet reality," and so forth. It was a good school: we soon began to understand what we were not permitted to say by name that which was taboo. Therefore, at the trial, in each of our speeches, as in Zhenya's, a sort of internal self-censorship was at work. And it is for that reason, in fact, that Gurevich in his speech neglected to discuss the real reasons and sources of his activity. Instead of his criticism directed toward society and the governmental structure, the minutes of the speech record such self-condemning clichés as "nationalistic attitude" (a criticism of anti-Semitism), "anti-Soviet activity" (activity directed toward the re-establishment of the rule of law), "anti-Soviet illegal assembly" (a meeting of young people), "anti-Soviet organization" (an organization for the struggle for human rights). Zhenya could speak of the philistinism of his own family, about extreme materialism, about the pursuit of personal gain by party members, but he could say nothing about the omnipresent lies that surrounded us, about the profound vices of the governmental structure. This is why we find in his speech such an emphasis on anti-Semitism. In his conversations with me, Zhenya, of course, touched on this problem, but rather as a private question. At the trial, however, it turned out that the criticism of anti-Semitism (which, of course, was called "nationalistic attitudes") was really the most important point. Like all of the minutes of our case, it is necessary to read Gurevich's speech critically, attempting to discover where the words show signs of self-censorship and where they have been adjusted by the hand of the KGB censor.)

Excerpts from the testimony of the accused, GUREVICH, at the judicial sitting of the Military Collegium of the Supreme Court of the USSR, 11 February 1952

I've known MELNIKOV since 1946. Our opinions developed similarly; we differ only in that MELNIKOV was calmer, and I more impulsive. The beginnings of my anti-Soviet opinions date to 1948. The first time I was strongly affected by conversations with ZASLAVSKY and KOSNELSON, about whom I held a very high opinion. KOSNELSON wished to enter the MAI [Moscow Automobile Institute] in its specialist faculty, but at the end of the summer it was apparent that he wasn't going to be accepted. The secretary of the selection commission rudely answered him that he could not enter because the personal information on his application was "not suitable."[32] ZASLAVSKY was also denied entrance to the Medical Institute for the same reason. KOSNELSON told me some other facts about the Jewish quota in the Institute. At that time we thought that the Jewish quota was based on the policies of the Party and the government, but we had some doubts about this. In order to explain these questions that bothered us, MELNIKOV and I formed a group and began to study philosophy and Marxism.

»   »   »

In 1949 I became acquainted with SHLEMERZON, who had graduated from the Institute of Economics with honours and wanted to go on to graduate studies, but was unable to because he was a Jew. While I had the occasion to listen to many nationalistic conversations outside my family, the nationalistic tendencies of my relatives were as influential on me. I was told that there was no way a Jew could progress in the humanities. At that time, when I could not imagine myself without philosophy, or philosophy without me, this troubled me deeply.

This was the first group of facts that helped to form my anti-Soviet inclinations.

The second group was related to philistinism. This, I believe, exerted a definite effect on the formation of my anti-Soviet views. I was brought up in a philistine, petty-bourgeois family, where everyone was narrow-minded and driven by petty-bourgeois attitudes. Not one of my relatives acted like a Soviet person. All were individualists and strove only for their personal gratification. MELNIKOV and I went so far as to consider the overwhelming majority of people to be petty-bourgeois and decided that we two were the only honest citizens. I constantly argued with my parents, as they always looked upon me as a child, and always bothered about keeping me from catching cold, crossing the street at the crosswalk, and so forth. They were philistines of philistines, they had no interest in my inner life, and only worried about whether I was hungry or healthy. My father, although he was a Party member and had a higher education, often had to learn from me about the Party's history. My animosity towards my father went so far that I announced to him that I did not consider him to be a Party member, that he had only joined the Party out of the calculation of personal advantage. My father was outraged at this and for a long time we would not speak to each other. In school there were only two out of twenty-six who were not members of the Komsomol, and I considered that in order to be worthy of the name of "human" one had to know philosophy, but of all these students only Kiryushin studied philosophy and he was one of the non-members. I was very struck by this complete passivity towards philosophy. All the girls I knew were interested in literature, but alongside this they knew nothing at all about politics. This also struck me very greatly.

Furthermore, the moral level of the youth, in MELNIKOV's and my opinion, had considerably fallen, and this also bothered me greatly. We were bothered by the opening of churches; MELNIKOV and I thought that, on the one hand, there was the question of freedom of conscience but, on the other hand, we were upset by the numbers in attendance, as a significant part were young people.

SHLEMERZON had a friend, a certain NIG. Once SHLEMERZON brought this NIG to my place and asked permission that he might join us. NIG behaved so amorally that I could not restrain myself and asked him to leave the apartment. He said wild things about his plans and dealings, that he spent 1500 rubles a day. Then SHLEMERZON came and even said that everything was in order. As it was made clear later they had acquired some streptomycin somewhere and were selling it at speculation prices.

This made a very shattering impression on me. At that time I told my sister that SHLEMERZON and NIG should be denounced to the office of the public prosecutor, but my sister dissuaded me.

The single person in my family with whom I had any sort of friendly relations with was my uncle, Samuel Abramovich TOLCHINSKY. TOLCHINSKY was a person with an all-round education but had never gone to school and declared that he, too, was a philistine. I liked this in him, and considered him to be an honest man. I often had conversations of an anti-Soviet nature with TOLCHINSKY. For example, we talked about the punitive politics of 1937, about Lenin's will, and other questions.

I arrived at August 1950 carrying such "baggage." In August 1950 I attempted to enrol in Moscow State University [MGU in its Russian abbreviation] in the Faculty of Philosophy. On the 20th of July 1950, I went to MGU for a foreign-language examination and met SLUTSKY there. We decided to prepare together for our geography examination. During our following meeting, SLUTSKY and I discussed where we might go after graduating from the Faculty of Philosophy. I said that the next step was graduate studies or Party work, or pedagogical work and declared that I was intending to do graduate studies. SLUTSKY declared that he would prefer to do Party work.

This conversation took place on the road to SLUTSKY's place. At SLUTSKY's apartment we read a couple of pages of the geography textbook and then started talking about philosophy, about the struggle of antitheses. Then SLUTSKY began arguing over which was more important in life, theory or practice. Then I said that my relatives were ninety-nine per cent philistines and ninety per cent capitalist remnants. SLUTSKY told me about his relatives, and that his relatives were no different from mine, and that only his father's relatives were decent people. He told about how his father had been reprimanded for belonging to the Trotskyites, and that at the beginning of the Fatherland War[33] he had volunteered for the front and perished there.

» » »

During one of our conversations, SLUTSKY asked me if I believed that the socialism present in the USSR was true, i.e., if socialism actually existed in the USSR. I told SLUTSKY that the answer was yes, the contradictions between labour and capital in the USSR had been overcome and that, probably, socialism existed. SLUTSKY said that he doubted in the existence of socialism in the USSR and that it was for this reason that he wanted to enrol in the Faculty of Philosophy, in order to elucidate whether it was possible to establish socialism in a single country.[34] Then we began to argue about the place of ideology in socialism. I always argued about all points, simply for the sake of arguing. Then SLUTSKY told me some of the history of the Party, in particular regarding the Treaty of Brest, and showed me John Reed's book with the preface by Lenin and Krupskaya.[35]

I told MELNIKOV about my conversation with SLUTSKY. MELNIKOV became interested in SLUTSKY and said that SLUTSKY was right. Then MELNIKOV and I decided to become more friendly with SLUTSKY. We would often walk along Gogol Boulevard and argue. I came to the conclusion that SLUTSKY was right, and felt the rise of anti-Soviet views within me. We met SLUTSKY daily and he told us that FURMAN shared his views and that he and FURMAN were intending to set up an anti-Soviet organization and that it was all waiting for FURMAN's arrival. When FURMAN arrived, SLUTSKY introduced me to him and at the end of August 1950 at our first assembly we established an organizing committee for the anti-Soviet organization, in which SLUTSKY, FURMAN, and I were the members. At this illegal assembly it was decided to have SLUTSKY draw up the preparatory program, to have FURMAN prepare the question on the relationship to war, and have me prepare the manifesto and book about the state. After this illegal assembly I shared my impressions with MELNIKOV and proposed that he join the anti-Soviet organization. MELNIKOV hesitated at first, but then said he shared our point of view and promised to join the anti-Soviet organization. Thus, on the one hand, I brought MELNIKOV into the anti-Soviet organization and, on the other, SLUTSKY and FURMAN brought in PECHURO. MELNIKOV and PECHURO became members of the organizing committee of the USCR.

In October 1950 when PECHURO and I were walking to SLUTSKY's for an illegal meeting, PECHURO announced in our conversation that the members of her group were burning with a desire for action, and there was no action. During the meeting at SLUTSKY's I moved that we proceed to terrorism. SLUTSKY and PECHURO spoke against my motion and it was defeated. At the next meeting, while we were discussing the program, I again raised the issue of terrorism. Moreover, I moved the creation of a thoroughly secret terrorist group, the leadership of which I proposed to take on myself. Members of the meeting disagreed sharply with me. SLUTSKY moved that no single terrorist in history had been justified, and that we were only spoiling the whole plan by my idea.

After our first anti-Soviet meeting, as I have already mentioned, the organizing committee of the USCR started recruiting PECHURO and MELNIKOV. MELNIKOV was assigned the leadership of the technical group. SLUTSKY said that in the USCR there were already fractions or groupings, already Bolsheviks and Mensheviks, and even terrorists. MELNIKOV announced then that he had a weapon. I knew that his relatives had given MELNIKOV a revolver, which they had asked him to get rid of, and therefore I asked MELNIKOV where he had got the weapon from. MELNIKOV smiled and said that he hadn't thrown away the revolver and hadn't told me so because you don't tell kids about such things. It was in September 1950 that MELNIKOV's mother discovered the revolver and MELNIKOV proposed that I take it into my care.

At the end of August 1950, SLUTSKY, FURMAN, and I went to PECHURO's and then we all went for a stroll in Petrovsky Park. The purpose of this visit was that SLUTSKY and FURMAN were about to leave Moscow and we needed to discuss certain questions about our anti-Soviet activities and, in particular, that all the work in Moscow was to be laid on the shoulders of PECHURO and me.

I enlisted MELNIKOV, REYF, and ULANOVSKAYA into the anti-Soviet organization, but I didn't intend to stop there. In October 1950, at the next illegal meeting, we discussed SLUTSKY's program and accepted it. The meeting was a very stormy one and we almost came to blows, but it was interrupted at its height by the arrival of MELNIKOV, who brought with him a transcript of the Fourteenth Congress of the Bolshevik Party,[36] and we began reading the speeches of various oppositionists at the Congress. MELNIKOV and I concluded that the program had not been accepted and it was decided to accept it at the next regular meeting at SLUTSKY's.

On 26 November 1950 I read out my theses at our meeting and declared, after the theses were rejected, that the program of the USCR had not been approved and moved its approval.

The very first point of the program called forth bitter argument and we were forced to abandon the attempt to approve the program and proceeded to read the theses point by point. The theses, as I've already indicated, were rejected. Then SLUTSKY read out the resolution in which he noted the existence of two tendencies in the USCR—the terrorist and the theoretical. SLUTSKY was opposed to terrorism and declared that terrorism could lead us into the camp of political murderers, adventurers, and spies. The meeting was stormy to the point of chaos. At the end of the meeting it was moved that we submit to party discipline.

The next day I told SLUTSKY that MELNIKOV, REYF, and I would not submit to party discipline and that we were leaving the anti-Soviet organization USCR. I also declared that there were twenty others with us. Then, at an illegal meeting at REYF's we formalized our own organization and established our own organizing committee, which consisted of me, MELNIKOV, REYF, and—as a member of the organization—ULANOVSKAYA. We also set up three sections: theoretical, organizational, and technical. I was entrusted with the leadership of the theoretical section, preparing slanderous anti-Soviet lampoons, and other matters. The organizational, and technical sections were united into one organizational-technical section. MELNIKOV and REYF headed this section. The organization was given the name Union for the Liberation of the Working Class. We then had an argument regarding the publication of our own newspaper. We decided to publish the newspaper in twenty copies and send them in letters to the members of the organization. The newspaper was basically intended for members of the group.

During my period of activity in the anti-Soviet organization I wrote anti-Soviet documents: a "manifesto," theses "On the Tactics of the USCR," and several articles for the newspaper. I placed the "manifesto" between the pages of my student workbooks and one day my father accidentally discovered it and began to read it. Seeing this, I tore the "manifesto" out of his hands and read it to him myself, telling him that it was a text by Bukharin and explaining that I needed it for my studies. That same day MELNIKOV, at a meeting of the organizational committee, declared that I had broken the rules of secrecy. My parents also asked MELNIKOV what sort of "manifesto" I had and he had great difficulty extricating himself from the mess. When I told my parents that I had broken off friendly relations with SLUTSKY and FURMAN, my parents were relieved.

I intended to write, together with MELNIKOV, a book entitled "State Capitalism," but later we rejected the enterprise and decided to write "The State" and after that, "Thirty Years." In these books we wanted to present Party history from the Trotskyite point of view.

Finally, the whole story had been told. They even allowed us the last word! The legalities of the proceedings were honoured. What did it matter that there were no witnesses, no defence, no glasnost—we were equated with military criminals, and judged by the Military Board of the Supreme Court of the USSR. This all sounded quite terrifying, but the whole tone of the trial promised nothing particularly bad. In fact, we ourselves set the tone and, it seemed to us, the gravity of the investigation reports evaporated as we told our stories ourselves. These wise, adult generals—"uncles"—should understand the noble motives of our actions and would not punish us harshly. We were all in a heightened state, laughing a lot, exchanging comments back and forth, and paying no attention to the threats to remove us from the courtroom. Our confessions contained so much naïveté that, a mature year later, we couldn't hear about our previous conduct and statements without breaking into laughter. The year before we had still been children, and the judges must have recognized that. I watched how the convoy, standing against the wall at the back, could hardly restrain their laughter when one of us was saying something funny or naïve. It seemed to me that almost everyone's spirits were cheerful—the very worst was behind us now.

As far as I can remember, the day on which they let us speak our final words was also the day the verdict was brought in. They took us out of the auditorium for our meal and then brought us back into the courtroom. The phrase rang out for the last time: "All rise!" The judges came in looking quite serious, and remained standing in front of the table. Their faces were redder than usual, but maybe it only seemed that way to me. The chief judge began reading out the sentence. We could not believe our ears!

"Boris Slutsky, Vladlen Furman, Yevgeny Gurevich are sentenced to the highest degree of punishment—death by firing squad!"

Several seconds elapsed before I could work out the meaning of what had just been uttered. My ears suddenly felt blocked up and the voice of the man speaking seemed to come from a great distance. I could understand the rest of the sentence only with difficulty—twenty-five, ten, five—what were these numbers, years of incarceration in prison, in the camps? What did "disenfranchisement" mean? It was impossible to concentrate. My eyes were fixed on the backs of those three young men. I saw Zhenya sway. Susanna lunged at Boris, but they dragged her away. I heard the concluding words of the sentence clearly enough: "Slutsky, Furman, and Gurevich have the right to appeal for mercy." (see fig 10.2)

The general and his colonels disappeared without my noticing somehow, and the convoys almost raced to the three who had been sentenced to be shot. An unimaginable noise rose in the room, everyone was saying something to someone else and, no longer afraid of the convoys, were shouting at the three as they were taken from the room: "Friends, appeal for mercy!"

The room quickly emptied. They led me away, as always, near the end. When the door to the cell slammed shut behind me I fell down on my cot in exhaustion. A terrible lethargy overcame me. I couldn't think about what had just taken place. It was all emptiness —no fear, no pain, no feeling at all.

Министерство Государственной Безопасности
Союза ССР

УПРАВЛЕНИЕ МГБ МОСКОВСКОЙ ОБЛАСТИ

ОРДЕР № Б-15

«7» февраля 1951 г.

Выдан сотруднику отдела Управления МГБ Московской области тов. _Староверову_

производство: _Ареста-обыска_

Рейф
Аллы Евгеньевны

адресу _улица Качалова, д. 16, кв. 140_

ПРИМЕЧАНИЕ: Все должностные лица и граждане обязаны оказывать лицу, на имя которого выписан ордер, полное содействие успешного выполнения возложенных на него обязанностей.

Начальник Управления МГБ
Московской области

Начальник Отдела

рест санкционирован прокурором — Васильев.

Зак. 23

» Fig 2.1 *Order for Arrest.*

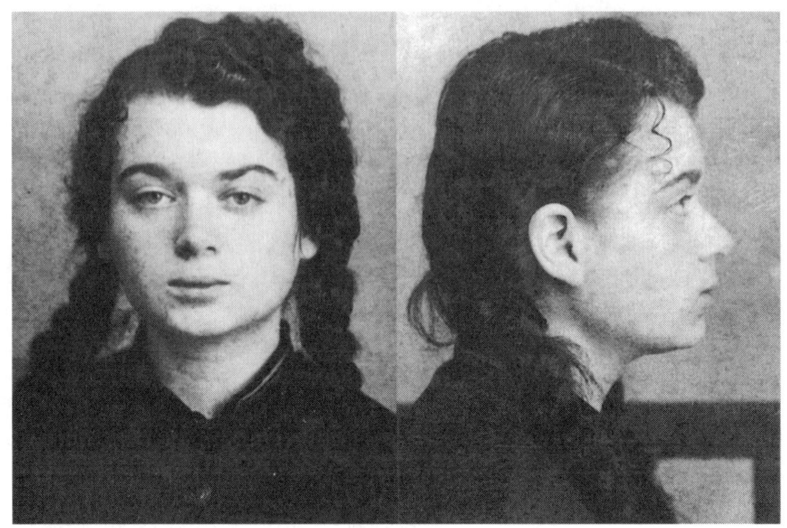

» Fig 6.1 *Case photographs taken after arrest in Lefortovo military prison.*

» Fig 9.1 *Alla's file from the KGB archives: one of thirty-two volumes.*

« Fig 10.1 Boris Slutsky,

» Vladlen Furman, and

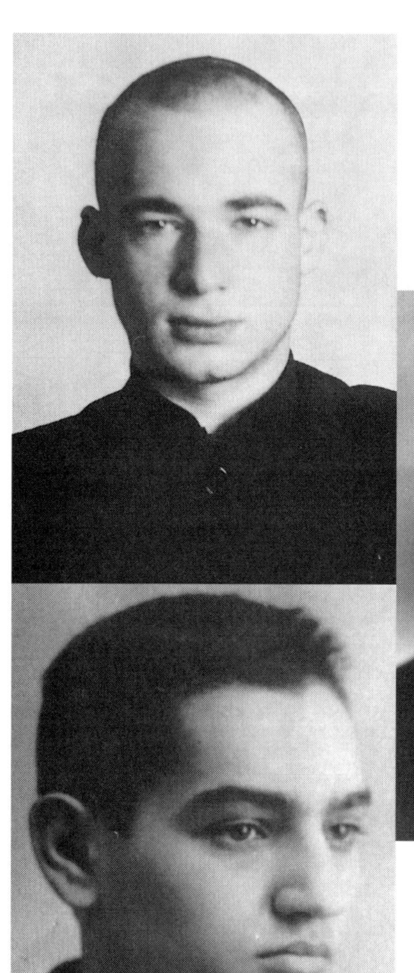

» Yevgeny Gurevich.

ПРИГОВОР

Именем Союза Советских Социалистических Республик

Военная Коллегия Верховного Суда Союза ССР

в составе:

Председательствующего *генерал-майора юстиции Дмитриева*

Членов: *полковников юстиции, Лебедкова и Семик*

При секретаре *лейтенанте Коноплеве*

В *закрытом* судебном заседании, в гор. *Москве*

06-13 февраля 1952года, рассмотрела дело по обвинению:

1. **С Л У Ц К О Г О** Бориса Владимировича, рождения 1932 года
сентября месяца, уроженца города Астрахани, еврея,
гражданина СССР, из служащих, бывшего члена ВЛКСМ
с 1946 года, не судимого, бывшего студента I-го
курса Московского педагогического института имени
Потемкина;

2. **Ф У Р М А Н А** Владилена Леонидовича, рождения 1931 года августа
месяца, уроженца города Одессы, еврея, гражданина
СССР, из служащих, бывшего члена ВЛКСМ с 1950 года,
не судимого, бывшего студента 2-го курса Рязанского
Медицинского института имени академика Павлова;

3. **Г У Р Е В И Ч А** Евгения Зиновьевича, рождения 1931 года мая месяца,
уроженца города Днепропетровска, еврея, гражданина
СССР, из служащих, бывшего члена ВЛКСМ с 1945 года,
не судимого, бывшего студента I-го курса Московского технологического института пищевой промышленно-
сти;

4. **М Е Л Ь Н И К О В А** Владимира Захаровича, рождения 1932 года
мая месяца, уроженца города Москвы, еврея, гражда-
нина СССР, из служащих, бывшего члена ВЛКСМ с
1947 года, не судимого, бывшего студента I-го курса
Московского химико-технологического института имени
Менделеева;

5. **П Е Ч У Р О** Сусанны Соломоновны, рождения 1933 года июля месяца,
уроженки города Москвы, еврейки, гражданки СССР,
из служащих, бывшего члена ВЛКСМ с 1947 года, не
судимой, бывшей учащейся 10-го класса 79-й средней
женской школы города Москвы;

6. **Э Л Ь Г И С С Е Р** Инны Леоновны, рождения 1930 года июня месяца,
уроженки города Москвы, еврейки, гражданки СССР, из
служащих, бывшего члена ВЛКСМ с 1945 года, не
судимой, бывшей студентки 3-го курса русского языка
и литературы Московского городского педагогического
института имени Потемкина;

» Fig 10.2 *Verdict*.

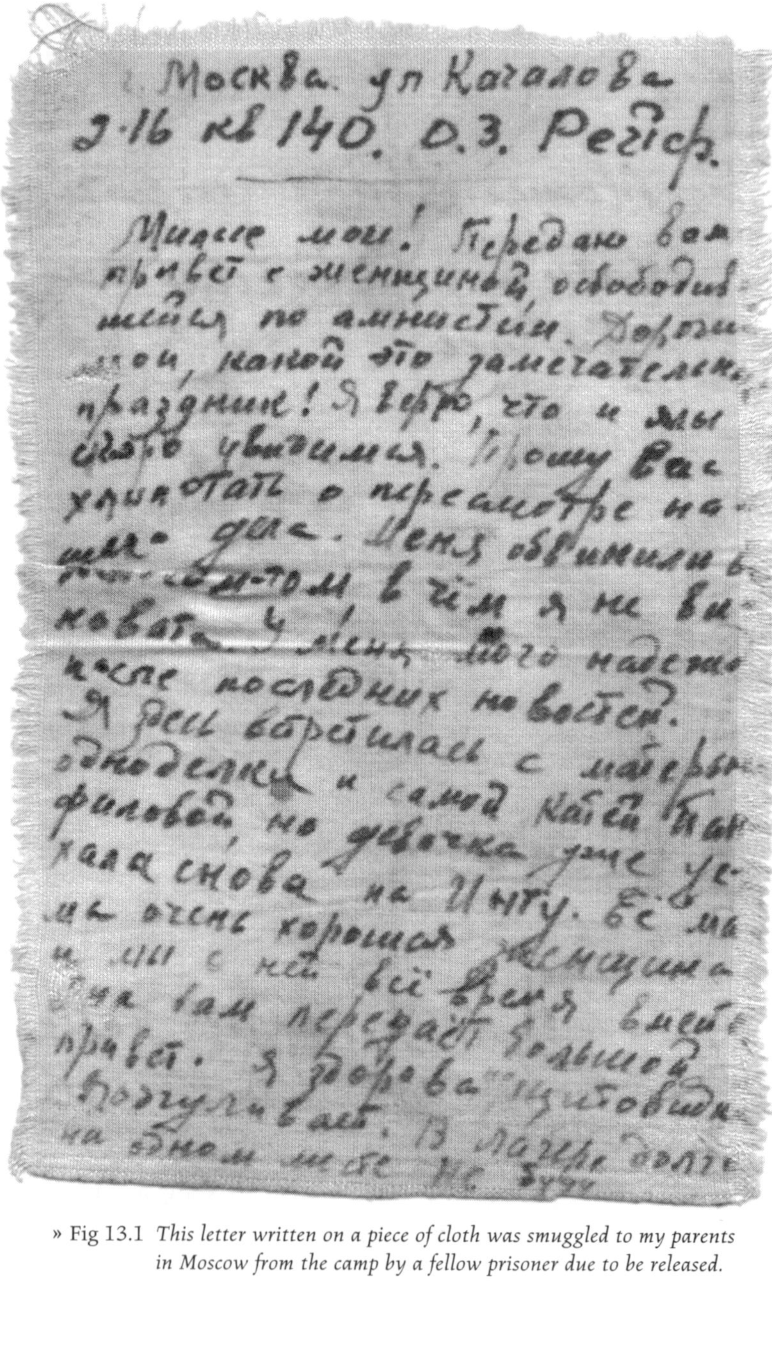
г. Москва ул Качалова
д.16 кв 140. О.З. Регистр.

Милые мои! Передаю вам привет с женщиной освободившейся по амнистии. Дорогие мои, какой это замечательный праздник! Я верю, что и мы скоро увидимся. Прошу вас хлопотать о пересмотре нашего дела. Меня обвинили в [illegible] том в чём я не виновата. У меня много надежд после последних новостей. Я здесь встретилась с матерью однодельцы и самой Катей [illegible] филовой, но девочка уже [illegible] кала снова на Инту. Это очень хорошая женщина и мы с ней всё время вместе. Она вам передаст большой привет. Я здорова [illegible] подгуливаю. В лагере долго на одном месте не буду [illegible]

» Fig 13.1 *This letter written on a piece of cloth was smuggled to my parents in Moscow from the camp by a fellow prisoner due to be released.*

» Fig 13.2 *Anna Ivanovna and Katya in a camp.*

» Fig 15.1 *Reciting the poetry of Mayakovsky for the inmates at a camp in the Inta region.*

» Fig 15.2 *Prisoners at the concert.*

» Fig 16.1 *Mother and daughter. Inta, 1955.*

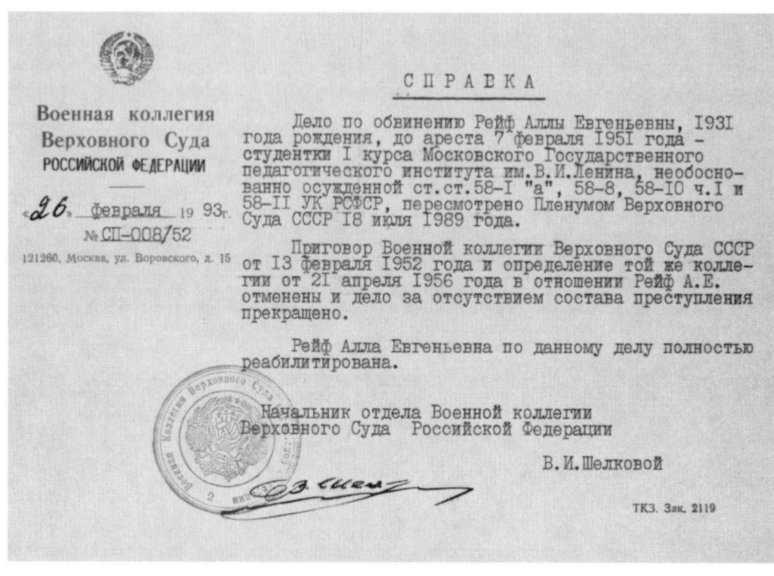

» Fig 19.1 *Affidavit of full rehabilitation.*

« *Alla Reyf before her release.*

11

Transport to the Camp

Much time passed before I recovered from the trial and sentence. Gradually a conviction was born in me that they had decided to scare the boys and would certainly not shoot them. But they had given most of the rest of us twenty-five years! Could this also be a warning? Did the legal code contain such astronomical lengths of sentences, or had they invented them specially for us? One obsessive thought never left me: only someone evil, weak, and unjust could deliver such a harsh sentence. Who was this "someone"? Our beautiful Motherland, our most noble Party, our wisest Leader? I thought in those words, or ones like them: those high-flown words didn't grate on me, I had become used to them since childhood. Only now, after this terrible blow inflicted on us, did these words sound wrong together, didn't match each other. Something began to change within me, as though a darkness was being replaced by bright, sober thought. What had we repented for? After all, we had made up nothing that had spurred us on to fight against the regime. They were afraid of us immature youngsters, this was the only possible explanation for the harshness of the punishment meted out to us. They were scared of us because we had been right and were thus dangerous. All the parts of the puzzle became clear to me and I found myself.

Pacing for hours in my cell, I didn't notice the passing of time. I mentally spoke with my "case fellows," my *odnodeltsy*, trying to prove to them how awfully we had behaved at the trial. Only Maya Ulanovskaya had shown herself to be a courageous person, while the rest of us had been pitiful chicks. I also spoke, in my mind, with the investigator and the judges and told them how cowardly they had been, how falsely they had prosecuted our case, all to gain favour with their superiors. It was shameful to recall the pity I had felt when my first investigator had had to rewrite his report so many times, in order to satisfy his bosses.

Gradually I acquired a certain freedom, strength, and good spirits from these mental conversations. I actually grew stronger and felt better. I diligently did my physical exercises and tried to make the time go quickly. If only I could get to the camp more quickly, to be among people! I was so tormented by my solitude that the camp seemed to be salvation, a chance for happiness. I was overflowing with love for all people without exception. I would be good and self-sacrificing. I would dedicate myself to those in need. I would never have my own family, not children or a husband. After all, no one would want to marry me. I would be an old woman when I got out of prison, and besides, everyone would be afraid of my criminal past. Well, so what! I would become useful to people and everyone would love me!

Deeply moved by such tender dreams, I fantasized about my life in the camp. I had not the slightest idea about the living conditions of the Soviet prison camps. No matter how hard I tried, I could only think of them in terms of my experience at the Pioneers' summer camps.

But day followed day and nothing happened. The most terrible thoughts crept into my head: what if I hadn't understood the sentence and they had sentenced me to solitary confinement for the full twenty-five years, or for a part of that term? I was so horrified by such a possibility that my legs gave way and I flopped down weakly on the cot.

Once the door to my cell opened and a man in a white coat walked in accompanied by an orderly. Apparently it was the prison doctor. He asked if I had any complaints about my health. As a matter of fact, I suffered from terrible headaches, but wasn't bothered by anything else. I don't recall if he listened to me with a stethoscope. I must have appeared to be genuinely ill. It is the only way I can explain why I was sent from prison to an "invalid" camp, as I learned about much later.

The exhausting expectation of the changes to my life continued for almost three months. The winter passed and the timid Moscow spring arrived. My last day in the Lefortovo Prison began like any other. Spring sounds drifted in from the streets in a special sort of way: the ringing of the trams, the birds singing, the roar of the city. I waited impatiently for my walk, but they didn't call me out. In the middle of the day they brought my suitcase into the cell. Its contents had grown significantly. I sorted through the warm things which, of course, Mother had brought. For a year and three months I had not worn normal underclothing. I had given up my regular clothes for a soldier's undershirt and a man's undershorts. Finally I could take off the dress that had almost rotted on me during this time (moreover, I had grown in the meantime and had difficulty getting into it). Having changed, I sat down on the cot, waiting for what was to follow.

Soon the *nadzorka* looked through the *kormushka*. "Get your things ready!" she ordered without emotion. Finally! One difficult stage in my life was coming to an end, and a new one beginning. For the last few minutes I walked around the cell that had been my home for so long. Everything is familiar, everything has grown hateful and yet, my God, how I have become used to it! And what if something worse was waiting for me? But this thought died away in a second. There would be nothing better, nothing better than to get out of here, no matter where!

Finally the long-awaited command: "Come out with your things!" I had become quite weak. My little suitcase that I had so recently taken with me to the summer Pioneer camps seemed so heavy to me now. I walked out of the cell. Once again, the familiar route along the narrow corridor, past the endless iron doors with their *kormushki* and spy-holes. The little flags clapped like dull shots as they regulated the traffic in the stairwell down on the bottom floor. The way is free. For a moment I found myself in the prison courtyard and immediately, almost from one door to another, I got into the back of a "Black Maria." The door slammed shut and I found myself in the pitch dark. I recalled my trip to "meet" with Abakumov. But my solitude this time was short-lived. The door opened again and into the back came a woman in a kerchief and quilted jacket. I couldn't make out her face in the dark. Yet how I rejoiced to see her! Had I ever rejoiced to have a new encounter before, as I rejoiced at that moment? I didn't care at all who she was, or why she was here; simply to have another person present, some-one like me, made me absolutely happy. We introduced ourselves. Her name was Lida. In my confusion I was silent, not knowing what one could ask her about. Lida was the first to speak.

"So, there you have it, the camp again. Damned life! What on earth made me lodge a complaint. So they reconsidered it! Now they've given me the works." Lida spoke angrily in a language I could hardly understand. What had they reconsidered? What were "the works"? I took courage and began to question her. What had she been arrested for?

Her history was brief and tragic. I had never yet heard such a one. She had been a nurse at the front and been captured by the Germans, then sent by them to a camp. In order to survive, she worked as a dental assistant there. When Soviet troops recaptured the camp, Lida was immediately arrested, given ten years and sent to Vorkuta,[37] beyond the Arctic Circle. She lodged complaint after complaint, explaining that she was guilty of nothing, that she had merely tried to save her life. Finally they called her in for a review of the case. Once again they tried her, but instead of ten years in the camps, this time they gave her twenty-five. Lida's story impressed me less than the sentence which they gave her: so we were not the only ones "honoured" with such a term. I am ashamed to confess that I was almost pleased at the discovery—I had thought that with my sentence I would never meet anyone. I embraced Lida and tried to comfort her with the fact that I had received twenty-five, too. That's what it meant "to get the works."

But Lida was an experienced "camper," not inclined to sentimentality, and the commonality of our fates did not cheer her up.

"We'll croak now! They have the strictest regime for the twenty-fivers in the camps," she sadly concluded. She wasn't interested in my case very much. When she heard my story, Lida said angrily: "And what were you short of? Pigeon's milk?"

I later found that such an attitude regarding our case was not uncommon. People who themselves were in the camps for no reason would sincerely condemn us and failed to see us as "strugglers for justice."

"We are suffering for nothing, and you, you pups, well, it serves you right, you could have left well enough alone." Ordinary people would say this, the ones who had gone through all the misery of the war and somehow, miraculously, come out of it alive. Many of them bore the eternal sign of Auschwitz or Dachau on their arms, and now on the back of their jackets was sewn the number of their very own Soviet camp. They considered themselves victims of the war, and expected that their cases would be looked into, and they would be released. For them, we were simply criminals, and they had no sympathy for our "good intentions." Lida was the first of many to condemn me. My *odnodeltsy* met the same response in the camps as I did. It was my first lesson: don't say too much about yourself or your case.

They drove us along Moscow's springtime streets. Through the smell of gasoline from the truck I could sense the fresh warm air. Whenever we stopped at an intersection, I could clearly make out the tapping of women's shoes on the asphalt and the many-voiced noises of the city. The sounds and smells of spring—this was all that Moscow could give me as a farewell present. If only I could see the city for a moment, the familiar streets! They unloaded us at some suburban railway stop, and I couldn't make out the city in the distance at all.

A soldier came up and took my suitcase and Lida's knapsack. We were led to the last car of a long train labelled "Mail." Lida and I crawled up into the car. It was an ordinary kind of car: a long corridor with compartments on one side, but with grating rather than doors. In the compartment we squeezed into, the space was filled absolutely to capacity. On the benches, on the floor, on the two full racks under the ceiling—everywhere people lay side by side or sat scrunched up next to each other. Dozens of curious eyes looked us over. With difficulty I found a place on the bench right next to the grating.

I was surrounded by strange women—crude, unlovely faces, half-naked bodies with enormous tattoos. They spoke in shouts, interspersing the words with profanity. For awhile it seemed to me that they were speaking a foreign language; I couldn't understand half of the words. All these loudmouthed women looked old, although their figures and their wild behaviour suggested youth instead. Lida whispered to me that these were *blatnyazhki*, thieves, and that I should tell them nothing about myself. But they didn't need any of our help to realize that we were "politicals." They asked me about something, shouting something down from the racks at the top, but I had lost the power of speech in this terrifying place.

"Hey, pinky, you mother fucker, don't be sulky. We're not going to bite you!" a large, half-naked *devakha* in a bra spoke to me pleasantly from the floor. On her stomach a dark blue snake wriggled at her every movement: the tattoo had been done masterfully. Pressing her face up against the grating that separated us from the corridor, she exchanged shouts with the male prisoners in the next compartment. From time to time the convoy bellowed back at her and, apparently knowing that there was no way he could cut off the conversation, continued on down the corridor. They brought us some salty fish *tyulka* in bowls and a ration of black bread, even less baked than in the prison. After such a meal we quickly developed a thirst, but no water was brought around until the evening. The prisoners shouted profanities at the convoy, demanding some water. The soldiers replied in kind. The worst kind of profanity hung in the air as densely as the stench of the place. It was impossible to breathe. Sweat ran down my body and my hands and feet went to sleep: it was impossible to change position due to the crowding.

I didn't even notice when the train began moving. Finally they let us go to the toilet in turn. First the men walked past. Many of them had the look of beasts. They all tried to slow down at our grating, shouting and laughing. Suddenly a bearded man pressed his face towards the corner where I was sitting. His burning eyes stared at me: "What's your name, girl? Let's get a little married!" The convoy dragged him off and thumped him in the back. On his return from the toilet he said something to me again. I shrunk out of fear and let my head fall so as not to look at his eyes. The bearded man took my behaviour as an insult and started to shower me with terrible swear words and threats from his compartment. "You just wait until we land up in the same camp, I'll show you, you Fascist! You sold off your Motherland, bitch! It's because of swine like you that we're rotting in here. Marukha, sweetie, give her one in the mug for me, and I'll add another when I get the chance!" He kept on like that for a long time, but I could hardly understand his language. Fear paralyzed me and my joy at finally meeting other people began to disappear.

Night came. The indefatigable *blatnyazhki* finally shut up. Everyone was overcome by sleep. By some miracle I managed to squeeze my way between the bodies onto the second shelf and stretch out my numb legs. A young girl with a pleasant, tender face was next to me. I started to speak to her enthusiastically and she answered me in German. So now I finally had a chance to use my miserable command of German. Her name was Helga Starke. They had arrested her for participating in a anti-Soviet student organization which was fighting for a free and unified Germany. They tried her in Berlin, gave her twenty-five years, and sent her to do her time in Soviet camps.

It was only the next morning that I managed to get a good look at my new acquaintance. In the den of thieves that surrounded us, Helga looked like an exotic beautiful bird: her delicate attractive face, the shock of fair hair, her bright summer dress. No prison could ever make the red in her cheeks fade. Helga told me that they had taken her when she was at the beach, and she had nothing except the dress and underclothes she had been wearing then. In order to keep from freezing in prison, she was given a long brown soldier's coat. That was the costume they had sent her off in. Her fiancé, Heinz, was in the next compartment. Through the wall they talked with each other quietly in German. The *blatnyazhki* abused the two foreigners in all sorts of ways but, fortunately, they didn't understand any of it besides the word "Fascists," although the hostility was clear to them both.

We arrived the next day after noon. I heard the name of the station, "Ruzayevka." Someone said that they had brought us to the camps at Potma. I was overjoyed—only five hundred kilometres from Moscow! But my happiness was premature. When we stepped out onto the platform we formed a huge dark crowd. We were ordered to sit down on the ground. Soldiers with rifles milled about us, counting the prisoners one by one. It seemed that I had become a part of some horrible herd of beasts. Scrunching down, I sat on the ground waiting for the end of this humiliating procedure. Then we were grouped into fives and the convoy shouted out something—I could make out the final words only with difficulty—which, this first time I ever heard them, sounded particularly frightening: "A step to the right, a step to the left, will be considered as an attempt to escape. The convoy will fire without warning!" How many times in the future was I to hear that "prayer"! It would slip past my accustomed ear, uncaught, leaving no trace. But this first time, each word penetrated like a nail into my consciousness.

The dark herd stretched out along the dirt road which had been made impassable by the spring weather. The line soon sprawled out while inside the crowd someone fell behind, someone pushed forward. Suddenly I heard next to me a hoarse voice: "Hey, beauty, let me take your suitcase. You're most likely tired!" It was the bearded man from the previous night. Now, when there was no grating separating us, he didn't seem quite so terrible. I thanked him but declined the offer, but he wouldn't give up. He was a comparatively young fellow with a dark, worn out face. His eyes shone with an unhealthy light. Later, I often saw such eyes in the faces of the drug addicts, and there were many of them among the criminal prisoners. But this fine April day in Potma I didn't yet have prison experience and the look of my "companion" seemed to me so strange that I would remember it forever.

"Don't be afraid of me," the bearded man said, for some reason using formal Russian. "I won't harm you in any way. And if we *do* turn up in the same camp, I would always protect you."

When he mentioned "the same camp" I began to shiver. It took my last ounce of strength, but I hurried on to join Helga who was walking alongside Heinz. I finally made it. Helga explained who I was to Heinz and he took my suitcase; we continued walking together. My persecutor fell back and I began to feel calmer. Suddenly our column of prisoners halted. Above our heads we could make out the barbed wire around the "zone" of the camp and the watchtowers with their guards. Someone nearby said that it was a transit prison—*peresylka*—and that they wouldn't keep us here for long. Thus the Ruzayevka Peresylka opened its gates to us.

The arrival of prisoners at a camp or at a *peresylka* was always accompanied by the strictest ritual. In a state where there were neither laws nor order, strict rules were observed only, perhaps, in the prisons. Life at the new place always began with a bathhouse, a *banya*. Even in prison a *banya* is a pleasure! It sounds strange, but the facilities were always, wherever I happened to find them, first class, even stylish: wash basins, hot water, and clouds of steam, just as they are supposed to be. For a couple of moments my anticipation was soured by the procedure of having to shave my pubic hair. I stood stock still when I saw the long queue of naked women standing in line. A male prisoner was doing the shaving. But when I saw how calm the others were as they approached him, even joking among themselves, I resigned myself to the prospect and came forward, like a sheep, for my shearing. After the *banya* they divided us into several large barrack rooms, with bunk beds along the walls. Not knowing the customs for these populated rooms, I didn't hurry to take the best place on the bunk, the way the experienced *zeki*—camp inmates— did, but stood waiting indecisively in the centre of the room. I found out later that it was important to take the upper bunk, where it was more spacious and airy. This time an unoccupied space in the very corner, on the lower bunk, fell to my lot. The darkness, stuffiness, and stench kept me from sleep—but only for a moment.

Life in a *peresylka* is not like anywhere else, neither in prison or a "real" camp. The Ruzayevka Peresylka was a transit point. All sorts of groups of prisoners assembled here and whole trains of goods wagons were sent out in all directions. Sometimes they went out not in groups, but individually in cars used just for transporting prisoners. These cars had been called "Stolypins" since pre-revolutionary times, after the Tsarist prime minister. In the room where I was there were about fifty people, but they were never the same fifty: people would suddenly appear and just as suddenly disappear. No one ever managed to get accustomed to a place or befriend any- one. They shouted out through the *kormushki* the names of the women to be taken away. The women would gather up their pitiful things and disappear out the door forever. The ones left behind waited for their own turn nervously—if not today, then maybe tomorrow. We all wanted to get out of this place as soon as possible, anywhere, simply to "get a place" for ourselves. It's true that not everyone was in such a hurry; the experienced *zeki* weren't in a rush, they knew that *kantovka*—dodging work—was easiest here, that nothing good was waiting for them in the camps, and that the greatest wisdom was something that I had not yet acquired: "A day of *kantovka* is a year of life!" They lived for the day, doing nothing to hurry time along, and created around themselves a sensation of comfort and warmth. I noticed such women from the very first day, observed them carefully, and couldn't understand how they could live here "in truth"! You had to experience what had befallen them in order to appreciate their wisdom.

Prisoners were not taken out to labour, received no books, and had absolutely nothing to do. Each of us occupied our time with what came to hand, mainly finding a suitable person to talk with for a long conversation, if we were lucky. At first I amused myself watching the mixed population of the room. It was impossible to figure out what kind of person might *not* be represented there! Village girls from Ukraine in their long skirts and wide blouses, some strange quiet women in white kerchiefs, all looking alike in their inwardness and rejection of everything that was going on around them (I later discovered that they were members of various religious sects). We had colourful Gypsies and thieving *blatnyazhki*, prostitutes and ageless, emaciated women who were completely unremarkable. I inspected this society with interest, listening in on their conversations. People were sitting about in groups or in pairs on the bunks, or simply on the floor, telling their unhappy stories to each other for hours on end. The need to talk was greater than the need to eat or sleep. The room was constantly filled with a dull hum of voices. There weren't very many *blatnyazhki*, but you could hear them above all the rest: they either shouted (and you couldn't figure out whether they were arguing or simply talking) or sang their own peculiar songs. I had never heard the like before: touching and passionate lyrics, accompanied by a simple, doleful tune. Each song told of a lost life, of grief and guilt towards a mother. They sang in sharp, hoarse voices, very much like moaning. Despite the fact that they were in a minority, the *blatnyazhki* considered themselves to be the masters of the room. They took the best places in the bunks, refused to take out the latrine bucket or *parasha* (which everyone was supposed to do in turn), swore at the convoys, hung out the windows and dropped little notes called *ksivy* down on string into the men's rooms. The prison was their home. These women filled me with both terror and curiosity and I followed their lives carefully, fearing lest they notice my interest.

Several of the women in our room had been sentenced to internal exile and had left straight from "freedom." They still carried foodstuffs with them in their knapsacks. The *blatnyazhki* would terrorize them for the food and, if they didn't give it up immediately, take it from them. For the first time I observed how a majority could unquestioningly submit to the pressure of insolence and power. Impunity made the *blatnyazhki* even more aggressive: they were proud of the fact that they had been sentenced in accordance with the criminal, not the political, code. "We're all Soviets, and you are all Fascists!" they shouted spitefully. We were "enemies of the people"—what could be worse! It seemed that the convoys sympathized with them in this; in any case, thieves were more acceptable than politicals.

During our few days in the transit prison, Helga and I were inseparable. It's difficult to imagine now that we could talk for hours on end with my miserable German, but talk we did: about art, politics, our families. Helga was a lawyer's daughter who lived in her own house in Potsdam. Her father hadn't supported the Fascists, but he considered the Soviet occupation to be a great misfortune. Helga became a member of an anti-Soviet student organization with the goal of a free, unified Germany. The activities of her organization were about as fruitful as ours, and all the members were caught just as quickly as we had been. We were the same age. What Helga just couldn't understand was why she was having to serve out her sentence in the Soviet Union: it was a court in East Germany that had tried her. And she was simply terrified of Siberia, thinking that there she would only find hard labour and shackles.

I taught her the most rudimentary Russian vocabulary, but one time I was careless and the *blatnyazhki* taught the lesson instead. All she wanted was some water. She went up to the door and loudly pronounced the most execrable profanity, sure that she was asking for something to drink. The watchman and the *blatnyazhki* all collapsed with laughter. It was painful to watch her look at us all with those perplexed eyes, having no idea what was going on.

As always, when we were "turned out" for our next journey, it came unexpectedly. This time the Stolypin car for prisoners was unoccupied, with only about ten people inside. I was happy that I was being taken with my new friend, but she grieved over being parted from Heinz. We travelled the whole night. Towards the morning we arrived in Gorky: I made out the name of the station through the window in the corridor. They loaded us into a "Black Maria" and drove us to the city prison. We were uneasy: why were they taking us to prison again? Where was the camp that we were to "settle" in? There was no one to ask.

The procedure for prison reception was familiar, but so demoralizing that it was impossible to get used to. A personal frisking into all parts of the body, hands combing through the hair and every item of one's things. In Moscow, in Gorky, the gloomy prison guards' faces were all the same, as though all born of the same mother! A *banya* again, but this time in shower stalls, like back in Lefortovo. Helga and I were the last to come out and then she discovered that her only pair of underclothes had disappeared. She was in despair, burst into tears, and kept repeating in German: "Who would take a stranger's underclothes?" Thank God I had an extra pair in my suitcase. Helga laughed through her tears, trying to picture how she would tell this story to her friends back in Germany. I laughed with her, but the humour of the situation was dimmed by my feeling of shame. Shame for my countrymen, for Russians, for how foreigners saw them. I would be ashamed again many times in the future for how these strangers learned to know Russia and her people as they travelled from prison to prison, from camp to camp. Many of them began to hate us all, both the torturers and their victims.

In a Soviet Russia that had been cut off from the world, mistrust towards foreigners had been nurtured since childhood. Spy-mania and xenophobia were encouraged from above. Chauvinism was blown up into a patriotism of monstrous proportions, a peculiar Soviet pride or, rather, arrogance. All this grew and flourished, destroying normal human relationships. An endless multitude of the foreigners who were prisoners in the Soviet camps experienced all that the authorities had sown in the souls of their subjects. They were shunted aside, despised wholesale, called "Fascists" and *burzhui* (bourgeois). And yet there were so many anti-Fascists among them, so many naïve communists who had come to help in the construction of "the world's first truly just society." And what "justice" did they find there! The Germans had it particularly hard. The Soviet prisoners who had suffered through the German occupation and captivity vented all their pent-up hatred on the Germans. They didn't have the strength to recognize that they were all victims of one and the same monstrosity. Of course I also saw completely different relationships, ones of friendship, with ardent attachments between Russians and foreign prisoners, but it rarely happened. And I'm not talking about the antagonism which, as a rule, the national minorities of the Soviet Union felt towards the Russians (and they were, all in all, a significant majority). In general, just as in the "prison outside" that was the whole Soviet Union, life inside the prisons and the camps was woven out of contradictions—hatred and love, fidelity and betrayal, friendship and hostility. Which emotion predominated would be hard to say—there are no statistics and personal experience is a subjective thing. In my own experience, I must say that in five years of the prison and camps I met much more goodness than evil. What sort of experience was Helga in for? How that girl withstood her sentence I cannot say: we were soon separated and never met again. Certainly our circuitous and long trip to the north, her first acquaintance with Russia, was not an easy initiation.

Together under a single blanket, Helga and I spent the night in the Gorky prison. There was no way to get warm in that dark, concrete cell. In the morning we were again put into "Black Marias" and driven to the station. There, someone let slip that it had all been a mistake, we were to have gone not to Gorky but in the opposite direction, north. That condition of instability, of life's indefiniteness —all that had tormented me in prison was continuing. No moment belonged to you, neither the last one nor the next.

And once again they rounded us up in the rooms of the Ruzayevka Peresylka. Each new day was identical to the one before. People kept coming and coming. Mostly they were Ukrainian women, often quite young girls. I tried to talk with them; I thought that I knew Ukrainian since we had had a Ukrainian nanny when I was a girl and I had listened to her speaking Ukrainian with my father. But these girls spoke a language quite unknown to me. Afterwards they explained that Western Ukrainian was different from the language of Eastern Ukraine, having borrowed many German, Hungarian, and Polish words, and that the intonation was different, too. At any rate, Ukrainian unexpectedly became a foreign language to me. Later, in the camps, I learned how to understand my friends from Lviv and the Transcarpathian region, but I never learned to speak their language. So we would chat on all sorts of topics in the two "fraternal" languages: I in Russian and they in Ukrainian. It didn't hold us up. But in Ruzayevka such communication was not yet possible.

Helga and I stopped feeling like the "babies" of the camp with the appearance of the "Western" girls. The Ukrainian girls looked just like children. Mariyika and Nyusya were both sixteen. For the past six months they had been shunted from prison to prison for investigations. Somehow I found out that they had been sentenced for connections with the partisans, the *Banderovtsy*. As a rule almost all the women in the camps from Ukraine asserted their complete innocence. Sometimes they would say that they had fed a relative who was hiding in the forest. But I didn't believe such stories very much, knowing how deeply the Ukrainians hate their Russian "liberators." I heard later about the cruel interrogations, the beatings, and the outrages. I had ceased to be surprised at the horrors. When our room was full to capacity, there was talk about a huge transfer. We tried to guess at where they would be taking us. Some mentioned Karaganda and Vorkuta. "Anywhere but Siberia!" Helga moaned. We were all afraid of Vorkuta, having heard the stories about the fierce frost there. Rumours swept the crowded room from one end to the other. We were all afraid, yet awaited the changes with some anticipation —life in the *peresylka* had become unbearable.

Once, when it seemed that not a single other person could be squeezed into the room, the door opened and a tall young woman entered. She was dressed in a fashion unlike ours and in our company looked completely unbelievable, as though she had landed here by accident, by mistake, and was about to leave. But the door slammed shut behind her and she remained standing, not knowing where to go. Helga and I were sitting on a bunk in the corner, not far from the door. I got up from my spot and called the novice over towards us. Just the few words she spoke in Russian left no doubt that she was a foreigner.

"*Sprechen Sie Deutsch?*" Helga asked hopefully. "*Ja!*" she exclaimed and they threw themselves into each other's arms. For several minutes they spoke rapidly, interrupting each other. They laughed and embraced each other again, as though they were sisters or old friends. It was difficult to believe that a few moments ago they had never met. I was happy that Helga had met a fellow countrywoman, but at the same time I was terribly jealous, understanding that our own friendship would now become secondary. Sitting next to them, I listened to their conversation and with some difficulty caught the sense of it. Then we were introduced. The young woman's name was Edith. She had been in a Soviet prison for a long time and had learned some Russian. Mangling her words in a funny fashion, Edith began the story of how she had come to be imprisoned. "A long tongue is dangerous. They put you in prison for chattering! But a short tongue is just as bad. They put me in prison for not reporting on my friend, who was doing something against the Russians." She told her story in peals of laughter, even though there wasn't very much funny in her tale. She was pregnant when they arrested her and after the baby was born in prison they immediately took it away and gave it to her mother. Edith grieved over the fact that they hadn't even let her put diapers on it. They had sentenced her to ten years, but she didn't believe for a minute that they would keep her that long. "Soon, soon *nach Haus!*" Edith said. Her white-toothed smile shone in her attractive face, and everything seemed a little bit better. Even the *blatnyazhki* amicably called Helga and Edith "our two little Fascist birdies," but the peacefulness didn't last for long.

Outside the days were sunny and warm. We were taken out in tens for walks, and I couldn't breathe in the spring air enough. In

     WHERE WE BURIED THE SUN

the room everything was stuffiness and stench. I tried to hurry the time along—quickly, quickly now, to the camp! I wanted to be working, to be doing something useful. The experienced "campers" taught me a piece of camp wisdom: don't hurry anywhere, don't show your any initiative, "stay sitting and don't make a peep!" You never know what's waiting for you ahead, it might be something worse. This line of behaviour was something which took me a long time to learn, for the time being I was like a young horse, unable to stand still and striving towards some activity.

And finally the long awaited departure came. We were lined up in fives, surrounded by guard dogs and guards carrying automatic weapons. The familiar "prayer" was recited once again—"A step to the right, a step to the left"—and then they took us off in an enormous column towards the station. I think that it was the first time they had taken us in a convoy with dogs. Despite their ferocious look, these dogs straining at their leads were attractive, especially for such an admirer of dogs as I was. I looked them over with pleasure and held myself back with difficulty from whistling a sweet one over to me—as I might have done in former times. Later in the camp I learned some verses, composed by a political prisoner (she had been a Socialist Revolutionary, an "SR," and had been in for twenty years but hadn't lost her sense of humour) in parody of the well-known children's verses by Marshak, *A Lady Registered her Luggage*. It might be out of place, but I very much want to preserve this parody from oblivion. I particularly remembered it as it takes a familiar, rather sweet story and suddenly infuses it with a sinister meaning: not unlike my own life. The original version told about a lady who registered her luggage, including suitcases, boxes and a little dog. Upon arrival at her destination, however, she received both her luggage and a great big dog. In explanation, she was told that her little one simply grew big during the journey. The parody told how the lady had registered a knapsack, not luggage, with no pictures, baskets, or boxes, and no one gave her a ticket at the wicket. She wore not an overcoat, but a *bushlat* of dirty-grey cotton wadding. The lady was accompanied by an armed convoy and was showered with the worst Russian profanity. The dog the lady had once held grew from a pug-dog into a German shepherd and was ordered to walk beside her, so that she herself wouldn't run away on the trip.

A train of cargo wagons was standing at the station. They divided us up into groups of thirty per car. Driven on by the soldiers' shouts, prisoners clambered up into the large, dirty cars. This mode of transportation was not entirely new to me, as I had been evacuated in similar cargo cars—*teplushki*—during the war. Then they had taken us to safety from Moscow to Stalingrad. My father's boss had chosen such a refuge for the families of his staff. Later we could hardly get out of there alive! Where would the *teplushki* be taking us now? The convoy didn't bother to hide the fact that the whole group was going north, to the Komi Republic. The Komi region was a place my imagination drew as endless and snowy. Reindeer, igloos, reindeer-drawn sledges—what else did I know about it? Ah, yes—permafrost and the northern lights! How fun it had been to stand in a warm classroom and with a thin pointer poke somewhere at the edge of the map. The capital city of the autonomous republic was Syktyvkar and the population consisted of the Komi people, who were primarily breeders of reindeer. About the other population, the one that was considerably larger in size and concentration compared to the indigenous people, no one told us in school. We didn't "study" that.

It was quite dark in the *teplushka*, the light barely making its way in through a tiny grilled window. I climbed up on the top bunk and pressed my face to the window. Anguish overcame my heart and I didn't want to talk to a soul. I looked at the land rushing past us—it was all grey and ugly. The sparse forests were still bare, the ground still brown, as though dead, and there were no other colours.

My thoughts turned to home. How were they getting along? Had my father been arrested yet (it was a constant fear)? How had they survived these hard fifteen months just past? It was inhuman that they hadn't been allowed to visit me. And now I was being taken further and further from Moscow. Would I ever return?

The train rumbled along the rails, and through this noise I could barely make out the buzz of voices in the car. When I turned away from the window it had begun to get dark. It was cold in the *teplushka*, despite the open stove nicknamed a "bourgeois" that had been set in the middle, its chimney reaching up through the ceiling. Women sat and stood around the stove, some of them roasting slices of bread over the coals. That scent of warm bread awakened my hunger: we hadn't had anything to eat since the morning. Finally the train stopped and with a screech the doors of the car opened. Two of the prisoners were ordered to take out the *parasha*, a heavy barrel on a pole. At the door there appeared a soldier with a bucket that had the savour of food. We each received a bowlful of oatmeal porridge. I don't think I had ever eaten such tasty porridge! Not a smidgen of fat, with husks of the grain—it disappeared in a second. The feast was topped with toasted bread and boiling water to drink. From then on, the smell of smoky bread would always be a delicacy in the camps and remind me of my first stage on the journey there.

It became completely dark in the car, with only a glow from the coals in the open stove. Now it was time to settle down for the night. The *blatnyazhki* claimed the best places in the middle on the upper bunks. Although they were in the minority, everyone—as always— accommodated them. With horrible profanity they ordered Helga, Edith, and me to "scram under the bench." It was most unpleasant to have anything to do with them and I immediately moved away. But the proud foreigners didn't want to submit. They didn't quite under- stand who it was they were dealing with, and they certainly had no idea to what lengths these barely human creatures would go. Their reprisal against the "dummies" only took a moment. I would have rushed to their aid but a soft-hearted Ukrainian girl grabbed me by the arm and wouldn't let me go. I watched with horror as my friends were thrown headlong from their upper bunks. No one lifted a finger to help them. The shame I felt for myself and all the women around me is impossible to forget. But it was a burning shame that was stronger than pity. Helga and Edith cried bitterly in their corner. I didn't have the courage to go over to them. What would they be thinking of Russians, what scorn they must feel for them! There were about twenty-five of us—simple, normal people who were peaceful and unaccustomed to fighting, to defending ourselves. And there were only five of these animals! And still they were more powerful.

"We'd rather sleep next to the Yid than with Fascists!" the girls bawled out, nodding over at me. No one answered. It was silent but for the sobbing from the corner. Then fatigue got the best of me and I collapsed into sleep.

In the middle of the night we were awakened by a terrible crashing—someone was pounding heavily on the roof of the *teplushka*. Then the knocking moved to the sides of the car and, finally, under the floor. Everyone sat fearfully on their bunks, deafened by the thunder of the pounding. Lida, who was there beside me, calmed me down: it was just the convoy beating wooden mallets against the car, checking if all the boards were whole, making sure no one was preparing to escape. The train stood still. Suddenly the doors opened and two soldiers jumped up into the car. The harsh glare of two flashlights cut into our eyes. No one understood what was going on, and we all just stared at the intruders.

"Everyone on the right, move quickly over to the left!" one of the soldiers shouted. The order was uttered with a ferocity that seemed to anticipate opposition. The half-asleep, frightened women began to stumble over to the other side. In the darkness we bumped up against each other and the women in the upper bunks almost fell headlong onto the floor, hitting others who were crawling out from under the bunks. "Faster! Faster!" the convoy pressed us. When the right side of the car was empty and all the prisoners, cramped up against each other, were crowded into the left side, they drove us back, one by one.

"One, two, three," they counted our heads. "All right, whatcha doin'? Turn about! You sleep walkin'?"

The prisoners, fighting against the torpor of sleep, moved from one place to the other. The flash lights illuminated individual faces and enormous shadows scattered across the walls. Again they herded us like cattle to the other side of the car. The convoys whispered to each other, checking that their sums tallied—thank God, they agreed, all were present.

"Get a move on! Go to sleep!" the soldiers tossed back as they left and clanked the doors shut. We returned to our places. I lay for a long time staring into the darkness, unable to fall asleep. There would be so many times in the future that I would have to jump up in the middle of the night, for a "frisking" or a "check-up." The half-literate guards would count the prisoners over and over again, for hours—and still the sum wouldn't tally! But an experienced *zek* lived her own life and paid no attention to what was going on around her: the longer they took counting, the better (if it was taking place in a barracks). When they counted heads on the way to work in a fierce frost or in the heat, when midges were tormenting you, it would be worse. But this first "check-up" was one that I never forgot.

By morning I was completely stiff. The stove had gone out during the night and you could see your breath in the cold. I had no desire to move—if I could only fall back asleep! But then someone began pottering about by the stove and then it smelled of smoke. The women began to get up. In the weak morning light they looked terrible, dishevelled, with pallid baggy faces, and wrapped in rags. A line formed for the *parasha*. Taking advantage of a freed space by the window, I climbed up onto the upper bunk and pressed up against the grill. The landscape had changed greatly during the night. The forests had completely disappeared and we were travelling through empty space with only the rare copse of bare, low-growing trees. The watch towers of camps began to race past in the distance, just like at Ruzayevka. There were more and more of them and I kept waiting for the train to stop—why were we going further when there were so many camps clustering here? The train eventually did stop. Several prisoners were called by name and were taken away. The rest of us were given some bread and boiling water. Conversation began as to where was the best place to serve your sentence—here, or further north. Lida insisted that there was better eating in the north.

They gave you fish, the vegetables were fresher, but here you would only get rotted cabbage and swell from the hunger. It appeared that we were lucky in our destination. But it was difficult to rejoice—the proximity of the north could be felt in the car and outside the window. Snow lay on the ground, and our teeth chattered from the cold. You could only warm yourself up a bit by the stove, and we crowded up close to it all day, face first and then back.

The days passed in endless conversation; it was the only way to forget, to take a rest from the overpowering melancholy and fear of the unknown. Edith told us the story of her life. She had undergone much hardship during the time of Hitler. Listening to her, I was even more astounded by her cheerful attitude. Her father was a Jew and her mother a German. For a time they didn't touch him—for some reason they never found out he was Jewish— but the family lived in constant fear of disaster. Her father was arrested for something entirely different, and then they learned he was a Jew. He was sent to a camp and they did not hear from him again: presumably he died there. Edith and her mother hid themselves away, constantly changing homes. They barely made it to the end of the war. Somehow their lives settled down and Edith married. And then another misfortune: she didn't report a friend who, according to Edith, was guilty only of having an affair with the wrong man. But Edith considered her "crime" so minor in comparison with her sentence that the naïve young woman had no doubt that she would be quickly returning home. She was remarkably beautiful, as though she had stepped out of a foreign fashion magazine: tall, long-legged, with golden locks of hair, and dark-blue, almond-shaped eyes. She laughed so infectiously that women who didn't even understand her German speech began laughing with her. I recall how amusingly she told about her "language of gestures" that she had used for a long time in prison to make herself understood, when she hadn't known a single word of Russian. It turned out that one could express almost anything without words. Then she began picking up some Russian words and it was so funny the way she would mix things up. I feasted my eyes on Edith—her beauty, grace, her special way of listening and talking. Now, for the first time, in the persons of Edith and Helga, I made acquaintance with people from the West. At that time I couldn't quite catch, or, rather, express, what the difference was: after all, hadn't these women grown up in a totalitarian state too? In order not to be obtrusive, I often consciously left my sweet German girls alone with each other—they had lots to talk about.

Whether our trip lasted a long time I cannot now say. At the time it seemed to me that an eternity had passed since I left my solitary cell in Lefortovo Prison. My memory of prison life had already begun to dim and seem distant, as though it were in another life. Could I really have been so tormented by loneliness? Had I really wanted so badly to be with other people? Here I am among them, squeezed between two other bodies on my bunk, and further off lie other bodies of people completely alien to me, people who are indifferent to my fate, or even hostile. They don't need me, nor I them. Each is busy with her own misfortune. Will I find any soul mates in this crowd?

I can't sleep. At night the car grows so cold that it is the same temperature inside as out. We hadn't yet learned to have someone stand guard at the stove. Instead, each one lived for herself and there was no collective feeling. And although everyone suffered from the cold, each one strove in the evening to clamber faster onto the bunks and fall into forgetful sleep. Toward morning the walls of the *teplushka* were covered in a grey sheet of frost. We had become accustomed to the midnight "check-ups" and the thundering of the wooden mallet against the walls of the car no longer scared anyone. When the convoy showed up, the women would mechanically move from one side to the other, almost without waking up; in the morning it was difficult to remember if we had got up in the night. The whole procedure became part of the inevitable routine of life, like carrying out the heavy, stinking *parasha*. Our train moved slowly, standing for great periods of time at the stations, which were always at a remote location so that we seldom heard the sound of human voices or the noise of a town. Through the window it became more dismal as the signs of spring completely disappeared, with snow covering the ground. The company of *blatnyazhki* diminished—three were let off along the way and disappeared from sight and memory. The remaining two girls quieted down and retired into the background. They spent the entire day on their bunk, droning on about something in their hoarse, bird-like voices.

One evening I climbed up onto their bunk and asked permission to look out the window. After their reprisal against the Germans, I had tried not to look in the direction of the *blatnyazhki*, they were so repulsive. But the desire to look outside our "cage" was overpowering. The *blatnyazhki* were quite pleased at my arrival: they felt their isolation and my attention changed the whole situation. But I didn't get a chance to look out the window. First they were curious about where I was from and, having found out that I was from Moscow and a student, they began to lament over me—how could such an educated girl become a Fascist? As far as they were concerned, anyone who hadn't been sentenced as a common criminal was automatically a Fascist. As I got to know the *blatnyazhki*, I quickly discovered that they considered themselves patriots, genuine Soviet citizens. They blamed no one in particular for their fate. Their grief was flavoured by the peculiar sweetness of vice and the sense of their own exclusiveness. In general, these people had made their own choices for themselves (of course, circumstances of some sort had started them out on their criminal way). Their home was the prison, or camp, to which they would return to time and again after brief periods of wild liberty. My new acquaintances' names were Lyuba and Ninka—at least that's how they introduced themselves. They were both young, but somehow worn out. They had grey and wrinkled faces that were framed by long locks of hair. And always there was a cigarette in the corner of the mouth. To me they looked indistinguishable, and I even asked if they were sisters. It turned out that Lyuba was from Rostov and Ninka was a northerner. The tattoos on their arms represented similar themes: there was one to "dear Father," that is, to Stalin, and another to "the Motherland." Later I saw tattoos with these standard incantations on the arms of many *urki*—the criminals in the camps: "I will die for Stalin!" or "I love the Motherland!" Sometimes the word "Motherland" was missing, and the criminal's love was pledged to her own natural mother. There weren't that many variants and the pictures used were common symbols: undulating snakes, pierced hearts, kissing doves. The primitiveness of the *urki* was shocking, especially in the way they religiously observed their own criminal laws while violating generally accepted laws of human behaviour without a qualm. You could write a series of studies researching the lives of this special class of society, its psychology, unwritten code of behaviour, folklore and, above all, the reason for its appearance and growth in number particularly in the Soviet environment. People hardly ever met such creatures in normal life. They were like a mirage, inhabitants from a distant planet, and it was impossible to understand them, no matter how hard you tried. Out of my naïveté and inexperience, I attempted to make some sense of their situation, imagining they had had a misfortune or been misled. I even tried to re-educate some of the *urki* (and I wasn't the first or the last to try). In the camp I almost paid quite harshly for my stupidity. But for now my earliest attempts ended in puzzlement and the loss of my mittens.

I was quite a find for these two talkative gals. They vied with each other for my attention, telling me stories and fantasies about their lives. Ninka confessed with inspiration about her homeless childhood, the gang of kids like her, the reformatory settlements she'd lived in. She went home rarely, and when she did she could only hope to escape—her father beat her severely and the neighbours kept their distance and avoided her. As an adolescent she had been passed from hand to hand and found no joy in it. She spoke of it without complaint; she simply told her story, as though it was quite ordinary, natural, that she was just like any other. I saw an endless chain of suffering and humiliation in the list of events she recounted from her life. For Ninka, it was simply a life. I can't now recall what banal truths I told poor Ninka when I had heard her story: probably, something like a recitation of the Ten Commandments. She thanked me and solemnly promised to change her life. She even swore a thief's oath: "I'll be a bitch if I don't break with the thieves." And, snapping her fingernail against her front tooth, she drew her thumb across her throat. We whispered together on the bunk until late at night. I was already making plans for our friendship in the camp: I would save Ninka and deliver her from the criminal world forever.

The next morning, at the first stop, they called her name and ordered to come "with your things." She scampered down from the upper bunk, grabbed her knapsack and, not looking at a soul, jumped out onto the ground. There was a thud of shutting doors and Ninka disappeared forever, along with my mittens. I didn't have a chance to be upset that I had failed as a Makarenko reformer[38] as several hours later, at the next station, the convoy called out my name among several others. I was glad that the journey had come to an end, although it was sad to leave Helga and Edith. We kissed each other farewell and I repeated once more Helga's address—I would write her as soon as I got out. It wouldn't be long, we were certain of it. They took my two friends further north, most likely to Vorkuta.

I was the last to jump out of the *teplushka*. "*Auf Widersehen!*" their two voices called out in farewell behind me. "*Do pobachennia!*" my Ukrainian travelling companions called out in turn.

The doors of the car closed. Before us an endless snowy plain stretched out to the horizon. The snow sparkled so brightly in the sun that you had to screw up your eyes. After the darkness of the *teplushka* it was difficult to look around. But in actual fact there was nothing to look at, nothing for your eye to catch hold of, nothing but sparkling blue snow and not a single dark spot anywhere. The convoy called the names of people from all the cars of the train. They came out onto God's earth and stood still, blinded by the sun as I was. We were driven into a single group, men and women together. I noticed that the people around me were mostly old and emaciated. There were about fifty of us. They took the men off to one side. We were put into groups of fives and the small column moved off into the nothing. On that white expanse, without anything to orient yourself to, it was impossible to imagine finding your direction.

After our many days on the train, we could barely shift our legs.

The column immediately lost its original outline. The convoys tried
to round us up with shouts, but it didn't matter. Some people stopped
to catch their breath, while many others were ill and exhausted in
the extreme. Nyusya and Mariyika, who had been travelling with me
since the Ruzayevka Peresylka, were walking with me. We tried to
keep up with each other. As we were the youngest, and therefore the
strongest of this troupe of "goners," we quickly overtook everyone
else and ended up at the head of the column. Where on earth were
we hurrying to? We were urged on by our curiosity; all that awful-
ness was behind us—prison, investigation, trial, the latest stage in
our journey. What could possibly be worse than what we had just
gone through? In youth everyone is an optimist. The tundra surrounded us, and we had never seen it before—it was already interesting! The crunching snow underfoot; the frosty, slightly sharp air
we inhaled with satisfaction—it was all new and exciting. Recalling
now that first "walk" in the tundra, I can hardly believe my memories: I was overwhelmed with joy! And with thankfulness—for something, to someone, someone above me, above us all, above the good
and evil actions of humankind, above the whole world.

+ + + + +

With these feelings, most inappropriate for the present situation, I approached the gates of the Abez Invalid Camp. Absorbed in
my thoughts, I almost didn't notice it as we came closer to the settlement. As a matter of fact, the settlement with the name Abez was
further on. It consisted of a single street with about ten little houses
which served as living quarters for the guards, convoys, and the
camp administrators. In the Komi language *abez* means "the Devil's
pit." According to the stories, an airplane had crashed near here and
from that time the place had carried this name. The column halted
in front of the wooden gates which were densely entwined with
barbed wire. Through it we could see long barracks constructed in
rows and surrounded by banks of snow. People shuttled between
the barracks, all of them alike as two peas in a pod, awkward in

their grey quilted jackets and kerchiefs. On the backs of the jackets I could clearly make out bright squares with numbers on them. At this sight, my inexplicable happiness began to evaporate. Although I had been warned about the numbers, seeing them with my own eyes was painful. The camp territory was large. Beyond a small square occupied by the barracks, wide strips of the "forbidden zone" stretched out, walled off with triple lines of barbed wire. In it, the untouched thin crust of ice on the snow sparkled in the sunlight. And at the corners of the zone, wooden towers stood out with their *popki*—sharpshooters—dressed in enormous sheepskin coats and armed with automatic rifles.

While I was looking over this frightening picture, the gate slowly opened. An officer stepped out of the guard house carrying a pile of papers and the reception began. Each of us in turn crossed that invisible line which separated freedom from captivity.

"Surname, first name, patronymic, year of birth, article of sentence, and term?" the man spoke abruptly. In his hands were the personal files of each prisoner entrusted to his care; he carefully confirmed the face of each of us with our photograph. His eyes were narrow and he had a blank face like a pancake. "Probably a local," I thought, mechanically reporting all my personal data. Crisply and loudly I pronounced my name and those terrible numbers now attached to it: article and paragraphs of sentence, and term. At first I felt that everyone was looking at me with horror, but I quickly realized that the prisoners were completely indifferent to these numbers, as were the guards. After all, many of them were there because of the same articles and term.

"Reyf, Alla Yevgenyevna, 1931, 58th, 1-a, 10, 11, 8. Term—twenty-five."

My "collection" of numbers, however, did elicit a certain interest: the officer took longer than usual to study my papers and a moment longer to inspect my face. "Pass!" the command finally came, and I crossed that invisible line. Several hours later, with the necessary sanitary procedures done, having changed my civilian clothing for a grey government-issue dress and a greasy and patched quilted jacket, I added one more important item to my personal collection of numbers: my camp number. That number belonged to me alone and would follow me along all the roads I travelled in the Gulag. The million-strong army of prisoners was increased by one more *zek*: number E-881.

That evening in the quarantine barracks, on one of the solid upper bunks, I carefully sewed the square rags with my numbers onto the back of my jacket and dress. I tried to attach it in the very middle, with even stitches and as firmly as possible. Why?! My character wouldn't allow me to do otherwise! I was just as conscientious in the labour I performed. What for? At the time I couldn't answer the question, and I was asked it many a time by some of my comrades. And indeed, I asked it myself often enough—why strive, why submit to the stupid rules, and work not out of fear but for the sake of one's conscience?

Many years have passed and now, as I recall my years of incarceration, I am able to explain the reason for my behaviour. In order to live, to survive, I had to embrace the absurdity of everything that surrounded me in actions reminiscent of ordinary, normal life. Any work I did had to make sense or else I couldn't do it. When I was stronger and was transferred to a different camp, one not for invalids, I had to perform various kinds of labour. For some time our brigade worked at a coal mine face. We had to lug waste heaps from place to place, shifting the smoking rock with shovels. The work was unbearable, and not only because we were suffocating and made ill by the clouds of reddish smoke, but because no one had bothered to explain why we should move it from one place to another. It was like a kind of torture, another punishment. But later, under different circumstances, when we loaded the smoking rock onto trucks that were laying a local road, it was much easier to accept. Still, it is difficult to imagine now how we managed to survive. For five minutes, our faces covered over up to the eyes, we would toss shovelful after shovelful, almost without breathing. Then we would race several metres away, tear the rags off our faces, convulsively swallow air, and then return to the scorching heat. I

can only compare this work to what I did later, when we were rooting out tree stumps, when the midges and mosquitoes were eating
us to death. Nevertheless, the work, even the most exhausting, if it
was done conscientiously and thoroughly, brought a certain happiness. I wasn't the only one to feel this way about our compulsory
labour; most were unable to change their ingrained conscientious-
ness, and this often saved us. Solzhenitsyn's Ivan Denisovich is a
good example of this attitude.[39] Of course, when the labour went
beyond our strength, the sense of its worth disappeared. The need
for self-preservation would compel the prisoners to do their work at
"half-strength."

The prisoners who were criminals had an entirely different attitude: any labour for them was accursed. These unhappy prisoners
were prepared to go so far as self-mutilation, as long as it got them
out of work. And what refined forms of mutilation they inflicted on
themselves! In the criminal jargon it was called "making a joint."
They would make as many injections as possible, with *any* substance,
under their skin, or swallow various objects, or rub the soles of the
feet or their hands with a certain solution to make the skin swell
and abscess. This often led to serious illness and, occasionally, even
to death. But nothing could stop the *urki* who would do anything to
keep themselves from being taken out to work. They wanted to be left
in the barracks where they played cards (something strictly forbidden
in the camps) the whole day long, chattered and slept. Complete idle-
ness, this is what their lives consisted of.

My own work life in the camp was put off for half a year. As soon
as I arrived at Abez I fell seriously ill and landed in the camp hospital, where I stayed for a long time.

12

The Sectarians

Spring in the tundra doesn't come all at once. It appears first in the form of a special kind of light which pours out of the skies and rises from the snow. The days get longer and longer and stretch out tediously before turning into night. This makes it seem that time has stopped, as if the reveille will never be sounded.

I still wasn't used to the white nights of the north—my first weeks were spent in the Abez Invalid Camp. They didn't take the newly arrived prisoners out to work. Instead, we lived in a separate barracks in quarantine. All sorts of people came to see me when they heard that someone had come from Moscow. They were mainly elderly women, also from Moscow. Our acquaintance developed through a fence: I wasn't allowed to go out. Everyone wanted to hear the latest news, but what could I tell them after fifteen months in solitary? They knew far more than I—to my surprise the camp had both newspapers and a radio.

Among my new acquaintances were those whose family connections were with the world of power and the world of the arts. One unassuming little woman by the name of Levando asked in a whisper whether I had heard the case of Molotov's wife, Zhemchuzhina. Rumours of a scandal had reached me, in fact, even before my arrest, when Golda Meir had visited Moscow. They said she had proposed that Soviet Jewish specialists go to Israel to help the young state. There turned out to be many who wanted to go and Polina Zhemchuzhina thoughtlessly gave Stalin a list of those naïve enthusiasts. They were all soon under arrest, including their lofty protectress. More arrests followed as they picked up the members of the households, relatives, and friends. As a great secret, Levando told me that she was Zhemchuzhina's cousin. The next lady from the "formers" was Frima Borisovna. She had quite recently held a solid, responsible position as director of the House of Culture of the Stalin Automobile Factory. Both these women were long-time members of the party, had worn red kerchiefs just after the Revolution, and had studied at the Rabfak.[40] They came from shtetls, out of poor Jewish families, and following the road that many, many others had trod, climbing the ladder up to this or that step of authority and then falling headfirst into the netherworld of the prisons.

Olga Ivanovna belonged to another class of society. She was a relative of the well-known cinema directory Kozintsev and, therefore, of Ehrenburg who was married to Kozintsev's sister.[41] Olga Ivanovna showed me a large, professional photograph of her grandson. She was the first to treat me with something tasty and homemade, something from a care package. I particularly remember several of these acquaintances from my first days in the camp. They reminded me of my family's circle of friends in Moscow. They looked at me as if I was a child, pitied me, and tried to help as much as they could. I am grateful to them to this very day.

I had already got to know the camp's security staff when I was in quarantine. These *nadzorki* were simple and vulgar, but much more like human beings than the robots I had known in prison. They would sometimes chat with the prisoners, telling the stories of their lives and would listen to our stories. The best of them, risking their own freedom, would even send off prisoners' letters through the public mail. It was a particularly valuable service as we had the right to send only two letters a year. The *operupolnomochenny* (the second top officer in command) came to talk to us in quarantine—he was a very important boss in the camp as he had responsibility for all the prisoners' personal files. He was as thin as a post and had a grumpy yellow face. I recall one of his remarks to me: "So what made you land up in a camp like this? This isn't where they re-educate you, this is where they punish you!" His statement contradicted all the slogans on the billboards hung around the whole camp: "Glory to the Communist Party!" and "To Freedom With a Clear Conscience!" and others in the same vein. The prisoners never paid attention to these displays, but they used them to find their way around the locale, you needed to know them to find the right barrack, otherwise completely indistinguishable.

My time in quarantine ended and our group of newcomers was dispersed into working brigades. In accordance with my term, I was put into a barrack for "twenty-fivers." Soon I landed in the BUR, Barrack of Ultrastrict Regime, no doubt so that I would more quickly discover the "attractions" of the camp. I was punished for a "terrible" infraction of the rules: I hadn't put my pair of ordinary blouses into the storage room, but kept them to wear under the coarse prison outfit. While I was sitting on my cot in the blouse a *nadzorka* crept up in secret and dragged me away to the punishment cell, as she called it, for five days. But the less strict superintendant of the camp prison decided, when he found out that I had just arrived, that I only had to stay two days in the BUR.

The BUR was divided into two parts: my part was "soft" and a kind of purgatory. It was slightly heated and the plank beds had rough mattresses filled with wood shavings and covered with a worn soldier's blanket. Once a day you were allowed a dish of watery soup. The other half of the barrack was truly a kind of hell. It was unheated, so that any difference in temperature between the outside and the room was made up only by the adjacent, heated BUR. There were no bedclothes and no mattress on the planks. The *zek*'s ration consisted of tough black bread and boiling water, given out once a day.

When I found out from the superintendant of the prison about all these "amenities," I counted myself fortunate and didn't worry so very much. All the more so as I had had the good luck to miss out on similar punishments in prison, making my prison education not yet complete. My new friends raced to the BUR and tried to persuade the overseer to take pity on me, a poor inexperienced *zek*, and let me back into the barrack. He confessed that he would have done so if the *nadzorka* hadn't first dashed off a report describing my "crime." They all feared each other and one false step could mean landing behind the fence yourself. The one thing that he agreed to, even though it contravened the rules, was to bring me a parcel. Not trusting the *nadzorka*, he himself brought me the paper bag filled with little presents that the women had hurriedly gathered together. I almost burst out crying when I saw all those candies all stuck together, the cookies, and bits of dried cake. It wasn't so bad to be put in the BUR if it meant receiving such loving tenderness.

But my friends left and I could only hear their voices as the door slammed behind the superintendant. As no other prisoners were in the BUR at the time, I was again left alone in my cell. Depression began its so familiar work on me. And although I tried to comfort myself that it was only solitary for two days, and at least it wasn't in the terrible Lefortovo prison but in a heavily populated camp, nevertheless, I understood precisely how the prison and the camp were an extension of each other, and in actuality were one and the same.

Immersed in these thoughts I suddenly noticed the sound of a low mumbling, almost like singing. In the afternoon, when my soup was delivered, I asked the woman who it was singing on the other side of the wall. "Sectarians," she said with venom, and unexpectedly added, "Do you want to see a show? Follow me!" I followed her to the door. She raised the cover over the peephole and told me to look inside. I pressed up to the opening. I will never forget what I saw in front of me. On two-tier bunk beds along the walls of the room were about twelve or fifteen women, all of them completely naked. In the half-darkness of the room I couldn't make out their faces. There were young ones, some no more than girls, as well as old women. Their long hair hung loose and they seemed to be trying to wrap themselves up in it, as if it were clothing. Women on their knees were praying and singing, barely moving their lips. There was something improbable to the picture, as though I were looking through a peephole at a theatre stage where some heart-rending historical drama was being performed. I quietly closed the peephole cover.

"What are you holding them here for? Why are they naked?" I asked the *nadzorka*.

"What, are you sorry for them? Don't be; they aren't even sorry for themselves. They keep rebelling, so now they're going to freeze and die. But they aren't afraid, these stubborn sectarians go on any way they like, just so they suit themselves. Well, that's enough. You've seen your show so now go back to your cell. I don't suppose you'll break the rules like they have!" She poked her finger toward the room where the sectarians were. She showed not a hint of pity for them.

For all the rest of the time I spent in the BUR I could hear the sound of the soft singing on the other side of the wall. I kept seeing their naked bodies on the bare boards. When I got out, into "freedom" in the camp's "general zone," I learned their history. A small group of "religious" had arrived. No one knew which sect they belonged to. In the camp they really didn't care who believed in what or how—if they were imprisoned for their religion, then they were sectarians. Just like all the other newly arrived prisoners, the women were taken to the *banya*. People usually look forward to the chance to bathe after the long journey, but these women refused outright to strip. It took brute force to get them out of their clothes and into the *banya*. After all their clothing was taken away, prison dress was put in its place. When the poor things emerged and discovered the exchange they quietly, without a fuss, explained that they couldn't put on the Devil's clothing. The authorities wasted no time trying to convince them but chased the naked rebels through the whole camp, across the spring snow, right into the punishment cell. Those who saw this procession said that many cried as they watched the sectarians being sent to a certain death. And yet the sectarians went calmly, not noticing anything around them, simply making the sign of the cross.

I don't know how long they kept the women in cold solitary on bread and water, but afterwards they all landed up in the camp infirmary. Many of them caught pneumonia which led directly to tuberculosis. Some of the women were soon dead.

After I was released from the BUR, I was assigned all summer to the brigade made of up "goners" who couldn't leave the camp area because of illness. We were put to work at all sorts of auxiliary jobs inside the camp. There were eight of us. We cleaned up the barracks, washed the floors of the guardhouse, delivered coal. Each morning began with a guessing game, where would we be sent today? One hot July day, when even the tundra was dressed up in bright field flowers, we sat in the sun by the barrack waiting to be sent out on a job. The women, worn out by the heat, were silent, enjoying a break from the used barrack noise. But, of course, they couldn't leave us in peace for long. A *nadzorka* arrived and, without telling us anything, led us toward one of the distant barracks. We followed slowly, making an unusual picture even for the camp. In Abez all the camps were for invalids. But within that monotonous identity there were various levels of squalor, infirmity, sickness, and so forth. We in the invalid brigade were the pariahs of the camp. Arrived but recently, we couldn't stand on our own and didn't know the laws of the camps. For that reason there were lots of people who ordered us about. It was especially the prisoners known as "shams" who would pour their fury out on us. They were the brigadiers, the work allocators, the ones in charge of the warehouses. They doled out third-rate clothing to us, the stuff that they had not yet managed to toss out as completely useless. Even taking into consideration how ugly the camp uniform was, it looked even more loathsome on us. The greasy jackets were in tatters and torn, with the dirty quilting hanging out. Our boots, enormous and shapeless, made us walk like tottery old folks. It was only the brand-new squares with numbers, so carefully sewn onto our backs, that could repair the impression that we were pitiful ragamuffins: we must be needed by someone, even at the bottom of that society, if we were given stock numbers.

We went out to one of the barracks for the ten-year prisoners. Figuring that we were fated to clean out the barrack, we followed our *nadzorka* inside. That was usually when her responsibility for us ceased and we were transferred to the woman on duty in the barrack. But this time the *nadzorka* took us right up to the bunks, pointed at the women lying there, and ordered us to carry them out of the barrack. In complete confusion we stood stock still. Why did we have to carry them out? Where to? Were they ill? The woman on duty briefly explained that these women were sectarians and had refused to go to the *banya*: it was a sin for them to bathe in public. So, once a month they were carried by hand to waiting carts and then from the carts to the *banya*. Although they could make their way back to the barracks on their own, they had to be brought back, since they didn't have the strength to cover the distance from the *banya* to the barrack. They had sentenced themselves to death and, since they were afraid of breaking their dietary code by eating government grub, would eat nothing except bread, water, and sugar. The *nadzorka* hurried us along: "Drag them by their legs and toss them right on the floor, they won't be hurt. It might make them come to their senses, though, and then they'll go on their own." The women in my brigade just stood there, with no idea about how to get started. I looked around the barrack in hope that help might be coming from somewhere. But there was no one else on the bunks. Everyone was out at work that time of the day. What if we said something to these poor, ignorant women? Probably no one had tried to convince them to go voluntarily to the *banya*. Only I would have such a naïve idea. All the others were older and wiser. I went up to the head of the bunk, intending to say something, even just to see their faces, to exchange looks. Eleven motionless bodies were lying on those bunks. They looked like corpses: sallow, swollen faces, tightly closed eyes and lips, hands crossed on their breasts. Only a barely noticeable breathing testified to their being alive. I was terrified and, without even trying to say anything, just stepped away.

In order to make us do something, the *nadzorka* decided to give us a demonstration. She grabbed one of the women by the legs and dragged her off the bunk. We were shaken out of our torpor by the hollow clunk of the woman's head as it hit the floor. At that point we all threw ourselves into the business, recognizing that we could do it without such harsh tactics, so that no one's head would break. They were a heavy burden indeed. It took four of us to move each woman off her bunk and then, struggling, we had to drag them across the entire barrack to the door. It was particularly difficult to heave these live "sacks" up onto the high cart. The sectarians looked to be old, but this might not have been the case—they were simply turning black and were probably quite ill. How could you keep your health when you tortured yourself in such a way? Our work that day turned out to be very hard. We dragged those bodies around until we dropped. And our exasperation at these ignorant, dirty, stinking, stubborn women grew as we worked. The pity that each of us had felt for them evaporated as we began to see ourselves as the real victims. What compassion could we have if we were the ones being tormented as we used such hateful violence against them? These sectarians were the ones at fault. We had already forgotten that it was the *nadzorka* who had made us commit violence against these, our sisters in misery. We ceased to recognize that chain of compulsion, in which we were the final link. The sectarians were rebels, stoics, and we were submissive nothings. We burned with shame and hated these women who had committed no crime against us. Prisoners coming back from work passed by and wouldn't even look in our direction.

In general, the camp population didn't pay any attention to such situations. When barbarity is the norm in a society, the victims of brutality elicit sympathy from only a small section of society. What's the problem if someone has it bad? Just leave me in peace, let me live my life, survive. There was no particular sympathy for the people who were persecuted for their religious beliefs. Their resistance was condemned: why shouldn't they have to go out to labour on Saturdays or holidays? Are we worse than they are? And if these believers were punished for breaking the rules, the rest simply saw it as a reasonable response. Subconsciously, perhaps, many of us envied the steadfastness of these persons.

There were so many sects in the camps! There was a constant migration as people changed their convictions, converted from one sect to another. Sometimes even an atheist would accept the faith of a particularly talented and persistent proselytizer. But more often the worlds of the sectarians and the other prisoners simply did not intersect. They had been strangers outside the camps, and remained strangers inside the barbed wire.

13

Anna Ivanovna

Our barrack for twenty-fivers was different from the others. The population density was particularly high. All the spaces between the bunk beds along the walls were laid with boards, creating a continuous surface of two-tiered bunks. Our barrack was locked up when the depressing sound of metal against a suspended rail rang out, announcing lights out to the entire camp. This too was different from the other barracks. Even in the coldest weather the rest of the camp had to race to a distant toilet during the night. The twenty-fivers had the dubious privilege of our own huge *parasha*, which stood by the locked door at the entrance. We greatly valued this convenience and the locked door didn't bother us at all: there wasn't anywhere to go at night anyway.

There was nothing else unusual about our barrack. There was the same grills on the little windows; the same semi-darkness and heavy, stuffy air in which, they said, you could hang an axe; and the same *burzhuika* stove in the middle of the enormous room. I don't know exactly how many people there were in the barrack as it was a "state secret." But there were a lot, a mob! I felt it most intensely when I once awoke because of some strange sounds. I was used to people crying out in their dreams, grinding their teeth, moaning and swearing, but this time I heard the harmonious sound of voices singing. I sat up on my mattress and looked around flabbergasted: I couldn't understand what was going on.

Women on their knees, in the middle of the barrack and on their bunks, were singing. It seemed they were a countless multitude for you couldn't see the walls or the floor of the room. The kneeling figures filled the whole space, from floor to ceiling. They sang in a low tone in beautiful harmony. Seeing my surprise, my neighbour explained that today was Easter and they were all rejoicing in the Resurrection of Christ. When the choir fell silent a single clear voice continued the service. Thus, for the first time in my life I was present at a religious service. The next day retaliation began. In the morning some *nadzorki* broke into the barrack, led by the chief warder, Prosvetov, an insistent dog of a man who terrorized the whole camp. They jumped up on the bunks and dragged off about a dozen women, shouting and swearing. Someone had apparently reported on them since the *nadzorki* knew precisely who they were taking away. That morning numerous prisoners refused to go out to work—they just lay on their bunks and waited to be sent to the punishment cell.

My day began as it usually did: while the prisoners went to their work outside the zone, we "goners" who worked inside the camp had no reason to hurry. We could rest awhile on the rough, bumpy mattresses stuffed with coarse shavings. Each mattress had its own peculiar depression, corresponding precisely to the curve of the body of the person who slept there, and only for her would it be comfortable. In my drowsy state I could make out the monotonous hum of the barrack. Then everything fell silent, but not for long—the rest of the population began to move. As soon as the others had left for work, the *nadzorka* would come to take us to breakfast. It was yet another "privilege" of the twenty-fivers, to be taken in a group to the dining barrack. All the other prisoners had to make their own way, whether in a crowd or by themselves.

It was the winter of 1953. The fierce Abez cold competed against the fierce regime of the camps. Could anything worse be imagined? Only two letters out a year per prisoner; you couldn't have a single thing of your own, not on your body, not on your bunk, not even a sliver of mirror. (see fig 13.1)

Before taking us out to work, the ferocious *nadzorki* crammed the prisoners' long hair under their kerchiefs so that any resemblance to a female human being. Then there were the huge numbers on the backs of our jackets and grey, shapeless dresses. But that wasn't enough: the people in charge kept looking for better and newer ways to tighten the screws. A few days before they had announced that it would be forbidden to visit other barracks, with solitary as a punishment, as usual. But threats couldn't stop us: what was solitary in comparison to meeting with those who were close to you in faith and spirit? If you could spend an hour before lights out in conversation with a friend, someone from your home, let come what may!

The mother of my fellow accused, Katya, lived in the barrack for the "ten-ers." Anna Ivanovna was remarkably beautiful—tall, stately, with deep-set, sparkling coal-black eyes. Her face was framed by black wavy hair with just a trace of grey around the forehead. By pure chance we turned out to be in the same camp. And then later, by the efforts of the prisoners themselves, Katya herself joined us in a large group of "goners" from a neighbouring camp complex situated in the city of Inta. It was a bitter meeting! The mother's joy burst through her pain, but to see her daughter in captivity! And the daughter's conscience tormented her—if it hadn't been for our activities, her mother would have still been free. (see fig 13.2)

Although Anna Ivanovna had been arrested because of Katya's case, her own case had been fabricated specially for her. They

    WHERE WE BURIED THE SUN

recalled the old "tradition" of the family: Anna Ivanovna's father, brother, and husband had all been arrested. The father and brother had been priests. I never knew what they had been accused of, and I never questioned my friends about it. The two men both died in prison. Just before the war Katya's father was arrested on the very same case. When the war broke out he was put in a penal battalion in which prisoners from the camps fought. Very few of the soldiers in these battalions survived: they were all condemned to death. Anna Ivanovna's husband, the father of two small girls, was one of the ones who perished.

It was difficult to raise the girls alone. Katya fell ill with tuberculosis and had to have special food and care. Anna Ivanovna worked as a bookkeeper and received chickenfeed for it, from which she took the means to help the two children of her late brother. Somehow the family made ends meet. They huddled together in a tiny little room in an Arbat sidestreet: the room was like a pencil case. The girls grew up and Katya was already in the senior class when disaster broke out anew: it seemed as though the family was destined for prison. They arrested Katya and, later, Anna Ivanovna as well. Only the younger daughter, Tanya, remained at liberty, and an old neighbour woman took care of her.

Anna Ivanovna's interrogation was very hard. The investigator wore her out in his attempts to get her to confess that Katya's real father was a Jew: why else did the girl look so Jewish? With her black hair and black eyes, her face like that on an icon, from an Orthodox and deeply religious family, she was a bone in the throat of the investigator. Every bit of our case led to the same conclusion: Jewish nationalists, renegades, and suddenly here was a woman with a grandfather and an uncle who were priests and not a single Jew in the family tree! A directive had obviously been sent out to force a confession from the mother that Katya's real father was that Jew the investigation needed.

Such people have a remarkable psychology that defies the elementary laws of humanity! It was in their power to twist any fact, to falsify events, or completely make them up, and—as a rule—they did so. How many invented crimes, recorded and bound into thick volumes, then stamped "Keep forever," rest in the archives of the police organs? Sometimes, the case might contain only a single sheet of paper. Why would the interrogators need confessions of guilt which were known to be false, bearing signatures acquired only after the torture or torment of their victims? After all, the interrogator would create the document by himself, without the participation of the accused. Often a case would not go to trial—the Special Commission could still function in the absence of the accused. And if the spectacle called a trial took place, the "truth" presented at it had no meaning; everything had been decided beforehand. The majority of those arrested, understanding that resistance was useless, signed the false records. But there were individuals from whom the interrogators could not force a signature. This minor detail changed nothing of their fate—they, like the others, would receive similar sentences, be sent to the same prisons or camps, be exiled or receive the so-called "ten years without the privilege of correspondence," which signified execution. Is it not this paradoxical union of lies and apparent legality that encapsulates the whole essence of the Stalinist regime?

For Anna Ivanovna the interrogations were particularly tormenting—she was pure in soul and in her thoughts; religion was her whole life, God an integral part of her existence. The interrogation broke her impressionable, spiritual nature, and she began to hallucinate. At night, in the small hours, when Katya and I had clambered up onto the top bunk, Anna Ivanovna would tell us in great detail about the miracles she had witnessed in the prison. She solemnly believed that everything she spoke of had indeed taken place, that she had dreamed up nothing, that God had shown her these miracles out of His grace, in order to support her in her time of testing. Once the sky parted above her head during outside exercise and she saw the Mother of God. Another time, the icon of Saint Nicholas, the saint she most revered, appeared in her cell and stayed for a long time. Nothing of this frightened her at all, but filled her with strength, and the surety that she had not been forgotten or abandoned by the Almighty.

Anna Ivanovna was completely devoid of national prejudices and hatreds. She represented the true essence of Christianity, showing kindness to all and was always ready to come to another's aid. She loved me from the beginning and at first—before Katya came to join us—she gave me all her maternal love and care. I was severely ill for a long time after arriving at the camp. A year and three months in solitary had not passed without effect. Thin and pale with my braided hair, I looked much younger than I was. The women treated me with great compassion. Many of them wanted to mother me, to fill that emptiness that had appeared with their separation from their own children. Although we did not have that much in common, I picked Anna Ivanovna to fill that role of mother. We were from different environments, with different pasts. But she had such an attractive strength, a simple and genuine spiritual beauty that I loved her deeply.

Anna Ivanovna appeared each evening in the camp hospital where I lay in the tuberculosis ward. She would bring flowers which she had gathered while working outside the camp. Sometimes she would bring something tasty to eat which someone had given her. She almost never received parcels herself, her younger daughter only rarely sending off something to her mother and sister. Anna Ivanovna had a need to share. And even more than that, she had, along with every deeply religious person, the need to share her own greatest treasure with the people closest to her—God. Anna Ivanovna was saddened that I was not a believer. But her mother would appear to her in her sleep and comfort her, promising that I would certainly find faith. Anna Ivanovna would tell me every time she had such dreams, may of which were prophetic. She would dream of people close to her and know precisely who had fallen ill and who was suffering from misfortune. When the camps began to melt away after the death of Stalin and hundreds of people were freed, Anna Ivanovna would often dream or have a premonition of who was next to be released. As often happens with very sensitive people, she was completely obsessed by her premonitions. Many of them in fact came to pass and the dreams were realized. It was at this mystical level that Anna Ivanovna became close to the Austrian fortune-teller and prophet, Inga Retenbacher, who was so well known in our camp and whose fate I will relate further on.

When I began to receive parcels from home, life became much easier. I remember how I brought lemons to Anna Ivanovna and she immediately ate up the whole fruit, including the peel, and didn't make a face at all. Camp life was hard for her; it was much easier for those of us who were young. I often saw Katya looking pained as she watched her mother going off to work. Wrapped up in her grey rags and moving her feet awkwardly in her crude boots, she looked at such a moment like an old woman. Her cheeks were sunken, her nose sharp, the only life in her face coming from her eyes. The grey lock of hair at her forehead had become greyer. But all the same, Anna Ivanovna remained beautiful. She only had to rest a bit, get a letter from her younger daughter, or chat with a friend, and once again her warm complexion would glow again, dimples would appear on her cheeks and her white-toothed smile would charm everyone.

There were many times that Anna Ivanovna was separated from her daughter—due to her transport to the next camp, or because of decisions of a commission—and a long road led the one away from the other. But it pleased fate to have them meet again and for some time remain together in the same camp. From Inta both were sent to Karaganda, where Anna Ivanovna was finally released in 1955.

Inga

The barrack for the ten-ers swarmed like an ant hill and gave off dozens of smells, all mixed together in a thick stench. The weak ceiling lamps illuminated only the centre of the long passage between the bunks. The bunks themselves were in semi-darkness, over which rose the steam of damp clothing drying on a clothes horse. We were sitting on the upper bunk, huddled close together and breathlessly listening to the fortune-teller who was forecasting my future. It would seem that my life contained no secrets, that everything to come was quite obvious —twenty-five years of corrective labour camps, then five more years of exile, and after that, well, there was nothing left to predict: life would be over. But that would be the prediction of a wicked witch.

Could you accept such a fate at the age of nineteen? Now it was a good fairy who was telling my fortune. She held my hand and carefully studied the lines on my palm.

"I see you as the mistress of your own large home. You are welcoming your guests in a long dress. You will be happy." The fortune-teller let my hand drop. I sat motionless, unable to tear my eyes from her face, barely lit by the glow of a cigarette. Her name was Inga.

She was a strange woman. Grey-haired, with most of her teeth gone, the few front teeth she still had kept her lips from sinking inward. But her cheeks were deeply sunken under prominent cheekbones. Small dark eyes drilled into her interlocutor, not letting her go. Her smile unexpectedly rejuvenated her face and I noticed her remarkably smooth skin. There was not a single wrinkle anywhere, not even in the corners of her eyes except when she smiled. My first impression, that this was an old woman before me, quickly evaporated.

Inga was Anna Ivanovna's friend and it was Anna Ivanovna who had introduced me to her. Inga Retenbacher's fate was unusual even for the camps, where you soon ceased to be surprised by anything. Her real name was Inge, of course, but in the camp she was called by the Russian form, Inga, and it is by that name that she has remained in my memory. I don't recall where she was born, but before her arrest she had lived her entire life in Vienna, Austria. She came from a well-off family, received a good education, and spoke remarkably fluent Russian. It was her impeccable command of the language that made people suspect, upon first meeting her, that she was actually a spy (this was what she had been convicted of). Inga herself explained her fluency in Russian by the fact that as a child she had had a Russian governess for several years. Anna Ivanovna believed in her completely, while the others did not. They did not believe her wonderful stories of her luxurious past life. In the black, stinking barrack these tales of balls, of fancy clothing, her beloved Vienna Opera, her travels—they just didn't sound real. It all seemed to be a retelling of stories from our favourite books—*The Count of Monte Cristo* or *The Three Musketeers*. But not many people worried about the accuracy of Inga's stories. It was simply interesting to listen to her and, briefly, to forget our harsh reality. Just like in the novels, Inga, young and beautiful (which was as difficult to credit as all the rest), dreamed of becoming an actress. For her aristocratic family such a career was unthinkable. So the seventeen-year-old girl ran away from home with some elderly gentleman and became an actress. I don't think she was on the stage for long. After a certain time, Inga married a great love and was very happy.

The war presented the crucial moment for her fate. Inga had no sympathy for Fascism. Like some Austrians, she was disdainful of those Germans who unquestioningly followed Hitler. She told us with pride that she was the pupil of a famous seer who had predicted Hitler's demise, for which he had been shot. The skill of fortune-telling was very useful to Inga in the Soviet camps.

Finally the war was over. The Austrians greeted the Americans and British as liberators, but they met the Russians with anxiety and fear. All the occupying armies felt comfortable in Austria. There were three zones of occupation in Vienna, three army headquarters with their staffs. At the time, Inga was the proprietor of a café (or bar). She called it "Honorary Proprietor." The café was famous for its association with so many of the great sons of Vienna, including Johann Strauss. The military men of all three zones liked the café and the highest ranks became regular customers. They became acquainted, and chatted over their drinks and the delicious Austrian food. They all had the good-humoured and contented temper of victors. Even Kliment Efremovich Voroshilov[42] himself often visited the place. Inga was proud of her friendship with him and during all her years of incarceration wrote futile letters to him, begging him to review her case.

I don't know what transpired in this café, perhaps nothing. But the rumour started that one of the Russian military men who frequented it had gone over to the Allies. Perhaps it wasn't true at all, but was used to stain the reputation of the hospitable mistress of the café, in order to explain her sudden absence.

Inga had disappeared without a trace. All the newspapers were full of stories about the mystery surrounding the whereabouts of the respected Frau Retenbacher. Even the Soviet representatives expressed their surprise and condolences. The papers fussed about it for a while and then fell silent. It was not a peaceful time. The war had only just ended and people were still being killed by a stray bullet here and there. How long her husband kept up the search for her, she never knew. Later Inga found out that he had offered a large reward for any information about her. But no one responded.

All the while, poor Inga was in a suburban villa not far from Vienna. She couldn't understand why she was being held there, why she had been snatched away. They had dragged her into a passing automobile when she was out walking one day, gagged her, bound her hands, and without explanation, drove her out of the city. She spent several days in a small, half-empty room under the vigilant observation of soldiers in Soviet uniforms. She demanded to know the reason for her arrest. She shouted and pounded on the walls. She spoke Russian well and could make her anger and perplexity clear. But her guards just watched her with indifferent eyes and kept silent, as though they couldn't understand a word of what she said. If Inga had not overheard the quiet words the soldiers muttered among themselves, she might have thought that they were not actually Russian soldiers, although their uniforms were Soviet. She was particularly burdened by this silence of her guards.

Several days after Inga's arrest, while she was being taken to the bathroom, Inga noticed in a mirror that her hair seemed to be dusted with some sort of white powder. She tried to brush the dust off with her hand and suddenly realized that her hair had turned grey. She was then thirty-six years old.

A seemingly endless week passed. Then, late one day, a Russian officer summoned her and, without asking her to be seated, handed her a sheet of paper. Several lines in German were written on it. Now Inga discovered that she had been accused of espionage against the Soviet Union.

I don't remember if she told us the details of her investigation, or if there was one at all. Shortly after she was forced to sign a decree of the Special Commission which stated she had been found guilty of espionage and sentencing her to ten years of imprisonment in Soviet corrective labour camps. Inga fainted. She awoke in the room of a

Russian hospital not understanding where she was or what was happening to her. The Russian doctor explained that she had suffered a miscarriage from the shock—she had been in her fourth month of pregnancy. Inga closed her eyes: she would never have a child. After that, it was all delirium: she barely remembered how long she remained on the hospital cot, how they took her out of the hospital, and set her on the train for Russia.

It took a very long time for Inga to reach her destination, passing through one transit point after another. Her past life seemed to be a wonderful dream, of which she sorrowfully told her chance and brief acquaintances. Thank God she had command of the language and was open to people—otherwise, in the midst of all these unhappy persons she would have felt even more lost and destroyed.

Inga told her story and listened to others that were just as bitter and no less tragic. With nothing to do in the transit camps or in the train cars, Inga began to tell the fortunes of her companions, making predictions from the lines in their palms, or from the stars. People thanked her for the distraction and treated her with tobacco from their own pitiful stores. Inga recalled her German seer-mentor more than once in the camps.

During all these long years of imprisonment she never once received a parcel or a single letter—none of those near or dear to her ever learned of her fate. But in the commerce of the camps, her fortune-telling was a valuable commodity: although Inga never had anything of her own, she always had tobacco. In her previous life she had travelled, but never as far as the Soviet Union. From her earliest days she had wanted to visit the country whose language she had known since childhood. And so she was fated to become acquainted with Russia by such a terrible route.

Inga didn't know where they were taking her, but the further the train proceeded, the greyer and more monotonous the landscape became. She could see it from the tiny grilled window in the *teplushka*. Sometimes the convoy would let slip that they were travelling northwards. The forests grew more sparse, the trees more stunted, and the sky hung like a low, leaden vault over the God-forsaken land. Then the watch towers and barbed wire of the camps appeared in the distance. There were so many camps that they began to seem like an integral part of the terrain. Soon the trees disappeared altogether and snowy expanses flowed by. It was a void with no people and no forests.

Inga's heart contracted in anguish—where were they taking her? Would she be able to survive or was she destined to perish in this God-forsaken land? When the train finally stopped and the whole group disembarked into a snowy field, the convoy announced that they had arrived at the place that was designated for their term. Only then did Inga catch a word new to her ears—Vorkuta. Perhaps she had heard it earlier, at the transit camps, but she had never connected it to her own fate.

So this was her new home! For long? For ten years—forever. She couldn't believe it. She would write Voroshilov, everything would be explained, they would free her and maybe even apologize, and she would travel around Russia as a foreign tourist. She would go to Moscow, to Leningrad. That's how she thought. And so she continued to think for a whole eight years of imprisonment!

Inga worked hard in the camp, was ill with scurvy, lost one tooth after another, but never lost hope. I read her statements to the procurator, complaints that were directed to Stalin and Voroshilov. They were written in the round hand of a student, in good Russian, although there were some grammatical mistakes. The answer was always the same: "The complaint has been considered. The case does not warrant a reconsideration." Inga grew accustomed to these answers just as she grew accustomed to everything else. But still she would stubbornly write again and again. At that time, up to Stalin's very death, prisoners were permitted to lodge only one complaint a year. And each year she sent off her letters to Moscow. Perhaps they didn't go any further than the superior officer in the camp, and the answers came from him, too—anything is possible. Her letters to her homeland remained unanswered and she understood that all correspondence was forbidden to her.

Inga met many foreigners in the camps; they came from almost all corners of the globe. Their fates were similar. Many had also been kidnapped and sent in all directions without so much as an investigation to Russia, where camps bristling with barbed wire were waiting for them. Russia's own citizens were, as a rule, better off. They could at least receive letters and sometimes packages; more rarely, visitors. Foreigners were deprived of all this.

I was very sorry for Inga. I liked her for her optimism and lively personality. Everything about her was illuminated by an interior light: from her hoarse, smoked-out, almost masculine voice, the ever present cigarette in her mouth, to her wheezy laugh and jerky movements. She never grew angry at life or at people. She even somehow contrived to love Russia, read Russian authors, and strove to get to know the customs of the country.

The prisoners loved her too; the only exceptions were certain "worldly" women of an intelligentsia background who thought that everyone except themselves was guilty, and that Inga was doubly guilty: first, as a German Fascist and secondly as a spy. I was warned by such "well-wishers": "Why ever do you make friends with that foreigner? She's guilty of something, all right, and you can't believe a single word she says!" But I trusted my intuition and kept visiting Inga and Anna Ivanovna in the ten-year barrack.

Today, an ordinary one in a series of ordinary days, at least had one exciting event: a large transport of prisoners arrived in our camp. The fact as such was not unusual—such groups arrived and departed often. Prisoners were mixed up and shuffled around so they wouldn't stay too long at one place, get used to it, and settle down with their friends. But we always expected that the next group would bring someone interesting, someone from our own area, with fresh news from the outside.

At that time the camps were bursting with newly arrived prisoners. Most of all they were filled with fresh *zeks* from Ukraine, and then from the Baltic states. These were the so-called nationalists. "Religious" also flowed from all ends of the country through the wide camp gates: sectarians convicted for their faith. Then there were the victims of wartime from the territories formerly occupied by the

Germans. You couldn't keep count of all the categories! From the capital cities, Moscow and Leningrad, came enchanting young women who had been convicted of being "with foreigners" (for the briefest of meetings or because of a legal marriage). The ladies of Jewish nationality from the intelligentsia were here because of "nationalism," and the relatives of Senoir Party members who had fallen from their high posts and were now considered "enemies of the people." In this multi-hued mosaic, everyone expected to find someone similar to herself, someone who was close in spirit, an intimate.

When I clambered up onto the bunk, Inga, as always, was sitting on Anna Ivanovna's mattress with her "hostess" and her ever present cigarette. Katya was there too with flushed cheeks from working in the cold, and between them a woman who was new to me. She was very pale and worn out, her age difficult to determine. She spoke quietly, almost languidly. Her frightened eyes darted about and betrayed her as a novice in the camp.

They introduced me to Natasha, who had arrived at our camp with this morning's group. It turned out that she was from Moscow! I immediately showered her with questions.

"When were you arrested?"

"A long time ago, eight months." (It was "a long time" for her, and for us only yesterday!)

"Where did you live in Moscow? Who's still at home?"

"Two children and grandmother."

"Which prison were you in? What is your term?"

The questions continued one after another. But we who are experienced prisoners only ask those questions permitted by camp etiquette. Of course we are interested in much more, but we know our place and aren't pushy. If our new acquaintance wants, and believes that we are worthy of her trust, then she will tell us what she thinks is necessary—about her case, what she is accused of, what is true and what is a lie, where her husband is.

Natasha told her story slowly, stopping to look fearfully into the dark faces of the prisoners. Below and on the neighbouring bunks they were listening to our conversation. We drank hot tea and ate chunks of black bread sprinkled with sugar. Very tasty! The warmth spread through my whole body and I began to feel drowsy.

But then the conversation suddenly became more lively. Inga, when she heard that Natasha and her husband lived in Austria after the war, fastened her eyes upon her.

"Did you live there for long? Were you ever in Vienna?"

"Yes, we went from the military garrison to Vienna for our shopping and simply to relax. What a wonderful time that was! The war was behind us and we were in Europe. Most people couldn't even dream of that before! We liked Vienna a lot. It was as if the war hadn't touched it at all."

"And did you ever get to that famous café on X-straße?" Inga asked unsteadily.

"Well yes, of course, my husband was often there with his officer friends, and I was there with him a couple of times."

"And do you remember the proprietor of the café?" Inga's voice was flat.

"But of course! Such a beautiful, bright young woman! I remember her very well."

We look at poor Inga intently. Her eyes had filled with tears. She dragged deeply on her cigarette and, choking, began to cough. Our new acquaintance realized that her words had caused a strange reaction and she fell silent. Looking around at all of us she asked if the woman wasn't a relative of Inga's. And suddenly the two images joined in her consciousness—that far away, carefree young Austrian and this pale, grey woman sitting before her.

"It was you, Inga? Frau Inge, forgive me, we are all so different now from what we used to be," she began to babble in apology.

We sat for a long time under the influence of this strange, bitter meeting. Inga smoked, absorbed in her own thoughts. I thought of how unjust others had been, the ones who didn't believe her stories about the past. Well, now we'd found a witness. Then Inga and Natasha began to share their memories of Vienna. And, to Natasha, it began to seem that Inga hadn't really changed all that much.

"Just colour your hair, get some new teeth, and you will be just as beautiful again! My word of honour," Natasha said, blushing. She too was transfigured, and it became apparent that she was still young and attractive. We were friends with her for a long time after, until the next transport of prisoners separated us forever.

Among all the days that were just like each other, only the day that mail arrived stood out as a real holiday. Letters brought the most joy. My relatives wrote often, although I could only answer them twice a year. Mother travelled outside the city to mail me food parcels—they would not accept them in Moscow. The arrival of parcels that had been packed by my mother's own hands was a special event. In the evening I would run to my friends with treats. We clambered up onto the bunks, spread out a towel, and displayed on it all the unthinkable riches she had sent—cold cuts, lard, cookies. It all disappeared in a flash, and then the four of us, Katya, Anna Ivanovna, Inga, and I, would sit until lock-up, dreamy from our exhaustion and the food we'd eaten. We talked slowly, recalling the past, listening to Inga's stories, and dreaming of freedom. Each of us believed it was somewhere close by, even though Stalin was still alive and no one was being liberated from the camps. It was 1953.

On one of those happy camp evenings—yes, I didn't make a slip-up, these evenings were sometimes truly happy—Inga suddenly proposed, "Let's tell your fortune, girl." After twelve hours in the fierce cold, we had enjoyed a peaceful and tasty supper with close friends. It was the height of blessedness.

Her eyes looked at me questioningly. Inga knew that I, as an atheist, didn't believe in those mystical predictions and would probably say no. But I agreed with pleasure. I had already heard so much about her remarkable ability to see the past of the person she was "reading." After studying the lines on a palm for a long time, she would always begin with a story about the person's past life. My life had been short and so simple that, even if she didn't possess black magic, she should be able to easily tell it all in a couple of words, and so Inga did. That a youthful distraction, "being in love," had played a great role in my "revolutionary" activity was easy to guess (and perhaps Anna Ivanovna had already told her something about it). This is what I was thinking while Inga, puffing on her cigarette, studied my hand through the smoke. Then the most interesting part began, the telling of my future.

I really didn't believe that you could know someone's life by the dates of her birth or the lines on her palm. But all the same a shiver ran over my body when I heard all that was awaiting me. I wanted to believe in all the good she forecast, while dismissing the bad. First, we were to expect freedom soon, all of us—me, Katya, Anna Ivanovna, and Inga herself. Something remarkable was about to happen, she didn't say what, and all of us would be freed. "There won't be hardly anyone left here at all!" Inga concluded and her eyes shone with happiness. Well, could you really believe Inga's words? She was simply trying to be nice and wanted to comfort us, support us. Around us was such darkness. The doctors' plot to poison Stalin had just been denounced[43] and in the newspapers it was apparent that the atmosphere outside the camps was getting worse. Inside the camps conditions were getting harsher day by day. New groups of prisoners kept arriving, among them people who had been convicted for telling a joke, for uttering a careless word, for having contact with a foreigner. And the terms were unbelievable —fifteen years, twenty-five years. Sofia Mikhailovna Bronshtein said that the Jews were the best violinists in the world and got ten years for anti-Soviet agitation and Jewish nationalism. All kinds of religious people and sectarians were being arrested as well. Among them were children of only sixteen or seventeen!

And yet now, this very minute, in the hubbub of the barrack, Inga pronounced the word "freedom" for all of us. Could we really believe it? Impossible! Yet we believed it! Katya and I were seized by such happiness that we hugged each other and tumbled about on the bunks, squealing and pummelling each other. When this outburst of joy had passed, Inga took my hand again, saying, "When you are free, two brushes with death await you." She had in mind the death of someone close, but expressed it with these words only. I will never forget them. I froze—my mother? My father? "I can't say who, precisely," Inga answered. "But then your life will be very happy. You won't go to school anymore. But you won't need to. I see you as the mistress of your own large home. You are in a long dress, greeting your guests. You will be happy." On this, Inga's predictions ceased. She let my hand drop and said nothing more.

The striking of metal on the rail signalled lock up. We had to immediately depart for our barrack, before the *nadzorka* caught us. Katya and I set off for home in a hurry. The biting frost didn't incline us to speak, and we silently made our way to the barrack for the twenty-fivers. We got there in time, just as they were about to close the door's enormous lock. After the cold, the barrack seemed cozy and warm. But not for long. Up on our top bunks we almost choked from the stuffy air. The mattresses lay in narrow strips, crushed up against each other. At night it was almost impossible to turn over, so tightly we were pressed together. Getting up at night was dangerous because you couldn't make your way back to your same place; the bodies had moved together, closing the opened space.

I lay for a long time, unable to sleep, cuddled up against Katya's shoulder. I thought that she wasn't sleeping either, but we didn't want to talk. Around us the others slept heavily after a long day of labour. So I will be happy! This I immediately believed uncondi-tionally. As far as the long dress was concerned, or my own home, or entertaining—well, that was just something out of Inga's past. She certainly didn't know anything about the way we lived in free-dom: communal apartments, queues, dresses mended over and over again, used clothing. For her such a life in freedom wouldn't be any better than life in the camp. So she told me the tale of Cinderella. It was silly to believe in fairy-tales.

But what about the two brushes with death? No, I'll forget about that. I will remember only one of the predictions—freedom is near! And with that joyful thought I fell asleep.

Two months after that evening Stalin died. Very soon after that the alleged doctor-poisoners were rehabilitated and Beria was shot, along with Abakumov and Riumin—all those who were connected with our indictment. Events piled up one after another, so quickly you couldn't get used to one before a new one came rolling along.

It was truly a joyful time! We were all full of hope. Soon they started letting people go, not waiting for the end of their terms. And then, after awhile, almost all of the foreigners were gathered together in a single camp and were fed much better food. Then they were sent to Moscow by train. Before their departure they were all given new clothing, so as not to frighten anyone with their appearance when they arrived home. Inga left, too. At her departure I brought her some final gifts from one of my parcels. She cried when she said good-bye to Anna Ivanovna, thinking that it would be forever. We received a letter from her soon afterwards. She was in Moscow, walking about the streets freely, and waiting to leave for home.

We all waited impatiently for the changes in our lives. The camps were melting away—Inga's prediction was coming true before our very eyes! Anna Ivanovna and Katya were taken away with a group of prisoners to the camps in Karaganda and, after a little while, I found out that Anna Ivanovna had been released. Mother wrote me that she had visited our home. My mother and the parents of the others who were convicted with me were petitioning for a review of our case. I received encouraging letters. But the bureaucratic machine moved slowly. Illegally convicted persons could only be released on legal grounds so we rebels had to wait longer than most.

It was only on the 25th of April 1956, that all of us were released into freedom, well after the Twentieth Party Congress.[44] "All of us" included thirteen of the organization's sixteen members. During the course of the review, the three that had been shot had their sentences reduced to ten years of incarceration. Even the dead had had their death sentences cancelled!

I won't write here of how we felt when we met our relatives again. I'll come back to that later. I will only say that the joy of our reunion was darkened by two pieces of news: just before my return, my favourite aunt, my father's sister, died in Kiev, and my mother's sister was mortally ill. She had been a second mother to me. Two months later we buried her. Thus another of Inga's predictions had come true—"two brushes with death" had been waiting for me when I returned to freedom.

As for her third prediction, that has also come true, although in a somewhat different way. Although I did graduate from the institute, I didn't particularly like my profession and only worked for a short time in my field.

But the most improbable part of Inga's prediction came to pass, years later, when I emigrated. Here I am, the mistress of a comfortable and pleasant home, actually standing at the top of the stairs in a long dress, greeting my guests. There would have been nothing extraordinary in this, if Inga hadn't seen it all from the bunk of that camp near the Arctic Circle.

Unfortunately, I know few additional details about Inga Retenbacher's life. For some time, during the period of Khrushchev's "indulgences," Anna Ivanovna kept up a correspondence with her. We found out that her husband, having given up the hope of ever finding her, remarried. Having survived this blow, Inga met a man in Germany whose fate had been similar to hers. But they were together only a short time. Then she emigrated to America. Her last letter and photographs were sent from there. In one of the photographs, a happy group of beautiful and well-dressed people were seated around a table. With some difficulty we located Inga among them. The blonde woman smiling at us from the photograph barely reminded us of our old friend.

Soon after that, Anna Ivanovna discontinued their correspondence. She was terribly frightened by some joking verses about Khrushchev that Inga had written in one of the letters. Obviously, Inga had completely forgotten where she had come from and believed that things had truly changed here. In a letter Katya requested that she no longer write. The fear was so great that when I myself emigrated, my friends did not wish to give me Inga's address—"Just in case!"

I am writing these lines from my home in Canada and Inga is, perhaps, somewhere in the United States. Our paths have never crossed and, probably never will! Unless I have forgotten another of Inga's predictions, and we are fated to meet yet one more time.

15

"Read and Envy"

The tundra at night is a magical wonderland. The black starry sky hangs ever so low over your head. The sparkling scythe of a moon illuminates neither the sky nor the earth—it just is, sharp and yellow. All of the light rises up from the ground, from the snowy, endless plain. It isn't even light but a milky, ethereal fog, which seems to quiver in the frosty air. When the sky is lit by the wisps of the northern lights, then your breath is taken away by rapture and a certain mystical fear. It is all like a fairy-tale: beautiful and awesome and incredible.

Two teams of reindeer race one after another along the barely visible road, marked only by the traces of the sled travelling ahead of you. We don't often get to travel by reindeer; usually they haul the prisoner-actors and all our baggage from camp to camp by truck. Then we shake about in the back, bouncing against the sharp corners of the trunks holding our costumes. In all the jumble of "civilized" sensations—the bright headlights of the vehicle, the roar of the motor, the stench of the fuel—the tundra's beauty is dulled. And really there isn't much time to admire the road—the truck moves so fast that we are already at the next camp in only twenty or thirty minutes. But when we have the good fortune to travel by reindeer we are simply overjoyed. You can barely hear the sound of the deer running, only the shout of the *kayur*, the driver, breaks the silence. The runners glide gently over the snow and we are silent, because to talk now would be a sin. Everyone understands this: Gerdas, the Lithuanian clarinettist who is not at all inclined to be romantic and looks like a boxer; Regina Tarasova, the refined Muscovite who preserves her elegance even in the camp's quilted *bushlat*; everyone in our multi-national *kultbrigada*—"cultural brigade." My friend Aldona Matskevichute, a singer, and I go completely crazy with delight. She and I are the youngest, each of us only a little past twenty, and therefore, of course, react to everything with special keenness. If only this wonderful sleigh ride would never come to an end! We are warm in our black sheepskin coats (a new and so far unheard-of item of clothing for prisoners—the "gift" of the chief of the cultural-educational section, Colonel Nikonov). We are wearing thick quilted trousers and felt boots. In such apparel you can hardly feel the cold. Right now it is probably about thirty below, but in the complete absence of wind and the dryness of the air the cold is different. The reindeer run slowly, barely tossing their horns, as if they feel as chipper as we people.

The route taking us from the women's camp to the men's camp which is expecting us isn't so very far—an hour and a half. We left early, about four in the afternoon, but it is already dark outside. There is almost no "daytime" at this time of year—at three everything begins to go grey and is quickly covered in darkness. By five o'clock the stars are shining overhead unless, of course, there is a snowstorm.

From the time that our *kultbrigada* began to serve all the camps in the area, we have travelled about a lot. At first we were accompanied by a convoy, then they gave us passes and we began to travel on our own. In those liberal, post-Stalin days (it was 1955) many prisoners received passes and some even lived outside the camps, while continuing to be counted among the prisoners. Miracles have indeed occurred in our lives.

After they shot Beria, Abakumov, and some other high-ranking masters of our fates, the camp administration didn't know what to do. "Who are *you* now?" "Who are *we* now?" "Who are *they* now?" a confused *nadzorka* kept asking, as she listened to the damning indictments lodged against her god and master, Beria. She stood in the barracks for twenty-fivers while a solemnly triumphant voice resounded from the loudspeaker, referring to Beria as "an agent of English and Japanese intelligence, an enemy of the people" and so on and so forth. The *nadzorka*'s gaze wandered across the faces of the prisoners. She didn't see us and wasn't directing her questions towards us, from whom she expected no answers. I will never forget that confused, pitiful security guard.

The camp administration, frightened half to death, began to make advances to the prisoners, thinking that today's *zek* might soon become tomorrow's boss, and maybe even an investigator. And he, today's "master," might soon (God forbid!) come under investigation. In such an unstable situation anything might happen. My trips with the other actors were only just the beginning. I fell into this privileged brigade at an unsettled time. The *kultbrigada* that entertained both the administration and the prisoners was being transformed into an *agitbrigada*—a propaganda unit. Previously, all political themes were forbidden, now—on the contrary—montages with songs about the Motherland, poems about the war which evoked patriotic feelings, plays containing the highest ideals, all became part of the repertoire. It was just such an educational entertainment that we were bringing on this journey. In front of us we could see the camp watch towers, illuminated by floodlights. From the world of wild nature we returned to the harsh world of humankind.

Today's camp was considered a hard camp. Healthy men were sent here to mine as much coal as possible. They were often transferred here as a form of punishment. The bestial camp commandant enjoyed an unpleasant fame throughout all the Inta camps. Experienced prisoners, who had spent time in many camps, knew well how much depended on the temper of the camp commandant, the security chief. Whether life would be bearable in the camp depended on the character of even the most junior "master." But everyone was fearful of this camp. The weakening of the regime here was taking place particularly slowly and the commandant allowed the *kultbrigada* to visit only rarely. This was my first visit.

The reindeer team halted at the wide gates of the camp zone, bristling with barbed wire. We tumbled out of the sleigh, moving our numb legs with difficulty. The men dragged out the trunks containing our costumes. The guards frisked us very carefully, shaking out all the costumes and making us unbutton our coats and take off our boots. It was the usual procedure—we watched the zeal of the guards with indifference. They knew, and we knew, that it was all *pro forma*, that we would bring nothing forbidden, except for tiny letter-notes, into the camp. But the notes, mail that was considered sacred in all the camps, would get through to the addressee, no matter how strict the regulations or how thorough the frisking.

Here the prisoners' resourcefulness had no end! And of course each of us was carrying those precious notes (in camp slang, *ksivy*) —from daughter to father, from wife to husband, from lovers who knew each other only by correspondence. Dozens of tightly folded, twisted, tied up bits of paper from people who yearned for someone. If the notes were discovered then it would be trouble for us—the upshot in such a case was the punishment cell and heavy labour. But the unwritten camp law required us to take the risk.

When the frisking was over, we proceeded into the camp. At that time of day or, rather, night, the camp looked like a dead townsite, deserted of people. The black barracks had been built in even rows. The tiny windows were barely visible and huge banks of snow stretched along the low barracks. During the long winter these banks were transformed into tall snowy walls, the paths between the barracks becoming white trenches. Here and there along these narrow roads dark, shadowy figures loomed, but you could make them out only with difficulty as the whole area lay in darkness.

Only the territory between the two stretches of barbed wire was brightly lit. Here the thin crust of ice over the snow lay white, diamond-like and untouched. This was where the vigilant gaze of the four guard-watchers was directed, their automatic submachine guns pointing inwards from the four corner towers of the zone. Neither man nor beast could crawl across this space unnoticed.

There was liveliness only at the dining-barrack, already a crowd was awaiting our arrival. For the male prisoners the coming of the *kultbrigada* weas a double holiday—entertainment, yes, but, mainly, a chance to meet with women, of whose company they had been deprived for many years. Tender smiles, happy faces—here they don't particularly appreciate our art, nor notice our wretched appearance. We represented for them all the women of the world, that certain beautiful female substance, each of us a woman-goddess. It was remarkable how these coarsened, tormented men, starved of women, were transfigured by our presence. They couldn't have welcomed us any better. We were idolized. They brought us gifts behind stage, bags with candies. They fed us special food, prepared just for us. Men always seemed to think that we suffered more than they, and many of them felt that they were to blame for the fate of their wives, sisters, or mothers.

These meetings with our brothers in misfortune were always full of the most conflicting of emotions—joy (after all, we too were miserable in the absence of men!) and discomfort over the worship they showered upon us, thankfulness, and a painful pity for these people who had it so much worse than us.

When it was approaching eight we hurried backstage. Now it was time to distribute those precious letters; sometimes we gave them all to one trustworthy *zek*. Then we had to get ready for the performance. No matter how much they heated the barrack up for us, the change into light, airy costumes was unpleasant. Our artist-designer, Alexander Sergeyevich, who had recently joined the brigade, was busy on the stage with the lighting, fixing up a luxurious background that depicted the sunlit landscape of central Russia —this was supposed to put the audience into a happy mood. "Shurik from Paris," as we called him (he had actually come straight from Paris ten years ago, right to Vorkuta, instead of Moscow where he had been heading), was a miracle worker: he dressed us in costumes in the style of Diaghilev's Ballets Russes—bright, original (they would have envied them outside the prisons!); he constructed unheard-of props out of.papier-mâché. Our concerts were designed à la Paris (so it seemed to us). "Shurik" is the diminuative form for "Alexander," and is usually used for a young man. Our Shurik, who was about to celebrate his sixtieth birthday, we all treasured.

The curtain was closed and we could hear the hum of the hall as it filled up. The tables had been taken away, and the whole space of the long dining-barrack furnished with benches. The actors were nervous (as they should be), but stage fright, as a rule, simply creates a special inspiration. As for myself, I had a very bad case of nerves— shivers ran up and down my spine. I trembled as if I had a fever.

Regina Tarasova is my mentor and tries to cheer me up.

"You are so pale, pale as death, you need more makeup," she advised me. "Don't be a coward, don't worry how you read your lines, they'll all be ecstatic. You could even just go out on the stage and stand there silently, and your success would be certain!"

Our music director, Nikolai Porfiryevich Klaus, once a concert-master and conductor in Minsk. A tall, thin, old man (to my mind, though he was only forty-five), was busy with our little orchestra. There was a clarinettist, a percussionist, a violinist, and Klaus himself in charge of the accordion.

Everything was ready to begin. To my bad luck, I was to be the first one out—that's what the administration decided, giving particular importance to my number. Colonel Nikonov, the head of the educational section, had lectured us for a long time, explaining our new tasks.

"You have to help these people come out into freedom not embittered, but loving their Motherland, as genuine Soviet citizens," this grey colonel tried to impress upon us in his quiet voice. The curtains slowly parted and I stood before the darkened hall. Now I was to fulfill the mission entrusted to me.

"Vladimir Mayakovsky's *Verses on a Soviet Passport*," I said in a voice muffled with emotion. Out of the darkness hundreds of eyes were looking at me. In the front rows I could make out the faces, lit with smiles. They were looking me over with curiosity: a youngish, nice girl, what's she going to tell us? The majority of the men in the hall didn't have a clue who Mayakovsky was—none of the Western Ukrainians, Lithuanians, Latvians, or Estonians had yet had the opportunity to become acquainted with "the best, most talented poet of our Soviet epoch," as Stalin once said of Mayakovsky. The foreign prisoners have never even heard of him, and our prisoners, the Russians, had forgotten all about him while they were at the front or in captivity, if they had ever known about him.

> *"I'd tear*
> *like a wolf*
> *at bureaucracy.*
> *For mandates*
> *my respect's but the slightest."*

I began with a voice that had grown more confident, entering into the role of the "agitator, the rowdies' ringleader."

> *"To the Devil himself*
> *I'd chuck*
> *without mercy*
> *every red-taped paper.*
> *But this..."*

My stage fright had disappeared. With my head held proudly, I took a step forward to the very edge of the stage. I was bursting with the feeling of patriotism, an unhealthy feeling of love for the

Motherland, the best one of all, and I needed to show this to all of those around me and, especially, to myself. I had never seen a single other country, but I was firmly convinced that only in my country did people live well. Just look at me! I was against all the injustice of the bourgeois world. I, *zek* number E-881, an enemy of the people, a Jewish nationalist, a traitor to the Motherland, a terrorist, sentenced to twenty-five years' deprivation of freedom—I would try to convince people just like myself, prisoners with numbers on their backs, how wonderful Soviet power was. There, outside the borders of our most just, most humane society, people hated each other, suspected other nationalities, spit on foreign passports.

> *"For one kind of passport—*
> *smiling lips part.*
> *For others—*
> *an attitude of scorn."*

Swedes, Norwegians, Poles—all are puny, unworthy of our attention.

> *"And without a turn*
> *of their cabbage heads,*
> *their feelings*
> *hidden*
> *in lower regions,*
> *they take*
> *without blinking,*
> *the passports from Swedes*
> *and various*
> *odd*
> *Norwegians."*

The police, the bureaucrats, absolutely everyone would be afraid of me *there*, simply because I was a representative of the first country in the world where people were happy.

"With what delight
*   that gendarme caste*
would have me
*   crucified on the spot,*
because I hold
*   in my hands*
*   hammered fast*
sickle-clasped
my red Soviet passport."

(see fig 15.1)

Not for a moment did it occur to me that I had chosen an inappropriate place for a display of my passionate patriotism. I didn't act even the tiniest bit against my conscience. The justness of the regime was ingrained in me, I was weaned on Soviet power, whose ideas had once fooled the mind of the very honest poet Mayakovsky. My ardent love for the Motherland did not suffer the least bit from the fact that I had just spent the past four years in prison, undergoing interrogation, trial, sentencing, and prison camp. Our youthful group wanted a just *Soviet* society. It would have the same power, only it would be good and kind, just as Lenin himself.

Nature had rewarded me with a fine, deep, ringing voice—it flew out into the hall, into each and every ear, into each and every soul. Forget everything that has happened to you. You are *zeks*, *zeks* with numbers, nameless, you are the happiest of all mortals! You know how they take such care of you here—they guard you with dogs. You have been behind the barbed wire for nothing—for ten to fifteen years. Your guilt is only that you remained alive when you fell into the war's meat grinder—had you died, it would have all been all right. You stood up for trampled national feelings and were sentenced as "enemies of the people." It's not important that your life has been crippled and that you—healthy young men—have become old and toothless; that the homes you might return to have disappeared, your families torn up by the roots and sent off to die in Siberia; that some of you are terrified of crossing that threshold of long-awaited freedom.

My hand stretched out its imaginary passport towards the prisoners: here it is, that passport they snatched from you! You haven't seen it for many years, and probably won't see it again soon. But that's all right, let them envy you, for you are prisoners of the Soviet Socialist Union! At that moment a just God should have struck me and turned me to ashes. But He allowed me to live, so that I would never forget my shame. (see fig 15.2)

The hall was quiet for a moment, and then a rather weak applause broke out. I bowed and then went backstage. My colleagues congratulated me on my successful début. During the rest of the concert I went out on stage several times in other numbers—in a jolly Ukrainian dance, and in skits. The first number was problably quickly forgotten, because I was met afterwards with quite thunderous applause.

The concert was soon over and those lucky fellows who already knew someone in the brigade, or were particularly bold and wanted to make friends, came backstage. I waited for the appearance of two young men whom I liked a lot. I had met them when we were constructing a road some distance away. They had waved at me from the column going to the mine, and had even written a note suggesting that we strike up a friendship. I watched for them everywhere in vain, for the young men never appeared.

Later, when I had acquired many friends in the men's camps, some of them told me that they had been shocked by my recitation, but had forgiven me. Those who didn't want to make my acquaintance, couldn't forget and didn't want to forgive.

I hadn't read Mayakovsky for a long time. We put on plays about the war, an opera, *The Zaporozhets Cossack Beyond the Danube*. I sang and danced, changing costume many times in the course of an evening. By the will of fate I was spared a repeat of my shameful début. But what if my fate had been different?

+ + + + +

The life of any person seems to me to be a long, long chain of transformations. If only it were possible to meet with the person you were at different stages in your life! A woman in her middle age could then chat with herself when she was a youth, or a grey-haired old man could argue with his younger self as he tried to make sense of his long life. How would you react to your actions in the past? After all, it was *you*, you yourself—only perhaps a more attractive, fresher, younger you. But my hands, my feet, my head, that birthmark on my cheek—all that I call "me," is the same. Your head spins from the memories, you catch your breath: what nobility, what audacity, how striking it all looked. From other actions you flinch, and try to push yourself away, to forget. Probably it is a good thing that you can't meet the you of the past. It doesn't matter that it is a green youth that stands before you. How could you have done it? How could you not have felt your own baseness? No matter how you try to justify it now, you can't return the past. *You* did it then, and *I* have to punish myself for the rest of my life.

Now my life is coming to its conclusion, but my memory does not fade and still returns me to my youth. You rub my nose in your actions, oh youth.

16

At the Arctic Circle

The camp uniform didn't fit everyone the same way. Of course it didn't "beautify" anyone at all, but the healthy and young ones often looked rather good in it. On the "goners," the ugly *bushlat* seemed to be appropriate, smoothing out the plainness and pitiful appearance of the wearer. And yet on Yevgeniya Alexandrovna the jacket, along with her formless dress, looked ridiculous or, in the Russian expression, like a saddle on a cow! She resembled Pierre Bezukhov, the character in Tolstoy's *War and Peace*, as he wandered through Napoleon's rear-lines. She was tall, plump, and a bit clumsy. Her arms were always sticking out, as if they were not attached to her body. Her mittens dangled below her sleeves on long tapes so that they (God forbid) wouldn't get lost

—this was a trick borrowed from children's apparel that Yevgeniya Alexandrovna was very proud of. In the centre of her round, red face was a short little nose, on which were perched round glasses with golden frames. Everything looked awkward on her: the *ushanka*, the winter cap with ear flaps, was pulled right down over her forehead and would from time to time slip over her eyes; the sleeves of the old, ageless *bushlat*, were too short and the dirt-hardened and crude boots were lined with dirty-white foot bindings. When she turned her head, Yevgeniya Alexandrovna turned her entire body —and then from behind those glasses her helpless, child-like eyes would be looking at us.

Yevgeniya Alexandrovna and I met at Abez, in the camp for the sick and weak, where I had been sent from the prison in Moscow. The camps in Abez, both the men's and the women's, were all "invalid camps." The tundra surrounded us and there was no particular work to do there. The small settlement outside the camps was inhabited by the military, the guards and security, and the convoys. Some of the "goners" from the Komi ASSR labour camps were brought here, as well as from other prisons. Many of them went straight into the camp hospital, which was always full to capacity. From the hospital, fate might send you either to a common barrack, or outside, "feet first." The mortality rate was very high.

My acquaintance with Yevgeniya Alexandrovna didn't happen at once. She wasn't among those softhearted Muscovite women who filed into the isolation barrack where I was briefly held after arrival. She was wary about striking up friendships and wasn't inclined to pour out her soul to the first person she met, as many prisoners in the camps were.

Soon after my arrival at Abez the whole camp was transferred to another location. These "great migrations" were a common occurrence —the camps were constantly shuffled around, moved from place to place. People were suddenly uprooted and transported hundreds of kilometres or perhaps only to an adjacent camp. This was not done without an ulterior motive: we were not allowed to become established in a single place, to settle down with friends—everything had to be unstable, short-term: only our captivity was forever. I was a completely inexperienced novice in the camp and thus my first "tramp" into the tundra almost turned into a tragedy. It was already the middle of June and it was very hot. The snow had melted everywhere. They told us that we would be moving to a nearby camp, only two to three kilometres away. I set off in my rubber-soled slippers, having forgotten all about the permafrost under my feet. It took about three hours for the convoy to check the prisoners into the new camp and by the next day I was in the camp hospital with a high temperature. The prisoner-doctors looked at me with pity— at first they thought it was an outbreak of tuberculosis, which often followed a long period of solitary confinement. After several days I could not move a single joint and my skin was covered with red lumps. But God had pity on me. The doctors joyfully announced that I only had acute polyarthritis and would soon recover. But this illness was followed by severe case of pleurisy. As a result, I disappeared into the hospital for the next six months. Many people thought I had struck it lucky to get into the hospital while not being fatally ill and be able to kill time. But I had no reason to rejoice over my supposed good fortune. The situation in the infirmary barrack was very bad: in one and the same ward, which resembled all the other barracks, were patients who were ill with contagious forms of tuberculosis and severe asthma, as well as many with venereal diseases. Among the latter were women who were completely insane, and others who were afflicted with various stages of syphilis. For the rest of us, these were the "untouchables." We all feared them. The poor wretches felt themselves shunned and some of them, becoming vicious, attempted to infect other prisoners. To do so they would dip their dirty rags into the barrels of drinking water—they were more than once discovered in the act. We didn't know how syphilis and other venereal diseases were transmitted and so we were afraid to even touch the handles of the doors. Even breathing the same air with them was terrifying. As soon as one of us was caught looking at these women, angry words would break out. "What are you staring at?" they shouted. "Just you wait till you've caught it!" I would sometimes watch them on the sly. Most of them were women who had been in prison for many years and had become infected with syphilis after they "shacked up" with other convicts whose terms were to an end at the same time. When politicals and common criminals served their terms together, the regime was lenient enough to allow such things. In reality, the danger of being infected with tuberculosis in these conditions was much more likely, but I didn't realize it at the time. Friends who were the same age as I—the Western Ukrainians who had passed through such terrible investigations, beatings, hunger, and freezing isolation—arrived in the camps half-dead from various forms of tuberculosis. The paradox was that the cold climate often saved them as it slowed down the development of the disease. Later I found out that once they had been released and returned to their homes in a warmer climate, many perished from galloping consumption.

Among those who were ill in the barrack were several epileptics. Sometimes we would be awakened by their animal-like howling and gnashing of teeth. Those of us who were strong would race to help—some would hold a woman beating herself in convulsions by the hands and feet, while others would put all their weight on the woman's body, preventing her from injuring herself. Those nights were horrifying; you wanted to cover your ears so as not to hear what was going on so close by. In the morning the victims had forgotten the entire seizure and lay quietly, worn out, and indifferent to everything.

During the worst period of my illness I paid little attention to my surroundings—I simply had to survive. But as soon as I began to return to normal, the thought of remaining in the infirmary barrack was unbearable. I could not wait until they released me into the "common" area. My endless, long days were made bearable by my growing friendship with Yevgeniya Alexandrovna Taratuta, who was for some time in the same infirmary. She was released before me and often came to visit. I had never had a wise, adult, friend. In my days of freedom I had been surrounded by girls my own age, while adults had only spoken to me in tones of condescension and, if they were not actually instructing me, would "simply" give good advice. It was all very boring! It seemed to me that it was impossible to be the friend of an adult. And now suddenly this dear new friend of mine, an author wise with experience, was talking with me as though we were equals. She questioned me about everything and even told me about her own life, about her family. In 1906, her father and mother had met in Siberia, in that famous city of exiles, Tobolsk. In the depths of one winter a party of exiles and convicts, some in shackles, had been driven in. One of those in chains was the twenty-six-year-old Alexander Taratuta. The group of new arrivals was met by the twenty-year-old Agniya Markova, who had come to visit her brother, a revolutionary who was finishing out his time in the city's central prison. It was only eleven years before the Revolution. The meeting was fateful and the young people vowed never to part. Together they took part in the revolutionary underground struggle. Yevgeniya Alexandrovna recounted how many sorrows had befallen her parents, how many prisons her father had known from the inside, how many parcels her mother brought to him! In 1911, Taratuta's escape from exile was organized and he made it to Paris. A year later Agniya joined him. During these years there were probably more Russian underground revolutionaries abroad than in Russia itself; in any case, the most active revolution-aries were living in Geneva, London, and Paris—all waiting for the right moment to return to revolutionary Russia. Taratuta met with many of the leading revolutionaries in Paris, including Lenin himself —which was to play a tragic part in his future: in 1937 he was exe-cuted along with many others who had been Lenin's comrades. I held my breath as I listened to Yevgeniya Alexandrovna's—real life stories about underground revolutionaries, friends with Lenin. This was her family! It was many years later that I found out that Yevgeniya Alexandrovna had been born in Paris: foreign birth was considered almost a crime, and you learned to hide such secrets well. After the death of her father, Yevgeniya Alexandrovna's mother was exiled with her two children. I eagerly awaited the con-tinuation of this intriguing story, but the storyteller fell silent. In a whisper she reminded me that Scheherazade's tales were always interrupted, cut off at their most interesting points, in order to heighten the suspense until the next meeting. "All the more so," Yevgeniya Alexandrovna added, "as mine is no fairy-tale but a true story that has no happy ending."

It was already late and the infirmary had grown quiet and was wrapped in sleep. From time to time the silence was interrupted by moaning, sobbing, and mumbling—our dreams returned us to the past and gave us no rest.

My "education," my growing comprehension of the unwritten laws of camp life, continued in the infirmary. All those things that are now well known to children in kindergarten I had to learn much later and in the most difficult of circumstances. My Ukrainian friends, students from Lviv, warned me that I should be wary of my neighbour in the next bed. She was a nice girl, with short hair like a boy's, and seemed to be drawn to me. Danuta joked and teased me, and even tried to wrestle with me on the cot. It never occurred to me that our relationship could be anything other than ordinary friendship. That is, until Anychka Ivanitska explained to me that there were women in the camp who lived as couples, like a kind of family, and that Danuta was well known among the prisoners as a lesbian. The *nadzorki* kept track of such women, and would send them into isolation or transfer the lovers to separate camps. I would later see so many genuine tragedies because of this—after all, their separation could be forever.

My friendship with Yevgeniya Alexandrovna had no sexual overtones, of course, but I was definitely in love with my older friend. How else could you explain the feelings that gripped me so? In the barrack I awaited her arrival impatiently until I caught sight of her and then I grew fevered and my heart began pounding and there was no end to my joy as a smiling Yevgeniya Alexandrovna sat down at my feet on the cot. What else could this be but love? This was like the infatuation young schoolgirls have for their teachers, no matter of which sex. They follow them, shower them with presents, and demand nothing in return. Once my entire class fell in love with our mathematics teacher, Nina Sergeyevna, who had nowhere to hide from thirty-two pairs of eyes, all fixed on her and full of adoration.

There was a great difference in age between me and my new friend, some twenty years—she was probably about forty when we first became acquainted. She seemed old to me, which is typical for one so young. Despite the fact that she was older and could have addressed me more informally, Yevgeniya Alexandrovna for a long time only spoke to me using the formal *vy* for "you." Such a usage, it seemed to me, distanced us from each other, and I asked her to address me informally, using *ty* or "thou." Yevgeniya Alexandrovna gently replied, "That has to be earned." Somewhat confused, I didn't pursue her remarks to find out what I had to do to earn her trust. In the evening, in the poorly lit barrack where I visited her, we would sit closely together and carry on our conversation almost in whispers, so as not to be overheard. I had already, long before, told Yevgeniya Alexandrovna all about my brief underground activities. And about the investigation, of course, the terrible isolation, and in general all the events of my rather short life. In return, Yevgeniya Alexandrovna did not rush to let me in on her secrets—she said nothing about her case, but mentioned that it had been fabricated from beginning to end. She told how hard it had been: the investigator had insulted and even beaten her. It was hard to hear of the humiliations she had to endure. I saw before me this intellectual woman, so gentle she couldn't even speak in a loud voice, and tried to imagine how that bastard of an investigator had beaten her. She wrote letters of complaint to the prosecutor's office, and other letters to Fadeyev, the General Secretary of the Writers' Union, whom she knew personally. Her letters were like literary compositions, attempting in their passion to evoke outrage over the lawlessness of those who were the authors of her unjust fate. Fadeyev never answered her, and the prosecutor's office replied that her case did not need to be reopened since Taratuta had been sentenced on a legal basis.

As a funny story, Yevgeniya Alexandrovna told how the investigator had written in his report that she had received a pair of gold eyeglasses as a reward for her espionage. With a bitter smile she showed me the gold-amalgam frames, which they hadn't even taken from her as material evidence. I looked at the photographs of her daughter, whom she had left in the care of the girl's grandmother. Yevgeniya Alexandrovna wouldn't mention the girl's father. Tanya, who was six at the time, bore her grandfather's patronymic—that's exactly how it was written on her birth certificate. From some of her remarks, I concluded that the girl's father was the same friend that Taratuta had been sentenced with. According to camp etiquette it was inappropriate to ask probing questions and I did not pose such questions to my friend. With the little money she had, my friend's mother sent parcels to her daughter whenever she could. I knew from my own letters that this was a difficult procedure: you couldn't send a parcel to the camps from Moscow. Instead, you had to travel outside the capital with your heavy burden. But the older revolutionary was hardened—from her youth, Agniya Dmitrievna had taken parcels to prisons; first to the Tsarist ones for her brother and husband, and then to the Soviet ones for her husband and now her daughter. Friends would help the little they could, without the knowledge of the authorities, of course. For instance, the children's author Lev Kassil, who was treated with such affection by the regime, would sometimes send books of his as soon as they were published. Yevgeniya Alexandrovna would recognize the sender by the familiar slight scent of perfume in the parcel.

No matter what story Yevgeniya Alexandrovna told, it was brightened by her sharp wit and fine observation. She was physically weak but possessed a rare strength of will and optimism. People were drawn to her and desired to become her friend, but she only allowed a chosen few to come close, by standards that were known to her alone.

At last, almost six months after I had been admitted, I was released from the infirmary. The prisoner-doctors often attempted, by the rules or against them, to retain those prisoners who had recovered, so the weak would not immediately by subjected to heavy labour. So it was with my case—I managed to regain my strength, settle in with new friends, and was no longer fearful of general labour, the burden of which I could not yet imagine. But since there was not much work outside the camp zone, the majority of prisoners were employed on maintenance work in the camp. The workers in the "zone" were called "crazies" in camp slang, which meant that they had managed to land light work. It was light only in contrast to the work outside the "zone," where prisoners suffered most of all from the cold. Among the "crazies" were the prisoners in charge of others. The camp elite consisted of the kitchen workers, and the ones who worked in the dining barrack and the bathhouse. There were less honourable "professions" but they were still desirable for those who froze in the cold for hours on end. Among them was sewage disposal. An enormous barrel on wheels hitched to a small horse made daily rounds of the camp latrines. Behind it slowly moved workers carrying long scoops over their shoulders. Taratuta began working in such a team and thought that her new profession was a great blessing: by the middle of the day she was already free from work, and after a careful washing, she would settle down comfortably on her cot and take up her needlework.

Fate also favoured me—after the infirmary I was taken into the brigade that cleaned the ashes out of the stoves in all the camp locations. To call this work "dust-free" (as any kind of light work was called in the camp) would be by any stretch of the imagination impossible, as those of us who heaved the full ash boxes were quickly covered from head to toe by layers of ash. We transported the refuse on a cart, but had no horse to help us—we were the horsepower, three of us hitched in front of the cart and three pushing it from behind. Passing from barrack to barrack we would meet with the sewage contraption, pulled by the horse. Hiding my envy of their horse power with difficulty, I would exchange smiles with Yevgeniya Alexandrovna.

It was the winter of 1953. The arctic night was barely broken by the coming of dawn. When the night was over it was succeeded by dusk, and after dusk again came night. The camp, covered in snow, was always brighter than the skies overhead. Sometimes we would see the northern lights. The transparent, greenish pillars of shimmering light joined the sky to the earth as though trying to console all of us swarming about in the constant dusk that there was still light in the heavens, that the arctic night was not eternal. The temperature went down to fifty degrees below zero. On such days prisoners were not taken outside the camp and were allowed to rest a bit. But such brigades as ours had to labour in all temperatures—during a period of bitter cold the stoves had to be cleaned out more often, in fact.

In the evening, or rather at the end of the day, since "evening" began at about three in the afternoon, before they banged the iron bar to let us know it was time to get into our barracks, after which it was strictly forbidden to move around in the camp, I would go into the barrack of the ten-year prisoners where Yevgeniya Alexandrovna lived. By chance, it also happened to be the focal point for the Muscovites or, as we joked, the "Moscow *bon ton*." The majority of the young women had been sentenced for "relations with foreigners." That was the rubric for those who simply had foreign friends, had accidently met them somewhere, who carried on long-term correspondence with a foreign acquaintance, or who were even legally married to one. Treated all the same, they were each given ten years without so much as a trial. This illegal process was termed "Sentenced by Special Conference" or SSC. The ginger-haired beauty Galya Wallace had legally married an Englishman from the embassy, I think. When he was required to leave the Soviet Union, his pregnant wife was not permitted to go with him. Soon after the birth of their baby she was arrested and the new-born daughter was left with Galya's parents. The clever and lively Margarita Werner, who looked like a little boy, was guilty of having been born in the United States. Then there was Ira Tsigarelli, a woman with a disagreeable and strange appearance, about whom rumours circulated that she had cooperated with the KGB in her editorial work on a journal—they even sent their collaborators to the camps! And many, many more women with similar stories come alive in my memory, where they ever remain just as they were half a century ago.

At last we were together. I had waited for this moment the entire day! The half-darkness created the illusion that we were separated from the rest of the barrack population. Yevgeniya Alexandrovna, in her soft voice, read to me a letter from home. I listened carefully, but my eyes were involuntarily fixed on a stranger in the far corner of the room. A tiny figure wrapped in what looked like a shabby, cat-fur coat (a strange bit of tolerance by the strict regime!), with jet-black hair and small bright eyes. I inspected the stranger with curiousity. She looked like a sick bird that had flown in from an exotic southern land. Her whole pose was filled with suffering: the lowered head, the helpless hands hanging at her sides, the bent back. I could not tear myself away from watching her, although I knew it was rude to stare. But the woman seemed to not notice how I was watching her. Her thoughts were surely elsewhere, in the past, perhaps. Catching my look, Yevgeniya Alexandrovna answered my silent question: "That's the new one in our barrack. Her name is Lina Ivanovna, she's the wife of the composer Sergei Prokofiev. She's a Spaniard." So I was right to imagine that she looked like a southern bird. Much later I discovered that during the happy days of their life together, Prokofiev had called his wife his *ptakha* (birdie). But that happy time was already long past shoved aside by years of discord and alienation. In 1936, after many years of life abroad, Prokofiev returned to the Soviet Union with his young wife and two small children. The new conditions of her life in a strange country were, it seemed, very hard for Lina Ivanovna, and soon after they arrived, their married life fell apart. At the time of his wife's arrest, Prokofiev had long been living apart from her and their sons Sviatoslav and Oleg were already adults. Lina Ivanovna was alone in a strange land. And now a new ordeal overwhelmed her. Taratuta didn't know why they had imprisoned her; possibly it was just to spite the famous composer who, though he was fully in the favour of the authorities, still might rebel against them. So, just as a warning, the mother of his sons was now in the camps. But maybe she had simply fallen victim to a new wave of repression. They said that Lina Ivanovna had met with foreigners. After all, she herself was a foreigner. Later I discovered that she had been arrested in 1948 and accused of espionage. Her arrest had certainly not just happened to coincide with the campaign against the greatest of Soviet composers, Prokofiev and Shostakovich. She was born Lina Llubera and in her youth had been a Lieder singer, often performing the premieres of many of Prokofiev's vocal works. They wed in Paris in 1923 and toured with great success in America, Italy and, in 1927, Soviet Russia.

At the time I met Lina Ivanovna she had been behind bars for four years. I don't know which camps she had been imprisoned in during those years, but she seemed to have just arrived in Abez. That evening, when I saw her for the first time, there was no introduction. Our next meeting took place a couple of weeks later, when our brigade was topped up by a new worker. She was dressed quite unbelievably: from under her patched, overlarge *bushlat* peeked a worn-out sealskin coat. Her face was half-hidden by her kerchief and only her sparkling, coal-black eyes could be seen. The novice introduced herself, weakly saying,: "I'm called Lina Ivanovna." I immediately recognized the stranger who had interested me so much and recalled Yevgeniya Alexandrovna's story about her. We welcomed the new member of our brigade warmly: the greater our number, the less work. And I was happy that I would have the chance to work with a Muscovite, a cultured woman. But it soon turned out that Lina Ivanovna was completely useless at her job. She didn't have the strength to lift the ashbox, she didn't have the strength to either pull or push the cart. In a weak, apologetic voice she would say something or other in her defence, while her watery eyes made it look like she was crying. We pitied her, not getting angry at all, and often sent her back to the barrack. "We'll get along without you, and if the *nadzorka* asks why you aren't at work, just tell her you are sick," we'd say. She would smile pitifully and depart, dragging her feet in their enormous boots with difficulty.

My life in the camp became much jollier when a new set of arrivals included Katya Panfilova, another member of my underground organization. We had not known each other until the trial, meeting then for the first time. But I had been very close to Katya's mother, Anna Ivanovna. Now the three of us made up a kind of family, Katya and I becoming great friends, almost like sisters. The two of us were in the barrack for twenty-five-year prisoners, while Anna Ivanovna was in the neighbouring one, for the ten-year prisoners. Katya and I worked in different brigades, so before we went to sleep we would exchange impressions of the day on our top bunks. At the time Katya worked in the maintenance yard. There were different sorts of work there, some harder, some easier. Some people were given shovels and other equipment, others were in charge of the storerooms or responsible for repairing vehicles and wheelbarrows. As the youngest, Katya was given the hardest job of sawing and chopping wood. No one looking at her strong physique, her bright-red full cheeks, and white-toothed smile, would imagine that she had been ill with tuberculosis. By some miracle, the tuberculosis had been cured in prison but could recur at any moment. She never complained of being tired but I saw that she would often fall asleep almost as soon as her head hit the rough pillow filled with shavings. I would fall asleep to the sound of her even breathing.

Once, at the very end of February 1953, just before going to sleep, we were talking about something in our usual whispers. The barrack was buried in the half-dark, the usual, many-voiced hum had ended but here and there you could still hear the soft whisper of a conversation. The last loud noise was that of the key turning in the enormous lock as the barrack door was fastened for the night: sleep tight, nothing threatens you, you twenty-fivers, except for your imprisonment. For some reason the reality of it was especially difficult that evening. During the day, at work, moving around, there had been no time to become pensive. But now, in the stuffy room, our bodies packed tightly against each other, lying like logs in piles, locked in until morning—if a fire should break out, no one would survive this common grave. It was at this moment that Katya and I most needed at least a shadow of a hope, a little thread that could guide us through this thick gloom. Could it really be twenty-five years ahead, twenty-five years of such nights and days? What could save us?

Perhaps a third world war would erupt and the Soviet Union go down in defeat. I don't remember which of us started talking about a war, but we both immediately rejected the idea—so many lost lives just for our salvation? Well, what else? A thought quickly sped through both of our minds, though neither of us at that moment had the courage to share it. What if Stalin were to die? After all, he was old and—imagine—not immortal. We didn't utter a single word but the thought rustled past and was expressed in our eyes. Was it possible to wish for the death of the Divine Being, the Moloch who ate his own children and yet was worshipped by millions of his blind subjects? The veil had already fallen from our eyes, we could see clearly, but the others . . . The unborn words died in our throats. With them we fell asleep.

In the morning it was our turn to take out the *parasha*, the huge tub that was used at night in place of a toilet by the entire population of the barrack. This pleasant job fell to each one of us in turn, but not often as there were more than one hundred prisoners in the barrack. At the gong announcing that it was time to get up we slid off our upper bunks. We had to hurry so we wouldn't be late for breakfast. With difficulty we hoisted the tub and its splashing contents onto the cart and dragged it to the door which was already open. The frosty, fresh air poured over us. After a night in the barrack we drank it in like water. Rolling the *parasha* to the appropriate place, we tipped it over with some effort. It was amazing how lightly we took this rather unpleasant obligation. We laughed when we couldn't move the tub from its place, and exploded into laughter as we jumped aside so as not to spill the repulsive swill on ourselves. All in all, we acted like ordinary young people, no matter what our situation was.

March began with a snowstorm. The air grew warm and snow piled up in walls. All the "crazies" were given shovels and we spent endless hours cleaning the snow off the paths between the barracks. It seemed that there would be no end to the snowfall. We slipped into the barrack to warm up a bit and again set off to shift the light cotton wool of snow. On one of our breaks we heard an unusually agitated announcer's voice coming from the speaker that hung by the entrance to the barrack. They were broadcasting a bulletin on the condition of Stalin, who had suddenly fallen ill. I held my breath —could our unspoken wish have been heard? Stalin was never ill, all his subjects knew that well. If they were broadcasting reports about his illness over the radio then it must be something serious. It never entered our heads that it was possible he was already dead and that his devastated satraps were simply gathering up their strength to announce to the people the a tragedy that had befallen them. Every two or three hours the regular radio broadcasts were interrupted and again came the tense, solemn voice of the announcer: temperature, pulse, rate of breathing. Picking a free moment, I raced to the maintenance yard where Katya was working. I knew that she wouldn't have heard the radio announcements there. Flying into the area where Katya was piling coal onto a wheelbarrow, I pounced on her, hugged her from behind, and whispered in her ear: "Stalin is seriously ill." We stood hugging each other for several minutes; there was no one around and no one could see our shining faces.

Two days later, on the 5th of March, the entire camp, from the lowliest "crazy" to the camp commander himself, was shaken by the announcement of the death of our beloved leader. For the whole day the radio speaker poured out funeral music. Of course, not everyone in the camp felt the death of Stalin as personal grief. The women from Western Ukraine, the Balts, the foreigners—anyone who had not lived through the normal ideological drill—none of them displayed any particular emotion. It is possible that they felt a certain joy inside, but almost all of them feared further repressions from an even stricter regime. In the camps any change was frightening—experience had taught that all change makes things worse. But most people, both in the camps and at liberty, mourned the death of the tyrant, believing that he had been like a "good tsar" who knew nothing of the abuses committed during his rule. I will never forget the two old women who sobbed to the sound of the funeral march music. They had been revolutionaries, taken into the party during the "Lenin Enrolment" after Lenin's death in 1924; it was said that they had been accused of Trotskyism. Precious few "Old Bolsheviks" had survived the numerous purges. Already in the camps for twenty years, the two women mourned the murderer of their party comrades, their husbands, and relatives to the seventh remove. You had to be completely blind, and so they were. Through their tears they kept repeating: "Now we are truly lost!"

A couple of days later Katya and I came upon an announcement in the local newspaper of the Komi ASSR. It was about a memorial evening held in Canada which had been dedicated to the memory of Sergei Prokofiev, who had died on the 5th of March—the very same day that the world had been told of Stalin's death. Well, who would have noticed such a thing as the death of that brilliant composer? We ran to the barrack with the paper to find the so-called Cultural-Educational Centre, or CEC. It was Sunday, when the amateur choir had its rehearsals, and Lina Ivanovna Prokofieva was one of the members of the choir. Not preparing her for the news, without thinking what effect it might have on her, we showed her the notice. She read it through once, raised her incomprehending eyes towards us, and read it through again. She broke down in tears, covering her face with her hands. In confusion, unable to say anything to console her, we thought only that she was mourning the death of someone she had once loved. Now, knowing her tragic life story, I understand that she was crying over her own terrible fate.

Several years later, in freedom, I met an elegant, unusually graceful and well-dressed woman at the Moscow Conservatory. I didn't recognize her at once. The friend who was accompanying me to the concert, Irina Nikolayevna Ugrimova, whom I had known from camp days, led me up to the woman. "Lina Ivanovna, don't you recognize this young lady?" she asked. "Oh yes!" the woman exclaimed in English and began to speak to me in that foreign language. She hadn't recognized me at all and I didn't have the heart to remind her about the boxes full of ashes.

Spring in Abez was in no hurry to give us warmth. But there was more than enough light, and camp routine didn't seem so gloomy when the days were sunny. The normal shuffling around of camp inmates began again. A commission of doctors, both prisoners and non-prisoners, selected the "working livestock" and decided who was to go where. Often completely ill people from the sick camps were sent to heavy-labour camps, where the work was completely beyond their physical abilities. They would suffer there for a time, and then, half alive, be returned to Abez. Katya was taken away first. Her departure was very sad as she bade farewell to her mother and to me. It wasn't long until they decided I was ready to go to the Inta heavy-labour camp. Taratuta left with me for the same camp. We were happy that we would be going south, into the forested tundra.

By the 1950s the Inta settlement had already taken on the appearance of a town. It had grown along with the growth in the number of camps around it. The prisoners worked in coal mines, on road and housing construction, and in the forests. This "free" labour force was far from efficient, but with an endlessly replenished army of prisoners, this northern region developed nonetheless. I managed to try out a number of professions there, since the brigades at the construction sites were always changing. We dug foundation trenches for housing, we rooted out stumps in the thin forests on the banks of the Black River, we spread still-smoking cinders on the roads, we even packed silage pits for the livestock during the summer. My hands, which had never known physical labour, became coarse and "proletarian" calluses appeared on them.

Sometimes the sites where the women worked were close to the ones where male prisoners were working. And at times, if the convoy was not particularly strict, we would exchange jokes at a distance and even strike up acquaintances. Such deviations from the rules were rare—the convoy might have to pay heavily for such a breach. I particularly remember one such site where we were rooting out stumps along the river. Our brigade was taken there over the course of many days. A little distance away prisoners from the neighbouring men's camp were felling timber. For them the work wasn't very difficult since the trees in that forested tundra had very slender trunks. For us, rooting up stumps was rather hard work. But what we all, both men and women, suffered from were the biting midges. These tiny, blood-sucking midges simply ate us up. Nothing, neither netted hats nor thick clothing, provided any protection— their bites drove us into a frenzy. Only by the bonfires could we have any rest from them. One young man, who always worked naked to the waist, stood out among his comrades, whose camp clothing otherwise made them indistinguishable. At first we thought that he was dressed strangely but, inspecting him more closely, we realized that it wasn't his dress that was strange: what looked like a shirt was in fact his bare torso plastered with midges. It was difficult to believe that he could bear such torture! But day after day he appeared at the site in the same way. It was said that even in the winter this young fellow went out to work half-naked. No one knew why he was so unkind to his body, until the rumour went around that he was preparing himself for an escape. At that time prisoners very rarely tried to escape, and there were practically none who succeeded. As a rule the local people would turn any fugitives in to the authorities. Long gone was the humane Russian tradition whereby the local population would leave provisions in deserted shacks for fugitives from tsarist camps or from exile. In these days, those brave enough to attempt flight ended up dead. And so it happened this time, too. Several days later they announced in the camps that fugitives had been captured and, of course, shot. We remembered this fearless young man for a long time, and how his life had ended so tragically.

Three times during these years my mother came to visit me. The first visit was very difficult, both for her and for me. The camps were still running on a strict regime; the relaxation of rules didn't begin until some time after Stalin's death. It was the first time in her life that my mother saw columns of prisoners marching under armed convoy and guarded by enormous German shepherds. It was not a pleasant sight. I was in the camp when they came running to bring me to the guard house. On the other side of the barbed wire stood my mother, grown thin and pinched, her hair gone grey at the temples, and smiling with a bitterness I had never seen before. Our meeting took place at the guard house. The *nadzorka* stood a small distance away but never took her eyes off of us. Right away they told us that we had been given only three hours for our meeting. I cried right through half of the time we were allotted. We were forbidden to talk about my case, as well as about life in the camp. Instead we talked about Moscow, about family and friends, about my father, and about my brother, who had been transformed from a little boy into a teenager during these years. It hurt to think that it was my fault that his childhood had been spoiled, that he had been forced to lead a double life, hiding the shameful stigma of having a sister who was an "enemy of the people." And what would be waiting for him in the future? Young people like him were not allowed into higher education and the threat of arrest hung over them all their lives. But I could not touch on this topic with my mother during our conversation. Our next two meetings took place during the Khrushchev-era "Thaw" in the mid-1950s, and did not leave me as depressed as that first visit. For her final visit I was even able to acquire a pass to go to the city and we had our picture taken together at the city photographer's. As I write these words this picture is now looking at me from the wall. (see fig 16.1)

The final place I worked before being sent off with the actors' brigade was a construction site for houses. We excavated trenches for the foundation. The snow had already melted away but the ground was still frozen. We struck our shovels into the soil with difficulty and broke into the clay-like ground in bits. I don't remember why, but each brigade member was excavating her own pit separate from the others. We had been hacking away at the clay for a week. My pit was up to my waist, but I was clearly lagging behind the others—their heads were barely visible above ground level. At the time they had started paying us a miserable little sum for our labour. What the whole brigade earned depended on how hard each member worked. Therefore, I tried with all my heart not to lag behind the others. But the deeper my pit grew, the more difficult it was to throw the soil out onto the surface. Finally the moment came when I no longer had the strength to toss out a layer of clay with my shovel, and it fell back onto my head. Hopelessly, I tried again and again to shovel out the clay, all the while becoming more covered with wet clumps of earth. My clothing, my boots, my hair—they all became sticky and wet. My repetitious movements made me look like a malfunctioning robot. At the moment of complete exhaustion, when I was ready to collapse onto the bottom of the pit, Olesia stretched out her hand to me: "That's enough, climb out!" There was no sound of reproach in her voice. Clasping the hand of my saviour, I somehow clambered out of the pit: my clay-covered boots probably weighed a Russian *pood* [16.38 kg]. Olesia jumped down into the pit and the clumps of clay began flying, shovelful after shovelful. A short time later the required depth had been reached. Olesia was a sweet young girl from Western Ukraine, the leader of the brigade, and spent all her free time embroidering a shirt for her fiancé in the neighbouring camp. I don't remember how I thanked her, perhaps I didn't even, I was in such a torpid state. And now, forty-five years later, I can't even recall her last name, although my heart is still overflowing with gratitude!

Thus my career as a "navvy" came to an end, and I began the more appealing career of "prisoner-actress." But not for long. The period of the Stalinist camps was coming to an end; indeed, they were later exchanged for Khrushchev camps and after that for Brezhnev camps, but those were other camps, with other prisoners.

In 1955 I saw one after another of my friends leave for freedom. Among them was Yevgeniya Alexandrovna. She promised to visit my family in Moscow. After my liberation we stayed friends for a long time, not meeting often, but we would always call each other on the telephone. I knew very little about Yevgeniya Alexandrovna's literary work: she had told me with great enthusiasm that she was working on a biography of Ethel Lillian Voynich, the author of the novel, *The Gadfly*. The book was well known in the Soviet Union. Many generations of Soviet youth had been raised on the example of the novel's hero, Arthur, known in the revolutionary underground as "the Gadfly," an inflexible fighter for Italian independence.

Published in New York and London in 1897, the novel was not widely read by the general public, but later became a handbook for revolutionary and radical youth at the turn of the century. During the Soviet period it took on new life and was republished countless times. Plays were based on it as well as a film, which included Shostakovich's remarkable music. The novel had everything needed to create a romantic revolutionary hero: all the clichés, sentimentality dressed up in heroic costume, melodrama, love and betrayal, rejection of religion—it was all there, but there was no living person at the centre.

After Stalin's death, when many Soviet ideals were beginning to fade, interest in the novel died away. It was then that Yevgeniya Alexandrovna began to work on her biography of the novel's author. In this single fact you can see a typically Soviet irony: yesterday's prisoner in Stalin's Gulag, sentenced to ten years for no reason, but still true to the ideals of the Revolution, works on a book which is destined to become yet another tool of Soviet propaganda! She had walked down the thorny Soviet path—the arrest and the execution of her father, exile with her mother and little brother, a brief respite, and then her own arrest, prison, a most terrible investigation and then the camp. And yet Yevgeniya Alexandrovna still naïvely believed that her fate and the fate of the prisoners of the Gulag had been determined not by the communist system as such, but by individuals who had perverted a fine idea. Even in her old age, describing her father's life story, she spoke proudly of his accomplishments in the "industrialization of agriculture"; that is, the forced creation of collective and state farms, in the process of which millions of peasants died and the Soviet Union's agriculture was completely ruined. I always felt uncomfortable when talk turned to Taratuta's writing. I respected her kindness, sincerity, and honesty, but I could not share her political beliefs, and we practically never touched on these themes when we were together.

I was in Canada when Yevgeniya Alexandrovna sent me her books, all of them affectionately autographed. One of them was devoted to the well-known Russian populist, the founder of the

People's Will party, Sergei Stepniak-Kravchinsky. He was a revolutionary terrorist who, in 1878, stabbed the St. Petersburg Chief of Police, Mezentsev, with a dagger. Having escaped abroad, Kravchinsky eluded inevitable punishment. He liked to show his friends the famous dagger, using it to cut up bread for their dinner. Taratuta knew that Stepniak-Kravchinsky was one of the inspirations for the hero of *The Gadfly*, but she didn't know about one interesting detail: the character of Arthur was also based on a certain Sidney Reilly. In his youth Reilly had somehow come into contact with some Russian revolutionaries, and met Ethel Voynich. She later used parts of his story for certain details of her hero's life. What later happened to Reilly was, from the point of view of the fate of the novel's hero, both symbolic and ironic: having become disillusioned with the ideas of the revolution, Reilly became an ardent anti-communist. He was celebrated for his work for British intelligence, took part in planning the assassination attempt on the Soviet representatives Krasin and Chicherin at the Genoa Conference of 1922, and perished at the hands of the Cheka. This is how the real life of one of Voynich's inspirations for the fearless revolutionary "Gadfly" ended. I myself found out about the life and death of Reilly and his links to the figure of the "Gadfly" only in Canada, and didn't dare write about it to Yevgeniya Alexandrovna. I still have the most affectionate feelings towards my old friend, and it hurts me to think of her fate, full of tragic shocks and trials. I recall our long conversations in the dark barrack, and I cannot escape the feeling that her life and naive belief in a good Lenin and in a beautiful communist future for all of humankind was in striking conflict with reality. In this sense Yevgeniya Alexandrovna was not alone. I saw so many like her in the camps and at liberty, people who remained true to the ideas of their youth, in spite of all that they had seen and experienced.

+ + + + +

At the beginning of January 1956, I too left Inta. Forever! Many years later, during the perestroika and glasnost years, my brother sent a letter to Canada with a clipping from the newspaper. The piece was entitled "To the Women Prisoners of the Gulag" and read, in part: "In Inta (Komi ASSR), in a former settlement of the Gulag, a memorial has been erected to the women prisoners who were repressed and sent here during the years of the Stalinist Terror. The modest stone monument stands next to a surviving camp barrack."

17

Liberation

It was 1956. For us the year wasn't just passing but racing by at a gallop, conquering the distance of thousands of kilometres, bringing us from the Arctic region, the tundra, Taishet, and Mordovia to our own Moscow. Then time stopped and threw us backwards, to that long ago year of 1951 and our arrest, as we were shoved back into the Moscow prisons, many of us again finding ourselves in solitary. At last they had gathered us from the various camps and brought us back for "review." Our parents had left no stone unturned in their long struggle with the government institutions. Finally they managed to get the office of the public prosecutor to agree to revisit the case of the "young anti-Soviet organization." The stunned "organs," weak ened by the execution of their leaders, were overwhelmed by a flood of applications for the review of cases in which there had been not a shadow of a crime committed. We, who had actually belonged to an organization, had to wait our turn. Commissions came out to the camps and freed thousands of prisoners on the spot, releasing prisoners who had almost served out their ten years and those who were considered worthy of liberation without a detailed investigation of their cases.

Trains from all corners of the country were packed with people wearing identical padded jackets or quilted coats, the dark spots where the stitching for their identification numbers had been snipped off still visible. But even if they had been dressed in ordinary clothing, their expressions would have somehow united them. There was something distracted in their faces, and at the same time their eyes shone with a joy that was hard to conceal. These people thirsted to talk about themselves, striking up conversations with their fellow passengers, trying to look them in the eyes and determine whether or not they were listening with interest and trust. But most often the strangers on the train were frightened and tried to get rid of the pushy story-tellers as quickly as possible.

In contrast to the former *zeks*, who had received permission to travel about on their own, I was transported in a prison wagon under convoy. Almost four years had passed since the first time they had shoved me into a tightly-packed Stolypin railway car on a deserted platform of some Moscow station. Then, the compartments were stuffed with bunks and people lay packed side by side, almost on top of each other. Then, the direction of the trains had been away from the large cities to the furthest reaches of the country. Now, everything was moving in reverse. And the situation in the wagon was completely different: I was entirely alone in my compartment, although the bars on the windows remained. The young convoy accompanying me kept trying to talk with me, trying to find out what I was imprisoned for. I, too, was completely different from what I had been when I started out on my first journey in the spring of 1952. From a frightened girl, almost transparent in my pallor, I had been transformed into a hardened veteran, with five years of experience of the prisons, transports, transfers, and camps. I had changed and so had the times! We had arrived at what one wit called "the era of delayed rehabilitation."

They took me quickly, without the customary transfers, straight to Moscow. When the train stopped at the small stations along the way, my convoy allowed me to stand in the corridor by an open window. Through the grating I could see the dirty ground and the grey sky. It was the beginning of January, but not much snow had fallen. There was only a dusting of snow on the ground and the rusty-black station outbuildings stood out here and there in their unkempt way, not brightened by a covering of snow. Women were working on the rails and in their dark, formless clothing they could hardly be distinguished from the trash which surrounded them. My wagon was marked with large letters: MAIL. But the railway workers knew exactly what was being transported in the place of the mail. Once, at one little station, some young women workers approached me at the window. Only recently, when Stalin was still around, people were afraid to even look in the direction of prisoners, dropping their gaze or turning their backs. But these girls looked me over with interest. Despite the convoy's cry of "All right, move on! That's not allowed!" and other such threats from his meagre repertoire, these curious women did not go away. One came right up to the window and began asking me what I had been sentenced for and where they were taking me. "You can't be a criminal," she said in a firm tone. And when I answered that I was a political, her eyes grew round and, turning to her comrades, she said loudly: "The girl's a political!" I tensed up, expecting to hear the usual shouts of "Fascist," but instead I heard words of compassion: "Such a young one! Why have they destroyed your life?" And someone else added, "It must have been a mistake!" I had not expected such a response and was deeply affected, moved almost to tears. When they learned that I was being taken for a review of my case, the girls were happy and wished me a speedy release. I remember this brief conversation well because in 1952, only a few years before, it could not possibly have taken place. Yes, indeed, I was smelling the scent of a fresh wind that filled me with joy and hope.

At another stop, workers resting on their spades engaged in a pleasant exchange of curses with my good-natured guard. "Why don't you let her go, soldier? She should be attending school! Let her have a little walk, she's not going to run away!" the young men shouted out in turn. For the sake of appearances, the guard chased my defenders away, but suddenly switched from his tone of command to a more gentle one: "Once I get her where we're going to, they'll look into her case and let her go free as a bird," he said, quietly adding, just for me to hear, "I know for sure." Could I believe him? Of course not! What could this nice guy know? But how much he helped me then! To the sound of the rumble of the wheels I dreamed about a quick release.

With each passing minute, Moscow grew closer. Finally the convoy warned me that it was time to get ready, the next stop was Moscow. I held my breath at the news. In just a few minutes I would greet my beloved city again, return to my past.

But I didn't get the chance to see the city, even from afar. Again a "Black Maria" appeared right beside the wagon—a single step onto Moscow's soil and I clambered into the familiar darkness of the truck's metal belly. Those old sensations were resurrected with a sickening clarity. My first year of incarceration. That had been the worst of times. I had lost my freedom and had almost lost myself. Then, in the camps, no matter how bad it got it was always easier than in prison. And the past year things had been transformed almost beyond recognition: the concert brigade, trips without a convoy, travel outside the "zone," going into the city with a pass. I felt as if I had stepped with one foot into freedom. And suddenly it was as if nothing had changed—my nightmarish year of 1952 was still dragging on! Again I was a non-person and no one addressed a word to me other than shouting and commands. There were no faces around me, no eyes, no people; just my guards, grey and angry. And again, as before, I was simply *zek* number E-881, sentenced according to an endless string of clauses in the penal code. They

 Where We Buried the Sun

passed me from hand to hand, like an object, an object worth nothing more than those clauses and subclauses.

A Moscow prison welcomes you according to certain rules and regulations. I drone in a monotone: surname, name, and patronymic, year of birth, article 58, points 1-a, 10, 11, 8. Was it possible, with all that "train" behind me, that they would let us free? I stepped through the prison gates and felt completely helpless. It would have been better to have stayed in the camp! Again I paced from corner to corner in my solitary cell, hardly different from my cell in the Lefortovo Prison. This time I knew that I was in the famous Butyrki Prison. Just my luck to complete my prison education in this ancient place!

I discovered that I was in the Butyrki when I overheard the conversation of two "criminals" in the reception box. Next to me in the same cupboard two old friends were chatting loudly; they'd just returned after a short period of freedom. I listened in curiously. In their colourful thieves' jargon, sprinkled with exquisite profanities, the two exchanged stories about their adventures during the brief time between one incarceration and the next. Both of them had been out for just over a year, but they had managed to make quite a splash in that short time. They had committed several more crimes and were now returning to their home, the prison. No regrets, no sadness! On the contrary, they were happy about meeting again, and kept interrupting each other with the names of friends, mentioning who was jailed where, and what jobs had been done recently. Without my transit camp experience I wouldn't have understood half of what they were saying. And not just because of their marvellous slang. I wouldn't have understood their psychology, their opinions about justice, about good and evil—their morality. What a strange, weird world of crippled people! And here I was sitting next to them, in the Butyrki Prison, where criminals made up the majority of the prisoners, and I prayed to the fates to grant me a solitary cell.

My prayer was answered and I was in solitary once again. But there was little to rejoice as my previous experience appeared to be no help at all. I had not learned to cope with the loneliness. The regime at Butyrki differed not at all from that at Lefortovo, except perhaps that you could hear the prisoners and their captors cursing each other. There was the vilest profanity on both sides and plenty of double entendres. "Come on, get out!" the guard would shout. "Come on, turn over! Come on, don't be slow!" The phrase "Come on!" was repeated endlessly. In reply, the women's voices would use the phrase provocatively: "Hey! Come on, come on, come on, but I'm not slowing down for you!" They would crudely flirt with the guards, or curse them to the skies. But the guards were accustomed to it and snapped back, not viciously, just for form's sake. The prison hummed with life—deep, gloomy silence had reigned at Lefortovo.

I wasn't in the Butyrki Prison for long. I don't think they called me for an interrogation once. The review of our case began in the most splendid of Moscow's prisons, the Lubyanka. It would have been unforgivable not to have at least once been kept in that world-famous torture chamber. But I landed there during its vegetarian days, when it would have been incorrect to call the Lubyanka a place of torture. At that time it was basically the location for the examination of previous decisions, which mostly ended with the release of the accused. Yes, indeed, it was truly the beginning of a new era, at least in comparison with 1951. They only called you for interrogation in the daytime. The prisoners signed in in a special journal which noted the times that sessions began and ended. I can hardly recall my conversations with the investigator, but the whole atmosphere was one of calm and even gentleness. They asked me to tell how the investigation after my arrest had been conducted and how, in my opinion, it did not correspond to the evidence in my personal file.

One of the important charges in the case against us had been "Jewish nationalism." In my case in particular it was based on the verses by Margarita Aliger found when they searched my family's apartment. During the preliminary investigation I had told the interrogator that I had never thought of myself as a nationalist. Aliger's verses were about the war and about anti-Semitism, and not about nationalism. The following is how it had been recorded in my file:

RESOLUTION

30 May 1956   Moscow

The military procurator of the Division of the Main Military Prosecutor's Office, Lieutenant-Colonel Onishko, having reviewed the material in the archives of case No. M-4727 concerning REYF, A. Y., sentenced on 13 February 1952 by the Military Collegium of the Supreme Court of the USSR according to articles 58-1 "a," 58-8, 58-10, pt. 1 and 58-11 of the Criminal Code of the RSFSR to twenty-five years at a Corrective Labour Camp,

HAS FOUND THAT:

During REYF's arrest and search in 1951, was discovered and confiscated a manuscript text of a poem, beginning with the words "How far from Egypt to Russia..." (cf. Vol. 34, personal file 174).

The possession and distribution of these verses were incriminating to her in the indictment according to article 58 10, pt. 1 of the Criminal Code of the RSFSR.

During subsequent investigation of the case, it was determined that these verses are an excerpt from the poem by M. Aliger entitled *Your Victory*, with certain emendations and additions.

Taking into consideration that, for a correct assessment of the manuscript verses taken from REYF, it is necessary to compare them with the author's text of the poem *Your Victory*,

HAS RESOLVED:

It is necessary to add to file M-4727 on the indictment of REYF the following excerpt from the poem by M. Aliger, *Your Victory*, published in the volume *Selected Works* of 1947, beginning with the words, "Mama, mama, neither cry nor wail..."

> [signed] Military Procurator of the
> Division of the Main Military Prosecutor's Office, Lieutenant-
> Colonel Onishko

»   »   »   »   »

An excerpt from M. Aliger's poem:

Your Victory

Mama, mama, neither cry nor wail,
Not your tears nor words will help.
Deprived of shelter in your old age
How can you accept this and survive?

+ + + + +

Lighting the oven and warming her hands,
Trying to settle down to life again,
My mother said, "We are Jews,
How dare you forget it?"
Yes, I dared, do you understand, I dared.
It was so cloudless all around,
I didn't manage to think of it,
From childhood there was too little time.
One doesn't choose his homeland.
When you begin to see and breathe,
You discover a homeland on this earth
Unalterably, like your father and mother.
The days were dove-grey, squinting,
Foul wind swept the streets...
I was born in Russia in the autumn,
And Russia took me in.

There isn't a single drop of nationalism here! What struck me most of all, I think, was that Aliger's poem wasn't, in fact, an underground effort, but had been published in the official Soviet press four years before I was arrested.

I don't remember the investigator's face at all, whether there was only one person or if several people conducted the examination. I do recall one person though our meeting didn't take place in an office, but in my solitary cell. Even now I was required to spend time in solitary. But what a cell it was! Heated, almost comfortable, with a parquet floor. And a library—you could only dream of such a thing before. I picked out books from a huge selection. My eyes were dazzled by the choices: Rabelais, Homer, Voltaire. I was able to hold magnificent, pre-revolutionary editions—you didn't see those often, even outside prison. My self-education would have suffered perilously without the book collection at the Lubyanka, filled with hundreds of books confiscated from prisoners.

Once, in the morning, when they didn't usually call me out for an interrogation and I could submerge myself in the complicated intricacies of the *Iliad*, the cell door opened. Outside were several military men. They entered and stood on the threshold. I stood up from my cot and looked my guests over fearfully. One of them stepped forward and stretched out his hand. I was flummoxed—not once in five years had I taken the hand of a free man, especially a man in uniform. "Hello," the officer said. "I am the inspecting counsel, my name is Terekhov. Do you have any complaints or requests?" I did have one request—to meet with my parents. And I managed one complaint—I wanted out of the solitary cell.

"You will be granted a meeting and we'll transfer you out of solitary," the man in uniform said briskly. "What are you reading?" he asked, nodding towards the open book lying on my cot. When he learned that it was the *Iliad*, he smiled and said that I was most likely intending to specialize as a philologist. I mumbled something or other in reply. When the door banged shut behind my unexpected guests, I remained still and dumbfounded for several minutes. Suddenly the simple and impossible thought came into my head: this man had just told me, in the special way available to him, that they were intending to set us free. After Colonel Terekhov's visit I had no more doubts that they were going to release me soon.

After I returned home, I found out from my mother that Terekhov was probably the only person who spoke with kindness to the parents who worked so hard appealing for a review of the case. She couldn't forget a phrase that Terekhov had once dropped: "I can look you straight in the eye, but how am I to speak to those parents whose children are no longer among the living?" My mother left in great agitation: people had long ago forgotten how to consider ordinary human feelings. I don't know how Terekhov's career had proceeded, but it was impossible for him to have risen to that rank without having somehow or other participated in some of the crimes. Yet he was able to show a conscience? Some of them managed to.

It turned out that you could live in prison quite well—I was rained on with packages from home. What didn't my mother send me? Such delicacies I hadn't dreamt of! Soon letters began to arrive and I was allowed to answer them. A pencil, paper—in my cell! Such things I had never been allowed before! Soon Terekhov's promises began to come true. One morning they told me to get dressed, but said nothing about exercise. That meant that they were going to take me somewhere. There was not a suspicion in my mind that there would be a meeting, since in my experience that could only happen here, in the Lubyanka. But prison laws have their own logic. They took me around Moscow for quite a long time, and I prepared myself to meet with the another official. As I got out of the "Black Maria" I had no idea, of course, where they had brought me to. They led me down a long corridor lined with a multitude of doors. My convoy opened one of them for me, and I entered a narrow room with a long, empty table in the middle. It was only then that they informed me that I was about to have a visitor. Whom I was to meet they didn't say, but strictly warned me about following the rules for meetings in prison: no embracing, no exchanging of items between us, no discussing the case, or the conditions in the prison—the conversation was to be limited entirely to domestic affairs. If the rules were broken, the meeting would be immediately terminated. I hardly listened to the regulations—I was well trained and knew them well.

My heart froze in anticipation of the meeting. I had no doubt that it was my mother who would had come to see me. This would be our fourth visit in my five years of captivity. The first three were beyond the Arctic Circle, and this one was next to my own backyard. I kept staring at the door. There were endless moments of waiting, and then on the threshold appeared my mother in a winter coat and fur hat. She took a step and suddenly, behind her, I saw my father. This was completely unexpected! I knew how much he was afraid. The whole family was afraid for him, too. During all these years he had written to me, but had entirely held off from taking part in the appeals and constant visits to various official places, or from even sending me any packages. I don't think that it made any difference, but by some miracle they never touched him. My father had continued to work all these years in a relatively responsible position in a ministry department. And now he was here. For five years I had not seen his face, not even in a photograph. I feasted my eyes on his face—saw each new wrinkle, the grey hair—all of it my fault.

My parents sat down at the table across from me and I couldn't keep myself from leaping up and kissing them. The guard remained silent and out of the corner of my eye I saw that he had turned away on purpose, so he could say that he had seen no infraction. But our disobedience didn't stop there: my mother immediately whispered that they had much good news, the most important being that they were going to release us soon. It was a joyful meeting, I kept wanting to break out in laughter, although we weren't talking about anything particularly funny. My father joked that I had hardly changed—I was still a joker, athough I had now grown up.

After our encounter it was not so painful to return to prison. I kept going over in my mind all the news. My parents had mentioned something about an unprecedented Party Congress. What was going on? What changes awaited me if I were released? I would soon find out, just hang on a little while longer, I told myself. At the same time, changes were also occurring in my prison life. Unexpectedly, I was told to gather up my things and my bedclothes. It was clear: I was being transferred to another cell. Terekhov's second promise was being fulfilled. I dragged my few things down the corridor. Stop. The guard turned the key in the lock. I was prepared to meet a stranger, and was prepared to be pleased, almost as much as if I was anticipating a visit with my parents. But when the door swung open, I couldn't believe my eyes: in front of me stood Katya! I threw all my things on the floor and flung myself around her neck. That "good counsel" couldn't have given me a better present.

My friendship with Katya had developed in a complicated way. We were very different in character: I was open and, basically, extroverted, while Katya was withdrawn and had a very deep nature. Our previous, pre-arrest, lives had also been different: mine was carefree and easy, hers was difficult, full of illnesses, and alienated from a society where religion was despised and you had to hide your faith. But, despite our many differences, we had become close friends and loved one another. We had been separated many times in the camps, and had longed for each other. Then Fate united us once more. This was yet another of those wonderfully unexpected moments.

We couldn't say enough to each other and quickly exchanged our news: Katya had also had a meeting with her mother. That evening we put together a veritable feast of all the great foods from home that we had not seen for so long. From the moment we were reunited we remained in a state of euphoria. We laughed at funny things, and for no reason at all; we struggled with each other, unable to channel all our energy; we chattered non-stop; there was no time to even think of reading. They completely stopped calling us for examinations, and daily we anticipated our release.

But several more days passed and, instead of our expected liberation, they took us to a large chamber with three cots. Soon they brought Galya Smirnova, another member of our group, into the room. Of course we recognized her immediately, although our acquaintance had been brief: during the trial we had sat side by side. With her long braids and child-like round face, she seemed not to have changed at all over the years. We welcomed her with joy. I think it was from Galya that we first learned that they had discussed Stalin's crimes at the Party Congress. It was hard to believe. We had no newspapers but, burning with curiosity we decided to ask our guard. We selected the nicest one and I (being the most daring) chose my words carefully, asking if it was true that the Congress had criticized Stalin (I couldn't say the words "Stalin's crimes"). The young man smiled wryly and answered evasively, saying that he wasn't supposed to be speaking with us, but that we ourselves would soon find out. Such an answer spoke volumes.

The prison spring arrived almost unnoticed—it was a spring of light. The exercise yards were located on the roof. They were concrete cages with the sky overhead. My heart caught at the city noises that wafted up. Somewhere down below was the real spring and April was almost over. Our cheerful mood was transformed by impatience—we just couldn't wait any longer. We greeted each day with hope, a hope that had faded by noon, and the evening dragged on endlessly. The morning of April 25 began like any other: exercise, breakfast, cleaning up the room. Having done all that, we sat down on our cots, waiting to be taken out for our walk. But instead of the usual "Get ready for your walk," we heard, "Get your things ready."

No matter how much you live in anticipation of freedom, when it arrives it is still hard to believe. In prison you learned to fear change: the old, accustomed ways are best. And now, "Get your things ready!" How many times had these very words evoked fear of the coming unknown? What was hiding behind these simple words this time?

Were they letting us go? Previously we wouldn't have dared to even ask the question. But we had quickly become accustomed to the new times and were bolder now. The prison guards smiled slightly as we looked into their faces—there could be no doubt about it, they were going to release us.

What happened next I can barely remember. One by one they led us into a room where we had to sign two papers, I think. The letters jumped on the page and the meaning of it all was slippery: something about non-disclosure and the review of our case. Back at home I understood that we had been amnestied, pardoned. They had changed the indictment, leaving in points 10 and 11 (anti-Soviet agitation and organization), and had withdrawn the rest. For these crimes they gave us five years. As we had already served those years, the most gracious organs decided that we could again live in Moscow and didn't even have to mention on paper our shameful past (they simply extended the recent amnesty to our case, too). With difficulty I understood that the bullets which had executed our boys had been replaced on paper by ten years of imprisonment. I couldn't understand the madness of the situation, but I got used to the Kafkaesque reality.

Classified

Supreme Court of the USSR

DECLARATION No. 008/52

The Military Collegium of the Supreme Court of the USSR

Consisting of: Presiding Judge Colonel Borisoglebsky

and members: Colonel Likhachev and Colonel Dolotsev

have reviewed, on the basis of art. 373 of the Criminal Code of the RSFSR, in a session held 21 April 1956, according to the decision of the Chief Military Prosecutor on the case of those persons convicted 13 February 1952 by the Military Collegium of the Supreme Court of the USSR, in accordance with arts. 58-1 "a," 58-8, 58-10, pt. 1 and 58-11 of the Criminal Code of the RSFSR—

....

The basis of the indictment of SLUTSKY, GUREVICH, FURMAN, PECHURO, MELNIKOV, and others was their depositions, given at preliminary investigations and in court, and material evidence: documents with anti-Soviet content, confiscated from the defendants during their arrest and search.

After sentencing, PECHURO, MELNIKOV, and others in their complaints and appeals asserted that they had undertaken no treasonable or terrorist activity, that the extent of their guilt had been significantly exaggerated at the preliminary investigations and in the court as a result of the employment on them of illegal methods of interrogation.

In connection with the above-mentioned complaints, the Chief Military Prosecutor's Office has conducted a supplementary review of the case, looking at the material which establishes that SLUTSKY, FURMAN,

GUREVICH, MELNIKOV, PECHURO, and others were sentenced by arts. 58-1 "a," 58-8 of the Criminal Code of the RSFSR baselessly, and therefore in conclusion the question of the repeal of the sentence in this particular area is raised and the discontinuation of the case by the following data:

At the interrogations during the supplemental examination, MELNIKOV, PECHURO, and others convicted denied the declarations they had given to the preliminary investigation and in the court, to wit, that the organization USCR and particular of its members had treasonable or terrorist intentions, declaring that such statements had been given by them under pressure or other illegal influences of the investigators.

The declaration of the convicted concerning the unobjective conduct of the preliminary investigation in this case has a basis for confirmation.

This review has established that during the preliminary investigation, certain violations of the law indeed took place, and that in this case measures of coercion were applied against the convicted, finding expression in systematic and lengthy night-time interrogations of the accused, by which they were deprived of their normal sleep and rest, in the deprivation of parcels, in the deprivation of the right to use the prison foodstore, and so forth. The declarations of the accused were taken down unobjectively, many of the interrogations were not minuted, verbatim records of the interrogations were fabricated in the absence of the accused, so-called "general records of interrogations" were used.

Former investigators of the case, OVCHINNIKOV and SMELOV, questioned during the supplementary review have confirmed the violation of the law and have declared that this was done on the orders of the former officers of the investigating section of the MGB of the USSR, LIKHACHEV and PUTINTSEV (both of whom have been sentenced for the falsification of investigative materials).

OVCHINNIKOV has testified that that SLUTSKY, GUREVICH, and others were at no time during the beginning of the preliminary investigation accused of terrorist intentions. Later, at one of the operative meetings, LIKHACHEV accused the interrogators of having failed to produce confessions of the terrorist intentions of the members of the USCR, although a weapon had been confiscated from one of them. OVCHINNIKOV then stated: "LIKHACHEV proposed that this be included in the following records of the interrogations."

OVCHINNIKOV also declared that during the preliminary interrogations, general records of interrogations were fabricated which were meticulously edited by SHVARTSMAN (who has been sentenced for the falsification of investigative materials) and only afterwards were they given to the accused for their signatures.

Concerning the revolver sequestered from GUREVICH, it is necessary to take into account that it was unusable and, as MELNIKOV showed during the supplementary inspection, it had been transferred to GUREVICH without any criminal intent.

GUREVICH, SLUTSKY, and FURMAN were not questioned during the supplementary review of their case in view of their deaths; however, their declarations at the preliminary interrogations and in the court concerning the terrorist intentions of the USCR and individual of its members seem to be extremely contradictory, and therefore cannot be accepted as proof of the guilt of either SLUTSKY, GUREVICH, or FURMAN, or any of the other persons convicted in this case.

Under these circumstances there is no justification for considering USCR a terrorist organization as a whole and therefore to charge its members under art. 58-8 of the Criminal Code of the RSFSR.

According to the materials of the case and the materials of the supplementary review it is also established that the activities of SLUTSKY, FURMAN, GUREVICH, and others of those convicted are completely devoid of a criminal character, as defined in art. 58-1 "a" of the Criminal Code of the RSFSR.

....

On the basis of what has been laid out by the Military Collegium of the Supreme Court of the USSR:

IT IS DETERMINED

that the sentence of the Military Collegium of the Supreme Court of the USSR of 6-13 February 1952 in part of the indictment of SLUTSKY, FURMAN, GUREVICH, MELNIKOV, PECHURO, and other persons convicted in accordance with arts. 58-1 "a," 58-8 of the Criminal Code of the RSFSR by reason of newly-discovered circumstances is hereby revoked

and the case in this part is to be annulled on the basis of art. 4, point 5 of
the Criminal Code of the RSFSR.

The following are to be considered convicted on the basis of arts.
58-10, pt. 1, 58-11 of the Criminal Code of the RSFSR: SLUTSKY,
FURMAN, GUREVICH, MELNIKOV, PECHURO, ULANOVSKAYA, REYF,
and SMIRNOVA.

In accordance with art. 58-10, pt. 1 of the Criminal Code of the
RSFSR, SLUTSKY, B. V., FURMAN, V. L. and GUREVICH, Y. Z. are
sentenced to the deprivation of freedom in a Corrective Labour Camp for
a period of ten (10) years each.

In accordance with art. 58-10, pt. 1 of the Criminal Code of the RSFSR,
the sentences of MELNIKOV, V. Z., PECHURO, S. S., ULANOVSKAYA,
M. A., and REYF, A. Y., are reduced to five years of the deprivation of
freedom in a Corrective Labour Camp each with disenfranchisement for
two years, and for SMIRNOVA, G. A., three years of deprivation of freedom in a Corrective Labour Camp without disenfranchisement.

All mention of the confiscation of personal belongings for those persons convicted in this case is to be erased, and as MELNIKOV, PECHURO,
ULANOVSKAYA, REYF, SMIRNOVA have served their sentences, they are
to be released from custody.

On the basis of art. 6 of the Decree of the Presidium of the Supreme
Soviet of the USSR of 27 March 1953, "On Amnesty," they are to have
their disenfranchisement withdrawn and to be considered as having no
previous conviction.

Original with appropriate signatures

        Seal   Corresponds accurately to the original

                      Court Secretary of the Military Tribunal

                          Senior Lieutenant (MARKOV)

But sensible thoughts came later; now we were dealing with
miracles. After the appropriate formalities were completed, they
took us to enormous heavy doors and threw them open before us. I
cannot recall that first momentous step outside prison. Probably few
remember. But even now I see the shining faces of my partners. We
slowly moved down a street that we hardly recognized, towards the

centre of the city. It was the middle of the day. A dense crowd of beautifully dressed people flowed along the street. No one looked at us, although we looked quite strange with our knapsacks, Katya in a quilted jacket and I in an old-fashioned coat with a small shabby suitcase in my hand. There was no train station nearby to suggest that we had just arrived. Later I realized that many such people like us appeared in this part of the city and passers-by tried to avoid noticing them. We, on the other hand, looked all about us. It seemed to me that the crowd was made up entirely of foreigners— the people were dressed so strangely. We listened to them and realized that no, they were speaking Russian. That meant that so much had changed in five years: fashions, colours, the expressions on faces. Perhaps it wasn't so much the five years of our absence, as the three years of Stalin's. Not only the people had changed, but the buildings looked different. Many of them seemed to us to have aged and become smaller. And here they had torn one down and were putting up an enormous one. Over the construction site was written in huge letters: CHILDREN'S WORLD. At Theatre Square we said good-bye to Galya who was going to take the metro. Katya and I continued together. We walked past the Alexandrovsky Gardens, and then one of us had the idea to turn up towards Red Square. One glance at the mausoleum and we would understand a lot. The empty square seemed hardly as big as it had once been. Not so very long ago I had come here on a holiday celebration. A sea of people heaved with banners, portrait of the leaders, and brightly coloured balloons. The enormous, moustachioed face of Stalin, repeated hundreds of times over, swam above the buzzing crowd. I had passed by the tribune of the masoleum many a time with my school. From far off we glanced at it, searching out the familiar service cap among all those standing there. You would ask the marchers in front of you if Stalin was at the mausoleum. More often than not, disappointment awaited us. But once I was lucky. The leader I idolized waved at us. He wasn't a painting, but alive, in the flesh—it was hard to accept such happiness! We shouted until we were hoarse: "Long Live Stalin!" "Glory!" "Under the Leadership!" and so forth. When had that been? The image of the people's exultation was so brightly preserved in my memory, and part of my own pride—I along with all the rest!

It was not time that separated the "me" of that time and the "me" of this—between us was a bottomless abyss. Katya and I went closer to the low mausoleum. It was closed to visitors that day and seemed particularly gloomy, withdrawn from the world of the living. The immobile guards looked as dead as the marble burial vault with its colour of dried blood. We couldn't make ourselves go all the way up to it, there had always been something scary about this place, but from the distance we could read the two names above the entrance: LENIN, STALIN.

But our mood couldn't be spoiled. We continued on our way home and at the corner of the Manège Square and Herzen Street we each bought a bouquet of spring violets, using the money we hadn't spent on transit. It was here that Katyusha and I had to part: her path went by the Lenin Library towards the Arbat, and mine, along Herzen Street to Nikitskie Gate at Kachalov Street.

I kept walking and no longer looked around me. My coat weighed down on my shoulders and the suitcase suddenly seemed so very heavy. Finally I dragged myself to the church where Pushkin had been married, as familiar to me as my own home. And behind it was Gorky's mansion and across from it an ambassador's residence. And there was the old manor house, where my school had once been housed. Further away stood an unfamiliar spire; they had erected a skyscraper at Insurrection Square, my mother had said something about it. Finally, my own building. Before it had been larger, newer, more attractive. But now it held within it my whole world, all my life. I had returned here many times in my daydreams and night-dreams, although at night the dreams were usually of being taken away. Passing the dark gateway I entered the courtyard. Oh, how small it was! And yet, on a bicycle it had been large enough to ride around in, and there had been so many secret corners to hide in. Children were racing about the garden pathways in the centre of the yard, and mothers and nannies were sitting on benches. Now someone might notice me, might shout out. Quickly I went up to my own entrance. I didn't buzz for the elevator, but walked up to the third floor. The door. A ring. On the threshold of the open door stood a tall, handsome young man with a shock of black hair— my little brother. This, then, was how many years had passed. How long my journey home had been!

18

"A Step to the Right, A Step to the Left"

(A Story with a Happy Ending)

On the middle of the laboratory table, bound by all four of its limbs, lay a large, grey rabbit. He was completely motionless and looked dead. His glassy, wide-open eyes, uncovered by lids and full of moisture, stared off into emptiness. Only his vulnerable stomach, covered with whitish fur, faintly stirred and heaved. The shaven middle line on its belly stretched out in anticipation of the knife. Two heads hovered over the little animal—one tousled and beginning to go grey, the other curly and closely cut.

Senior scientific researcher Aron Yevseyevich thought that he was on the verge of a world-shaking discovery. He always thought that when he approached a new experiment. There was no greater happiness in his life than this. And now, preparing to kill the unfortunate rabbit, he felt no pangs of conscience, nor did he even see the animal—he saw instead before him the unsolved secret of life, the mystery of the synthesis of protein. He would destroy another creature and create something of his own—to do what no other mortal had accomplished! Aron was in ecstasy. Tiny drips of sweat covered his forehead. In a low and nervous voice he gave me orders: "Clamps, scalpels, test tubes." I mechanically played my role of assistant, experiencing none of the emotions that were transporting the scientist. I was nauseous and my head spun. The rabbit gave off a warm, rather unpleasant aroma. But it was the aroma of life, of a living body, and I had become used to the smell of the animals.

Three months before my new life had begun. I entered a biochemical laboratory, knowing nothing about biochemistry. The laboratory's small collective greeted me with extraordinary warmth. They all knew my story, although only parts of it: I had been in prison and released in the flood of rehabilitations. There were a lot like me at that time, and the country was fragrant with spring, with new ideas. Hearts were thawing after an ice age of thirty years. I was beginning my life again, picking up from the moment my ordinary life had been ended by that night-time arrest. Indeed, I was five years older now—eighteen years old then, twenty-three now; but that wasn't so very important. You can make up for what's been missed. I was already beginning to work on my re-admission to the Biology Faculty, where I had studied only half a year. Meanwhile, I began working in the laboratory of a large scientific institute.

Now the most important task was to try to forget everything that had occurred—the years in prison, the transfers, the camps. I was still beset by nightmares, but they had grown less frequent, without the painful details that make a terrible dream seem real, so that in the morning you can't believe you only dreamt it all. But I still felt an undefined something. I had no name for it but it was so oppressive, so heavy. In the morning, the light of sun pouring into the room, the visions would disappear as soon as I opened my eyes. And then the work day would begin—a day just like all the others before. Springtime in Moscow, the crush of people in the buses, the human flood along the streets. Then with my co-workers I would walk through an old park to the institute, hidden behind huge trees. It was a fantastic sensation. I was going to work like any other ordinary person, no longer trudging in a column of prisoners. My position was junior laboratory assistant and, although the pay was miserably small, I was satisfied with my junior status. Slowly, I acquired a sense of the stability of life.

The most important thing was to be like everyone else, to not stand out, to disappear dissolved in that mass of humanity. Fate had already marked me, and that mark had been like a crucifixion for all of my family for five endless years. Now it was all to be put out of our minds. It was that simple: nothing had happened, the arrest and imprisonment had never taken place. Make yourself not think, forget. My experience in the Komsomol had trained me to subordinate all my emotions to reason. Man has it in his power to do anything, if only he desires. And life is pure and beautiful in its simplicity. There isn't even very much to wish for when the most ordinary things bring joy. It is so easy to walk down the street, straight ahead, straight ahead, turning nowhere. Not so long ago it was an unrealizable dream; pacing from corner to corner in the Lefortovo solitary or going around and around in circle until my head began to spin in the prison courtyard, so that I was ready to scream out. I had so wanted the obstacles in my way to disappear, to see the horizon that was denied me, to walk towards it without stopping. Now, in a crowd, I felt the happiest—which one of them, these young folks and old, could attain such indescribable pleasure just by moving about in public? A step, another step, a hundred steps—and not a single obstacle, not a single cold and damp stone wall, not a single fence.

My work in the laboratory also brought a certain satisfaction as each day brought something new. Aron Yevseyevich was always in a mood, while preparing for the experiments. "Now, Allochka, is the time to rejoice, as you predict the answer to the question posed in the experiment. We will always have time later to doubt and be disappointed," he said, rubbing his hands with satisfaction and slyly glancing in my direction. His strong, fat fingers performed the most delicate work with fragile test tubes and microscopic quantities of chemicals which he weighed on miniature scales. I followed his movements with fascination, admiring my boss' agility and precision. Our relationship established itself at once: I delighted in his quick mind and knowledge, his inventiveness, his absorption in science; he liked my youth, my curiosity about everything new as well as the past. This was unusual for such a young woman. He didn't hide his happiness at my presence and was displeased when I was assigned to assist some other researcher in the laboratory.

Occasionally, afraid of offending me with his curiosity, he would cautiously question me about my arrest. He would lead the conversation onto the theme as though by chance or accident. I had no doubts about Aron's compassion and his sympathy for the cause I had been sentenced for. So I readily and in detail told him about our youth organization, how it had decided to struggle against an unjust government, and how we had been caught like baby chicks, and how I had spent a horrible year in solitary. Aron listened and thought that he too could have been in my place, joining such a group of young boys and girls, as he had long resented the lies which ensnared our lives. He had seen through it all, as so many others had, when he returned from the war and looked at the world around him with completely different eyes. He was astonished at the ease with which I talked about those tragic events. Could he have preserved himself, not become embittered, not have lost that easygoing nature that was a quality of youth, having undergone all that had fallen to the lot of this girl? Aware of my boss's attitude towards me, I worked for him with particular satisfaction.

Only one thing disturbed the harmony of my new life: I could not comfortably watch the laboratory animals as they died. These sweet little animals—guinea pigs, rabbits, white mice and the nicest possible red-eyed white rats—were losing their lives in order to prolong the lives of humans. The rational explanations, the iron logic that Aron employed to justify the immutable laws of life both in nature and in human society—where the death of one could bring life to another—it just didn't help. But what could I say against it? Yet, as soon as that slender thread separating life from death appeared before my eyes, and I myself had to undo this thread, destroy its continuity, of my own will transform the warm, living creature into still stoniness, I experienced such pity that I had to force myself not to start crying and just continue the experiment. At such a moment I would dislike Aron. His usually kind grey eyes would grow cold, and his busy hands working on the animal would look like the hands of a butcher. Especially ugly were his big fingers with their short nails. I had even heard somewhere that such hands were a sign of denegration. Sweet Aron would turn into a vicious vampire. I would hurry so that the torture would finally come to an end, both for the rabbit and for me. Now we had located the pulsing carotid artery. The stretched-out clamps exposed the red interior of the wound and a small incision was made. "Cannula!" Aron commanded. "Beakers!" And the thick, dark red blood poured through the small glass tube and into the heavy centrifuge beakers. I moved the beakers, arranging them so that not a single drop would be lost. One, two, three—they were drawn up in order on the stand. Now is its last seconds of life, the rabbit's flow of blood had slowed down, and would now stop. At that moment the rabbit lets out a desperate dying shriek. My heart breaks to hear this oppressive sound. I wanted to cover my ears, but tried not to display my torment. Aron pretended that he saw nothing—I would get over it; after all, it had taken him awhile, too.

The first part of the experiment was finished. The rabbit's lifeless eyes remained staring at the ceiling. I tried not to look at the operating table, and put the blood into the centrifuge. Now we would have our lunch break and I could rest, let my tension go. Unexpectedly, the "gofer" from the director's office stuck his head through the door: "Alla Yevgenyevna Reyf, you are requested to come to Personnel." It had been some time since I had been addressed by my full name and patronymic. I felt something stab me in the chest. Personnel was an unpleasant place for all of us, even for those who had no blots on their past. Personnel was a section wrapped in mystery and it held in its hands the threads of life for all the workers in the institute. In its hands were the power to fire, the power to promote. But someone else, in different, much higher spheres held the threads of Personnel as well. All the instructions to Personnel descended from there.

I asked Aron to put the centrifuged blood into the refrigerator and descended the staircase to the first floor. Zinaida Pavlovna, the head of Personnel, had a rather unmemorable personality and you seldom saw her. I could only just recall what she looked like. Her voice responded to my knock on the door, inviting me in. I stopped on the threshold in surprise—a woman's voice had answered my knock, but it was a strange man who sat behind the large desk. Across from him, sat another man with his face turned to the door. The two of them like two peas in a pod. Which of them had spoken with Zinaida Pavlovna's voice, I wondered, inspecting the two strangers. At that moment the head of the section arrived from somewhere off to the side.

"So, Alla, I will leave you with these comrades. They would like to have a chat with you." She seemed to be completing a previously begun conversation. She slipped through a side-door, and closed it carefully behind her.

"Please be seated, Alla Yevgenyevna," the one behind the desk said to me. For several seconds I could not move a muscle. A storm of thoughts raged in my mind: This is an arrest! But they only just released me! I have done nothing illegal. Still, they can put you in prison even when you're completely innocent, as long as you've fallen into their hands before! So, is it prison again? Freedom had been so short.

I had no doubt that the men before me were from the KGB. The two of them were indistinguishable from my interrogators, or the three that had come for me that night five years ago. I slowly sat down. That familiar trembling, which had so tormented me in the interrogation rooms, seized hold of my knees. I met the stare of the man sitting across from me. Ginger eyes with speckles, whitish eyebrows and lashes. The very same eyes and hair that the last Lefortovo interrogator, Colonel Shilovsky, had possessed. He had also stared at me the same way, coming right up to the edge of the little table in the far corner of the room, where I always sat.

The ginger eyes came closer to my face, and stared at me. Then the lips began moving and I could hear some sort of angry mumbling. His speech cleared and I began to understand the words. "When, where, and how did you intend to kill Cabinet member, Beria? Here is the paper, write everything down in detail, sketch out the plan of Beria's house." The lips are still moving, but I have stopped making out the words. Why are they asking me again about Beria? He's already been exposed as an enemy of the people and a spy for foreign intelligence! Even more, he is no longer alive—they shot him long ago.

I look into the face of the ginger-eyed man, but he is silent, his lips not moving. With difficulty I turn my head to the man sitting at the table and with surprise catch him smiling. Getting up slightly, he stretches out his hand to me.

"Alla Yevgenyevna, I am pleased to make your acquaintance. My name is Pyotr Sergeyevich, and this is my assistant, Ivan Ivanovich."

I shake his hand and try to smile in reply. In fact, everything is in order after all. They have no intention of arresting me, no reason to panic. They simply came to get acquainted.

"We are operatives for the KGB and have the obligation to be interested in the lives of those persons who, one way or another, have had some connection with us," Pyotr Sergeyevich said softly, still smiling. "We know your history and are pleased that you have repented, understood your guilt, and are now living the life of a good Soviet person." I have regained control of myself, and my knees have stopped trembling.

"What, in fact, interests you about my life right now?" I asked, trying to sound indifferent.

"Absolutely everything," Pyotr Sergeyevich began quickly. "Who your friends are, what you talk about, what your colleagues at work talk about, what jokes they make when people are around. We would like you to tell us all about everything." Coming out from behind the table, he deliberately paced about the room, from the window to the door, from the door to the window. His steps were accompanied by a slight squeaking, and for a moment I imagine that it is the words slipping out of his lips that are making the sound. "We are concerned about your future. Once you committed an irreparable mistake. You trusted bad people, chose bad friends. Now we want to help you so that you won't make such mistakes again. You will tell us about your acquaintances, and we will explain to you which ones are good and which are bad." Halfway to the window he unexpectedly turned sharply, in a military way, and quickly came up to me. "We don't need your help, Alla Yevgenyevna. We want to help you!" The last words are said in a rather high, barking voice.

So this is what they want: these two agents want to sign me up as a *stukach*, an informer. I have only seconds to think about it. How can I answer without putting myself in danger? Once before in my life I had had a similar experience, when the boss in the camp had tried to tempt me with early release. At that time I had refused outright. No threats could frighten me. And what could be worse than my sentence—twenty-five years in the camps? The boss gave way immediately, realizing that he'd been dealing with the wrong person. And now, if I didn't agree, they would begin their revenge, chase me into a snare. In the camp I had heard of many such cases. But where did that word "if" come from? There had been no "if" before, there had been nothing to lose. Now? Immediately, at this very moment, I had to come up with something that would help me out of their trap. It seemed that an eternity went by before I heard myself saying: "I cannot cooperate with you because I am deathly afraid of you." I surprised myself with the sound of my changed, broken voice. The second red-haired man who hadn't dropped a word up to now moved towards me on his chair. And again those eyes of Colonel Shilovsky were looking at me. This time he would strike his fist on the flimsy table: "Get up! Enough twisting about! You are all little snakes, you Jewish nationalists!" My head shrunk back into my shoulders and my knees began jumping up and down.

But Ivan Ivanovich hadn't shouted, on the contrary. He leaned forward and, shining with kindness, began to quietly explain that there was no reason to be afraid of them, that this time I wouldn't be against them, but with them.

"Our organs will defend you from danger," he said, as though talking to a sick person or a child, and I realized that I had chosen the best course—they had believed my fear to be genuine, the only reason I was unwilling to become an informer. After all, they knew about fear better than anyone: out of fear, a person could do the meanest things; out of fear, a person wouldn't do the meanest things. Fear is the only motivation, they knew that well enough! I spoke of my fear so sincerely because it was a sacred truth. An icy horror grabbed hold of me at the memory of the investigation, the court which sentenced the three young men to be shot, and all the others of us to the unbelievable sentence of twenty-five years in the camps. Having escaped by some miracle, I would always live with the sensation of a noose around my neck.

"I cannot overcome my fear; it is stronger than I am. It has grown up in me and become my second self. You will get no satisfaction from me. You would do better to leave me in peace, and I will protect myself against my mistakes, from dangerous acquaintances." I spoke more and more loudly, with growing confidence, as if I felt solid earth beneath my feet, a path through the boggy swamp. "In the camp I met many *stukachi* who were helping you, your 'organs', they had informed on the innocent and the guilty. And it made no difference—your own reliable *stukachi* were in prison, too!" What was I doing? I had just used one of those contemptuous nicknames for their collaborators! My cheeks were flaming and, I heard my voice ringing, as if it would break. If only I could hang on to my nerves, dear God, don't let me break down before these scum!

"Settle down, Alla Yevgenyevna, there is no need to get excited. You should decide for yourself if you want to demonstrate to the Fatherland that you have not been released in vain, forgiven for such a crime," Pyotr Sergeyevich entered the conversation again. His mumbling, rasping voice didn't carry the words well. I followed his movements from the door to the window, from the window to the door. How many hours had I, like a pendulum, paced my solitary cell, carrying on that same endless, interminable dialogue with myself. Who was right? The boys with their criticism of the regime or the investigator, who so easily demolished their arguments? At that time I could still have doubts.

The squeaking steps stopped at the window and for a moment tense quiet reigned in the room. The red-haired broke the silence.

"So what are we going to do, Alla Yevgenyevna? Time is flying, and we are still where we started," his voice had a metallic sound. "Stop making youself sound like a frightened little girl. What are you afraid of? Enemies ought to avoid us, but genuine Soviets have never refused to show us assistance when we ask for it. Such work is considered honourable in our country. What sort of silliness are you telling us, that we would put our own assistants into the camps? That is nonsense! Now, if they had been in conspiracy with the enemy, that's another business. Your behaviour is suspicious. Were you given the right to live in Moscow, to work in such a fine scientific institution, too soon?

My eyes cast down, I listened to his menacing words. Now he would read in my face how much I hated them all. It was better for them to think that I was afraid. And if they should guess the truth? Then, "We will crush you like cockroaches!" one of my past interrogators had shouted, spluttering with saliva. I think it was the one who was later shot, together with Minister Abakumov, after Stalin's death.

"Don't you really want to live in Moscow?" I heard the agent ask. I had to react somehow, say something. But what? I wanted terribly to just ask what would happen if I refused to collaborate with them. What would they do with me, arrest me again? What was the red-haired hinting at, exile? That wasn't half the problem. But if he meant to hide me in a "closed camp" in Vladimir, a camp which people said such terrible things about!

I felt so sorry for myself, just thinking about prison, about my life that was already ruined, that I began to sob. My head fell down on the table and my shoulders shook. Biting my lips, I tried to stifle the sounds that were tearing out of my throat, but instead I just sobbed louder.

Such a turn of events was apparently not what the agents had anticipated. Such a scene was no good here. In the corridor they might hear these strange noises coming from Personnel. The red-haired poured me a tumbler of water, but I didn't raise my head. Pyotr Sergeyevich began speaking softly, imploringly.

"Alla, may I call you simply Alla? After all, I could be like a father to you. Listen to what I'm saying. We are not here to threaten you, to force you. We want you to voluntarily agree to collaborate with us. You will directly benefit from the decision—no one will ever be able to drive you off the right track again." I didn't answer, still shaking as I wept. So this is what they call the right track!

Oh, how that woman had screamed when they strangled her in her bed. I heard the squeezed, abdominal shriek from somewhere in the corner of the room. That night I pressed my ears shut with my hands... I no longer heard the words of the agent, but the shriek of the *stukach* they were killing just kept getting louder.

Earlier that evening, the whole barracks had been whispering about something that was supposed to happen that night. Verka, a sharp *blatnyazhka*, climbed up to the top bunk where Katya and I made our miserable beds on narrow mattrasses filled with wood shavings. Looking about conspiratorily, she motioned us to her and, putting her round red face up close, spoke in her deep smoker's voice: "Don't make a move tonight. You know nothing, and will hear nothing. We've had enough of this spy's snitching. We're going to sew up the bitch today. You, my sweethearts, heard nothing from me, and I wasn't here. Got it?"

Verka slipped down and disappeared. The savage night-time reprisal was swift. But I could never forget what happened, as though I myself had taken part in the murder.

Trying to put the memory out of my mind, I bit my fingers until they hurt. You mustn't open old memories. If you carelessly reach back to the past, it will gnaw and tear at you. By sheer force of will I swallowed my tears and raised my head. Why had I collapsed for these two? They weren't the ones who would be deciding my fate. Yes, it had probably all been determined beforehand. Right now only one thing was important—to get away from them as quickly as possible, get outside, and breathe the fresh air. I drank the glass of water in a single gulp and stood up.

"I think that we have talked about everything there is to talk about. I have explained my refusal to you as best I know how. I have nothing more to add." I turned away so they wouldn't see my tear-stained eyes. "It is late now, and I have to go home. My parents will be getting worried." Pyotr Sergeyevich handed me a piece of paper.

"About your parents: tell them nothing about our conversation. And not only them, talk to no one at all. Sign here that you will not divulge our conversation to anyone."

I read the form and signed. Once, when I left prison, I had signed a form saying I would not expose the secrets of the KGB, and immediately, not even thinking about the strict warning and the threat of punishment, I started telling everyone who showed any interest in my case about life in the prisons and camps.

"So now I can go?" It was in their power to do anything: they would arrest me immediately. Suddenly, the scene of my nighttime arrest five years before flared up in front of me. The things strewn all about, furniture moved from its rightful place. On the table in the dining room, next to a jar of cookies, lay the warrant for my arrest. Now one of them could pull the same sort of paper out of his pocket.

It was several only before the red-haired spoke but it seemed like an eternity.

"We will be the ones to tell you when you can leave. This is a state matter, and we have the right to make demands of your time. Please, be seated!" he pointed at the chair and I obediently took my former place. My head was pounding with pain and I was having trouble breathing. My thoughts were getting all mixed up. Would there be an end to this torture? Why was it so difficult for me? After all, they were torturing not me, but the rabbit. I could always get up and leave the room. It was the rabbit that had its paws bound, and its eyes, full of fear, strained up towards the ceiling. Aron would be coming now and save the rabbit. I turned my head at the sound of a knock at the door. But instead of Aron, the head of Personnel stood on the threshold. "I've come to ask the comrades if they would like some tea." Zinaida Pavlovna sang in an oily voice. By this trick she managed to free her things from the office, so that she could finally leave for home. The institute was empty. The "comrades," as if by command, rose.

"It's a good thing you looked in on us, Zinaida Pavlovna. We've been talking so much with Alla Yevgenyevna that we've lost track of the time."

The guests put on their coats turning into two indistinguishable twins and shook the woman's hand. At the door, Pyotr Sergeyevich—or was it Ivan Ivanovich, I couldn't make them out anymore—turned and shot at me: "Until next time, real soon, Alla Yevgenyevna!"

I grabbed the back of the chair. The head of Personnel left after the agents. I sat numb for several minutes—I had no feelings, no thoughts. How much time had passed since I walked into this room? The clock on the table showed it was five. So, the working day had finished. They had called for me at the lunch break, at two. They had tormented me for three hours. And it wasn't over yet. "Next time, real soon!" I remembered the agent's parting words. Where would that next time be? In Lefortovo Prison, the strictest military prison, my one-time home of fifteen months, or Butyrki Prison, where I had also had to sit in solitary "on the edge of freedom," as I waited for the completion of our case review? Or perhaps in the "comfortable" Lubyanka, where just four months ago they released us into the noisy streets of Moscow, into a sea of people? It had been the happiest moment of my life! All my troubles had remained behind the heavy doors that slammed shut behind us forever. It was clear, like the bright April day that greeted all of us, now more mature, smarter, but more or less the same. Today I realized that the prison doors never completely shut behind the backs of those who have once been on the other side. And indeed,

"You can't give up either prison or the begging bowl" is one of Mother Russia's wisest proverbs.

I walked down the empty, darkening corridors to my laboratory. In some places light shone from under the doors—particularly industrious colleagues would be working until late at night. "What if Aron still hadn't gone home?" The thought made me stop. "What would I tell him, how would I explain my being away for so long? I couldn't lie—I would have to tell him everything, exactly as it was, and his sympathy would make me feel better. I even decided to run up the stairs to see my good, wise boss all the sooner. But having taken several rapid steps I stopped again: what if he would be afraid, wouldn't believe that I had refused, or understood that the KGB would never leave me in peace, and that it would be better to have nothing to do with the likes of me.

The corridor leading to the laboratory was completely dark. I even bent down to make sure that there was no light under the door. "Thank God!" I said to myself. Somewhere in the depths of the old building, a weak echo replied.

I opened Aron's office and smelled the familiar aroma of rabbit. But the rabbit was gone from the table. "Liberated, poor thing! The rabbit has died and no one will ever bother him again. Lucky thing, now that he is dead! He is free!" I suddenly realized that I was speaking out loud.

My God, you could go out of your mind this way. Get outside, as quickly as possible. I took off my laboratory coat and put on my raincoat and then remembered that I should call home or else they would be worried. "Mama, I've been kept late. The experiment isn't over yet, eat without me," I tried to fill my voice with confidence and I think I overdid it. What if I couldn't hide my condition at home? My mother wouldn't take her eyes off me—she had waited for her little girl! I remember my mother calculating how old she would be when I completed my sentence: fifty plus twenty-five— seventy-five years old! Would she live that long, would I live that long?

The past four months had been pure happiness, free of darkness.

How could I tell them at home about what had happened? I would just be reviving more of the old fear.

There was a light, warm drizzle outside. Looking down, not seeing the puddles, I walked along Pirogovskaya Street, along the boulevard's iron railing. People rushed past me, or toward me, sometimes bumping me with a heavy bag, or briefcase, or shoulder. No one apologized—it was crowded on the narrow sidewalk and I was walking slowly, not in the normal rhythm. My route lay straight down Pirogovskaya Street, then Kropotkinskaya, and then along Gogol Boulevard to Arbat Square. Of course, I could have taken the trolley as I usually did, and get home in about half an hour. But I wanted to walk and walk and walk down these familiar streets, along the boulevards I had loved since childhood. So I was walking, as I had dreamed of doing not so long ago. On and on and on, I could walk this way all evening, all night, until I decided to turn towards my home, my very own home.

At Nikitskie Vorota I did not turn towards my own street, but continued on to Tverskoy Boulevard, which brought back vivid childhood memories, and then crowded Gorky Street.

Once I found myself in the dense crowd, I felt that I had lost the strength to go any further. But I was terrified of going home. It is a strange thing, being alone in a crowd! I heard snatches of conversations, the shouts of passers-by, car noises. A familiar sensation filled my whole body. It was difficult to move my heavy feet and my back was breaking from fatigue. How many more kilometres to the camp? We are walking in groups of five women, joining our hands together. Great gobs of mud cling to our huge boots. The heavy, quilted coats press down on our shoulders. There is a roar rising up from the column—the noise of steps, entwined in a muffled sound. It was forbidden to talk loudly during transit. You aren't allowed to move from one group of five to another; convoys with automatics and huge German shepherds walk alongside the column. The parting words of the convoy commander at the beginning of the march are always the same, ending with the phrase, "A step to the left, a step to the right, will be considered escape! We will shoot without warning!" This convoy "prayer" was one I heard twice a day—on the way to work and before returning to camp. We grew used to the words and they ceased to frighten us, although in those dark Stalin days they indeed often shot without warning. They announced such incidents as a deterrent: "Shot during attempted escape." I walk not seeing the road. My thoughts are in faraway Moscow.

Suddenly a powerful jolt stopped me—someone hurrying had run into me and then rushed past. Looking around, trying to return to the present, I shook my head and rubbed my eyes. How fancy the Yeliseyev Delicatessen is! A crowd flowed in and out of its wide doors. The crush of people flowed around me, like water around a stone.

I just had to go into the shop and buy something tasty, I thought, but I was fixed to the spot. My God! How could I break free of the past? It seemed more real to me than the present. But perhaps the past and the present didn't need to be separated? One passed into the other and back again. People around me rushed into their tomorrows, worrying, fussing. Their past was always right at their heels. How many of them who look so free right now, have been linked by their fate to a prison, were imprisoned themselves or had relatives or friends who were in prison, or who still are? After all, there were millions of prisoners! Thus we were all connected by a single thread—prison had stepped up to the very threshold of door after door of our homes.

The morning had been so fine and it had been so easy to go to work. I had walked straight ahead, just like now. An abyss lay between the day's sunny morning and now, this rainy dusk. Would I ever be free, if only for a moment!

The column of prisoners was ready to march. Soldiers ran along the grey ranks making their last inspection, the tally. The vicious German shepherds bared their teeth. Far-away at the head of the column the familiar command rang out: "Ready! A step to the left, a step to the right, will be considered escape! We will shoot without warning!"

19

Thirty Years Later

One clear cold April day in 1990 I chanced to receive a package from my far away homeland. In it was the certificate, issued by the Military Board of the Supreme Court of the USSR, concerning my complete rehabilitation. The package was brought to me from Moscow by the first Soviet tourists who dared (and this was a time when these "trial" trips were still quite rare) to visit their relatives in Canada. Here it is, that remarkable document, exactly as I received it: (see fig 19.1)

CERTIFICATE

The case concerning the indictment of Reyf, Alla Yevgenyevna, first-year student at the Moscow State Lenin Pedagogical Institute before her arrest on 7

February 1951, was reviewed by the Plenum of the Supreme Court of the USSR on 18 July 1989.

The sentence of the Military Collegium of the Supreme Court of the USSR of 13 February 1952 and the decision of the same Collegium of 21 April 1956 in connection with Reyf, A. Y. are rescinded and further action on the case is to cease.

Reyf, A. Y., is by this to be rehabilitated.

> [Signed] Head of the Secretariat of the Military Collegium
> of the Supreme Court of the USSR,
>
> Law Colonel A. Nikonov.

It was with mixed feelings that I read the lines of this apparently standard text. After all, such certificates were being issued in the thousands, if not tens of thousands. Still, there seemed to be reason to rejoice, to finally breathe freely. Could I have imagined in 1956 that the day would come when they would revoke those horrible accusations against us?

On the other hand, the certificates were written out for all of the members of the organization, both the living and the dead. Did this mean that the organization was no longer considered to have existed, as though it had arisen only from the fevered imagination of our interrogators? And does one state have the right to absolve us of our sins against another state which no longer exists? Indeed, we had not been "enemies of the people," but we had certainly been enemies of that system, that regime. The all-powerful punitive machine had allowed some of us to slip out from under the iron millstones. But only by accident. After all, during the same time it dealt severely with much more important people, those who were known internationally, including members of the Jewish Anti-Fascist Committee—Mikhoels, Markish, Kvitko, Zuskin.[45] And there was no fear then, no hands shook from signing false accusations which led the innocent to be shot "according to the law." It's true that for Mikhoels they didn't bother with "according to the law."

And I ask myself one more question: how would the three dead young men have reacted to this indulgence? Would they have rejoiced? Or, perhaps, only laughed wryly? Who knows. It is possible now only to question the air, the earth, and sky into which they have disappeared, not having even left graves behind them. Yes, they were children of their time and acted in accordance with values instilled since childhood. They were simply ignorant of the existence of any other ways, nor could they find out about them. The light of knowledge could not penetrate through the thick folds of the iron curtain. But millions, tens of millions of much more mature people, those wiser in life's experience, had obediently marched in the holiday demonstrations, sat through the required hours of celebratory meetings, clapped wildly until their palms ached when the "great name" was mentioned. And if they saw something, or didn't accept something, they would keep it to themselves, preaching the "truth" known from the beginning of all time: "You can't fight guns with sticks."

What if someone, all knowing and prophetic, had addressed our boys then with the words: "You don't have to do anything now, because no matter what, nothing can be changed. Just simply wait: first wait two years for Stalin's death, then for the Twentieth Congress and Khrushchev's "Thaw," and then another thirty years for Gorbachev's Perestroika." Would they have listened to this clairvoyant? You can accept such wisdom when you are fifty, or maybe even forty, but when you are nineteen? Imagine wasting all your life, the only one you'll ever have, on this endless, desiccating anticipation, so that when you're sixty your tired breast can finally inhale the air of freedom that you've desired for so long. No, for people of this type of temperament, such a prospect would be beyond their strength. For them, entering their age of consciousness in the years after the war, when the inhuman face of the regime was finally exposed, life in such stagnant, poisoned air was unbearable. Therefore they chose the path of action, the path that led to their own destruction.

The rest of us, the ones who passed through the camps, were fated to live. And we lived our lives in our own ways, although there was much that we had in common. Almost all of us, who were burned once in our youth thereafter, with a few exceptions, steered clear of politics. We lived for our families, our work, and took the so-called stand of "hidden oppostion" to the government. But each year on the 25th of April, on the anniversary of our "second birth" we assembled together, and once gathered, recalled the memory of those who had perished. And even when the bonds of our shared prison and camp fraternity weakened over the years, and many of us were scattered across the globe, this date remained holy and inviolate, and is celebrated by each of us, at least in the family circle. Yet it is a bitter celebration.

They say that time heals all wounds. For my part, I dream less and less of that burning scene of my arrest, and the tormenting night-time interrogations in Lefortovo. Those five years of prison and camp seem to be covered by smoke, and sometimes it seems that it didn't happen to me, but to somebody else, and I was just watching from the sidelines. And it is only the final scene in the court, with those terrible words of the sentence, that flare up in my memory now and then and make my heart contract. Apparently I still cannot reconcile myself to that fatal irrevocability, although almost a whole life has passed by since then.

We know how we passed those years. But how would those three have lived them, separated from us by their implacable sentence? What did society lose with their untimely and violent deaths? That something was lost there can be no doubt. Do we know much about the cases of resistance to Stalin's regime? You can count them on the fingers of one hand. Compare these numbers to the millions who applauded the regime or silently assented. It was no accident that twice a month Stalin was personally informed about our case. Most certainly he personally sanctioned the sentence which was obediently rubber-stamped by the judges. It turned out that they missed the dawn by barely a year.

In this book I have told the story of just one small episode in the war between a totalitarian state and its people. I have told of what I have witnessed, and which I myself passed through. The theme is immense and inexhaustible, as inexhaustible as the suffering and grief of the millions of people who fell under the wheels of the government's powerful chariot. But if, in this tragic mosaic of the past, I have succeeded in illuminating an unknown page of history, it means that my efforts have not been in vain. I understand that no matter how much detail is added, this chronicle will remain unfinished. The final word can never be written.

Epilogue:
March 1999

This year the winter was absolutely extraordinary. So much snow had heaped up that it was as if the city was covered with a white eiderdown. The streets, the houses, the trees were all garbed in white. The snow muffled the sounds, and the silence was broken only by the crunch of snow under our boots. We walk in the ravines, Sasha and I, and in front of us runs our ginger-coloured golden retriever, Timosha. We take a walk like this every day and can't get enough of the beauty that surrounds us. The coniferous boughs bend under their burden of snow, the tops of the trees, heavy with ice-covered needles, dip down to the road and, from time to time, we are sprinkled with snow disturbed by the squirrels jumping from tree to tree. Sometimes in the distance we see a long-eared white hare and come upon lonely coyotes who disappear like ghosts when they catch sight of us. And this is all only a couple of steps away from our home, a ten-minute ride by car from the university and downtown Edmonton. We have been living in this western Canadian city for the past seventeen years and each time that we return from a distant journey we experience a special joy to be back home.

Our family has recently celebrated one of the most important events in our life—the twenty-fifth anniversary of our emigration from the Soviet Union. On an overcast, damp day of 21 March 1974, the three of us—Sasha and I and our twelve-year-old son, Vladimir —had passed through customs, and were on the second floor of the Sheremetyevo Airport in Moscow. Down below us, separated by a glass wall, our closest relatives—my mother, father, and my sister-in-law—were waving their farewells. I couldn't hold back my tears: after all, we were leaving forever and there was almost no hope of ever seeing them again. And we weren't just leaving, we were fleeing, saving ourselves and our son from the double life which we had been leading for such a long time. Emigration from the Soviet Union was only just starting. Under pressure from the US Congress, from Senator Henry Jackson, and Henry Kissinger's negotiations on détente, the exit of Jews, the numbers of which were unprecedented, to their "historical homeland" was beginning. This opportunity, to leave for a "historical homeland" excluded other national groups, except for two other categories: Volga Germans and Armenians. These latter had been repatriated to Soviet Armenia from the Middle East after the war, and were now streaming back into their "unhistorical" homeland. The Iron Curtain had parted but only slightly. One had to hurry to jump through before the hole was closed up again. And that, indeed, was what happened: from time to time, for long periods, emigration was almost entirely stopped.

It was not easy to decide to emigrate, especially for me—I would be leaving my elderly parents and a brother who was ill. My heart was torn between the feeling of obligation towards my relatives and the selfish desire to escape to freedom. A single incident, however, served as a catalyst. Among the flood of forbidden literature known as *Samizdat* (literature "published" by the author) or *Tamizdat* (literature published abroad) that flowed from person to person and opened our eyes to so many events of which we had had no idea (Nadezhda Mandelshtam's *Memoirs*, Zhores Medvedev's book about Lysenko's crimes in the field of "socialist" genetics, Pasternak's *Doctor Zhivago*, among others), we obtained the memoirs of Maya Ulanovskaya, who had been arrested along with me. My brother brought us this thin booklet: he was carrying on the work of his elder sister and was closely connected with dissident circles. Through him, Maya passed on the suggestion that each of our group should write his or her reminiscences, and put them out in a single volume. Thus a fuller picture of our story could be created. It was a very sensible suggestion, but my blood ran cold from the single thought that I would again be under threat, in the underground, exposing my family to danger. Maya's memoirs, a slim, typewritten notebook really, were about our trial. At night, when it somehow seemed less dangerous, Sasha read her restrained, emotionless account. The scene of the trial that Maya described was accompanied by a small schematic drawing or plan of the trial hall, with little squares showing where each of us had sat. In each little square were the initials of the accused. Going to the end of the last row, where in one little square were the initials A. R. (Alla Reyf), Sasha suddenly realized that at this very moment, somewhere in a brightly lit KGB office, someone could be reading the same thing as he was. There was no thought now of sleep. It was illogical but he suddenly feared another arrest. And yet, there was a certain "Soviet" logic in his fear. After all, many people who had served their sentences and returned to freedom had quickly been put back behind bars or exiled. The next morning Sasha said that we had to emigrate before it was too late. Where to? Wherever we could get to, only right out of this country. At that time it was possible to go to Israel so to Israel we would go. It made no difference that we had been Russified to such a degree that we were reminded of our Jewishness only by the constant anti-Semitic jabs; nor had the existence of Israel, while pleasing us, ever called forth any desire to move there. We could no longer waste any time.

I knew that Sasha was right. The situation in the Soviet Union was clearly heating up. Fresh in our memories were the protests in Red Square by small, banner-waving groups condemning the invasion of Czechoslovakia. We knew how they had been dealt with. "Signers," scientists and artists who had signed open letters in defence of the dissidents, were being attacked in the newspapers and defamed in public meetings. Recently the trial had been held against the famous dissidents Krasin and Peter Yakir (son of the general who was shot in 1937). They had also arrested Petro Grigorenko, the rebellious general who had been demoted. He was soon sent to a psychiatric hospital (the most horrible of prisons). My brother Igor had become his constant correspondent and filled the role of domestic physician in the household of the disgraced general. Their friendship lasted until Grigorenko's death. My brother feared arrest himself and had given us all his papers for safekeeping. Among them was a copy of Solzhenitsyn's novel, *The First Circle*, produced on photographic paper. "Do with it as you wish," Igor told us. Thus, a bomb was planted in our home. After we had read the book, it was imperative for us to dispose of it.

But it wasn't an easy task: the book was in the form of photographs, each page of which was fourteen by twenty-two centimetres (six by nine inches) and it looked an appalling sight: on the table it rose up in dense mountain of photographic paper. Following a longstanding tradition, coming from the distant and near past, we decided to burn the dangerous book. But it was not so easy—photographic paper doesn't burn, but smoulders, giving off an asphyxiating stench which would soon attract the attention of our neighbours in the building. Then we had another, equally absurd, idea: we would tear the photographs into tiny bits and flush them down the toilet. We began cutting up the sheets of paper, shearing them with scissors, tearing them apart; we were ready to use our teeth! For a bystander the sight would have seemed quite ridiculous, but there was no laughter on our lips. As we worked the heap of pages grew smaller, but around us rose a mountain of torn pieces of paper many times bigger than the original book itself. It was already well past midnight when we realized that even the smallest piece of this trash would immediately block up the toilet. At that point we could imagine how the plumber, called to fix the clog, would find some of the pieces and immediately denounce us to the proper authorities. What in the world could we do with our dangerous trash? Every little bit of it, on which you still might read a couple of words, would be a piece of evidence against us.

Then we reached our final decision: we would make up several small packets of the bits of paper and throw them into trash bins in various parts of Moscow only not, of course, in our own. It took us till dawn to do the packaging. Our son slept through the night in the next room, completely innocent of the danger that was threatening our family. In the morning Sasha and I loaded ourselves up with the packets, each with our own bag, and set off by bus in different directions. I recalled that large garbage bins stood in the courtyard of a building close to my place of work. I quickly slipped through the gate and, having made sure that no one was nearby, threw away part of my burden. One stop further on the bus route I looked for another bin and was finally rid of my dangerous load. With a light heart I continued on to work. I had no idea that Sasha's mission had not turned out as simple as mine. That evening he told me what had happened.

At the square by the Tanganka metro station, on the opposite side of the street from his usual exit (this was Sasha's route to the Ippolitov College of Music, where he had been teaching for the past two years), stood several enormous, shoulder-high trash bins. The square by the station was full of people, as usual, but Sasha was late for work and decided not to look for a different place. Quickly he approached the bins, slipped his hand into his bag and threw his two packets into that dark womb. By the hollow thump they made as they hit the bottom, he knew that the bin was almost empty. The job was done. Now he could forget everything that had happened and return to his normal life. But first, he needed to phone one of his students. There were telephone booths next to the metro station. Going up to one of them, Sasha began rummaging in his briefcase for his datebook, but it wasn't to be found. The first thought that came into his head was terrifying: he had thrown the book into the bin along with the packets. Now, at the bottom of the trash bin, lay the ID of a state criminal who had read an anti-Soviet book and, of course, had let his friends read it and had been trying to cover up the traces of his crime. Completely panicked, Sasha ran back to the enormous bins. But when he arrived there he realized that there was no way he could look inside the bins without calling attention to himself. He stood there for some time with no idea of what to do. His very appearance might call forth suspicion: a well-dressed citizen shifting around the trash. Then he had a hopeful idea—what if he had left his datebook at home? He raced back to the telephone. Vladimir's calm voice announced that yes, his datebook was lying on the table next to the telephone at home. Sasha took a deep breath of relief.

This episode clearly shows what nervous stress we were under. Having passed through the first circle of hell by reading Solzhenitsyn's book, we continued our journey through the succeeding circles of fear and panic. It was a familiar experience for Soviet people. Now we may laugh at our helplessness, our irrational behaviour. But only *now*. At the time it wasn't funny at all. We had lived a double life for many years, in fact, a life of internal exile, attending the incessant meetings at work (*politchasy*), keeping our mouths shut. We knew which joke could be told at work or socially, and which ones might cost you twenty-five years of punishment, or those that might only be worth ten years. We experienced anguish over the open trial of Sinyavsky and Daniel who had dared to publish their books abroad. And before that there had been the mocking and persecution of Pasternak and the exile of the young poet Joseph Brodsky. Just like during Stalin's time, the people silently approved of all that came from the authorities. The newspapers were filled with hysterical lies, just as they had been during Stalin's Terror. The Khrushchev "Thaw" which had brought the hope that the regime would be democraticized had long been over. They were even talking about the rehabilitation of Stalin! The latest incident was Solzhenitsyn's forced exile to the West. Despite the constant jamming, we regularly listened to the foreign radio stations that broadcast in Russian, trying to catch some particle of news through the noise of the jammers.

It was a strange sight that our son would see: his papa pressing his ear close to the radio speaker, listening to garbled speech through whistles, howling, and what sounded like witches' laughter. He would bend so close to the radio that it looked as if he was trying to crawl in, head first. Vladimir was ordered not to disturb his father and to just get out of the room. So far the little boy had not yet asked any difficult questions. But the time would come when those questions would shower down on us as from a horn of plenty. We understood that our boy was growing up. Now we stood before a dilemma: should we tell him the truth how we feel about the Soviet state, warning him to keep silent? That would mean that our twelve-year-old would be forced to live the difficult double life that his parents were already leading. He would immediately have to learn how to lie, to say one thing and think another, but he would grow up to be our friend. If we decided to keep him ignorant of our convictions he would be in harmony with the reality that surrounded him but might grow up a stranger to us.

An unpleasant incident had already taken place. I had torn up a little book about the famous Pioneer hero, Pavlik Morozov, in front of our son's very eyes. I had good reason for that! The "hero" had denounced his own father and had been killed by his family for it. The story was familiar to all, young and old: according to the legend, Pavlik reported on his father out of his sense of patriotism and loyalty. No one at the time knew the actual truth about Pavlik and his motives; it emerged only during the perestroika years. At the time of collectivization in the 1930s, when the *kulaks* were being "destroyed as a class," the State would seize the peasants's stores of grain, leaving them without any food and condemning them to hunger and death. Peasants who hid their produce that was to be handed over were cruelly punished—whole families, including infants and the aged, were sent to Siberia. Many were shot in cold blood. Pavlik Morozov was just fourteen when he decided, after an argument with his father, to take revenge and denounce him as a hoarder of grain. The father was arrested and his furious relatives made short work of the boy. Pavlik was murdered and immediately resurrected as a hero-martyr in the cause of communism, a model worthy of imitation. His name was given to streets, Young Pioneer detachments, and parks in which monuments to the heroic denouncer stood in marble and bronze. The spread of his story took on unheard-of proportions: books were written, songs were composed, and study of the heroic denouncer became a required part of the school curriculum. Thus an example to be followed was created, and the practice of children reporting their parents to the police became not only the norm, but an obligation. It is not difficult to imagine how our family reacted to Pavlik's "feat." But how were we to explain our point of view to Vladimir and avoid coming into conflict with what his teachers were telling him at school? There was no way out—we resolved to tell our son the truth, and did so with repeated warnings of what was and was not permitted to be spoken of beyond the walls of our apartment.

Vladimir already suffered from the sickness of anti-Semitism, which was increasing during these years. It had always been present in society, but was especially virulent during periods of crisis. The authorities had decided to finish off the dissident movement once and for all. Among the dissidents were many Jews, and this fact was exploited during the reprisals undertaken by the KGB, journalists, and party functionaries—all those who were interested in safeguarding of the regime. "Rootless renegades" and "anti-Soviet elements" were the labels of the time, recalling the campaign against "cosmopolitanism" in the 1950s! Children caught the mood of their parents and, using their inherent cruelty, began to poison by degrees the lives of playmates little different from themselves. Vladimir would come home from school depressed: "How do they know that I'm Jewish? Aren't all our faces the same?" His Russian surname couldn't save him. The teacher's classroom journal listed all the students' ethnic identities in an appropriate column.

Anti-Semitism was active at all levels of society. At the Institute of Gynecology, where I worked in a clinical laboratory, almost all of the Jewish doctors were let go. N. A. Verbova, the dean of the Vocal Faculty of the Gnesin Institute, where Sasha had graduated, took him aside one day and confidentially informed him that because he was a Jew he had no hope of going on to postgraduate work. The situation grew worse as emigration took off. Employers were afraid to hire Jews because they were potential emigrants. Once you presented your documents for leaving the country, a stream of curses would shower down on your head *and* on the head of your boss, who would be accused of "poor ideological work." At public meetings that all workers had to attend, the unfortunate future emigrant would be smeared with accusations of preferring hostile, Zionist Israel, with which we had broken off diplomatic relations, to the "happiest country on the face of the earth." Some people decided against emigration because of the humiliation they knew they would face.

And still, because of all these events and our own thoughts, we decided to emigrate. Of course we had to receive the blessing of my parents (Sasha's mother had died a year before our marriage, and his father had died when he was still a child). I foresaw a difficult conversation: because my mother had been sick for several years, I wanted to speak with my father first. In the kitchen, I softly asked him what he thought of our decision: "Just one word from you, 'no,' and we won't go," I said. He embraced me and said something that I will never forget: "If I were twenty years younger, I would leave on foot myself." And this from a man who all his life had occupied important positions, who had never been in material need, who outwardly submitted to the regime, expressing his dissatisfaction only in a whisper among his family. Nevertheless, he was worn out by the constant lying and by his role of "cog" in the wheel of the state machine. Mama also approved of our decision.

Thus the blessing was received. Relatives in Israel, who had left a year and a half before, had already sent us the invitations we needed to be considered for immigration. We took our documents to the Visa and Registration Office (OVIR is its Russian acronym), having already quit our jobs to avoid the nasty recriminations at the public meetings which all "departers" were subjected to. We soon made new friends who were also waiting for permission to leave, and joined the new social category of "those who are waiting." We found out from them that there was no obligation to go only to Israel. There were several countries which were accepting refugees —although we were officially emigrating we were given refugee status. From the letters of our friends who had left earlier and were awaiting their visas in Italy, we learned that our first stop would be Vienna and that there we could declare our wish to continue on, not to Israel, but to any one of four countries—the United States, Canada, Australia, or New Zealand.

After some reflection, we picked Canada. I can't say that we knew much about the place. We knew the names of the three largest cities, the hockey triumphs, the Montreal Summer Olympic Games, and that the climate and vegetation were like those of Russia. But our decision was really based on something which might appear rather strange: our acquaintance with several Canadian musicians. My husband, a professional singer, had worked for the past ten years in the well-known Moscow ensemble, Madrigal. As a student he had become acquainted with the Canadian singer Lois Marshall when she performed in the Soviet Union. Her concerts were a tremendous success and Sasha was so taken by her artistry that he wrote his diploma paper about her. At the time he was a freelance correspondent for the magazine *Soviet Music* and proposed to his editors to write an article about the famous singer. There followed a series of meetings and interviews with Marshall and her accompanist, Weldon Kilbourn, and a personal friendship developed. After Marshall another singer came from Canada, Donald Bell, about whom Sasha also wrote. Not long before, Muscovites had been staggered by the performances of Glenn Gould and Maureen Forrester. We were not often treated to guest artists from North America and it seemed to us that Canada was a centre of musical culture. Later, after we arrived in Toronto in 1974, we realized that our expectations and impressions were somewhat exaggerated. Of course there were other, more fundamental reasons to choose Canada. We had heard that Canada had significantly fewer social problems than the United States. And Australia and New Zealand weren't even in the running—they were just too far away.

The last days before our departure took place as though in a fog. We said our farewells to our relatives, visited our friends. Persons we knew and even those we didn't know stopped by to take a look at these daring people who had come to such a decision. They eyed us with curiosity, with surprise, and with envy. A new tradition had been established: those who were departing would set aside a day for an open house, opening their doors to everyone. From morning to evening we received people who came by to see us off. They all considered it necessary to give us a farewell gift, but some, it seemed, couldn't even take the simplest step—to drop in and say goodbye. The apartment of anyone who was emigrating would be under constant surveillance. Our neighbours told us that a policeman had stopped in and questioned them about us: were there many people who visited us, did we live luxuriously, did we have any valuables, any gold, or diamonds? The neighbour answered that she had never noticed anything suspicious about us. Every person who was brave enough to come see us that day would perhaps turn up on some blacklist. But the majority overcame their fear and those who couldn't, called us on the telephone. Late in the evening, under the cover of darkness, the last ones came, the old friends who were scared to death yet, nonetheless, proud of their own heroic action.

On one of the last days before our departure we decided to buy some clothes so we could dress our son in a "western" style. The three of us set off for the Children's World store in Dzerzhinsky Square, named in honour of the first leader of the Cheka, "Iron Felix" Dzerzhinsky. His monument towered in the centre of the square against the background of the Lubyanka—headquarters of the KGB and a prison whose infamy was even known beyond the borders of the Soviet Union. It was from one of the doors of this building that I had stepped into freedom some eighteen years before. Usually, as I passed this place, I felt ill at ease, as though some threat were again hanging over my head. I would turn away and walk even faster. But this time we deliberately stopped and Sasha, pointing towards the building, told Vladimir to remember this place well. Vladimir was surprised, saying, "What's so special about it? It's a building like any other." "I won't tell you now, but when we're gone you'll learn all about it." Vladimir pondered for a moment and then happily announced that he had guessed the secret: "That's where they issued our visas so we could emigrate!" "You've almost guessed it," Sasha answered, "but there's a bit more to it which you don't know about, and we'll tell you later." It was only when we arrived in Vienna that we told our son about what his mother had experienced in her youth.

And finally the day of our departure arrived. It was morning when the taxi drove up to our building to take us away. A final look at the building, at the trees that had grown up around it, planted only six years ago when we had settled into this new region of the city, Davydkovo. It was famous for having been the site of Stalin's *dacha*, his fortress in the countryside. It was here that he had died. Each of us was wrapped in our own thoughts, but one was common to us all—this had been our home, and despite Soviet power, or (perhaps) in opposition to it, we had been happy there. Now, at this moment, crossing the threshold, we were without a home and without a passport (they had taken our passports away and in return gave us pink slips of paper that stated: "without citizenship"). Our spirits were anxious. We got into the taxi without our luggage, which had been sent on earlier. I was carrying our dog, a white English fox-terrier with a black snout, called Lada. No one had told her that we were leaving our homeland forever, and she settled comfortably into my lap. Lada hadn't the slightest idea of what was happening. "What airport are you going to?" the driver asked. "The 'socialist' one or the 'capitalist'?" "The 'capitalist'!" we all shouted and set off for Sheremetyevo, from which flights took off only for the *kapstrany*, or "capitalist countries." Finally the painful separation from my parents. The last smiles, the last farewells. We are flying off to Vienna.

The flight didn't last very long and it seemed to me that my tears hadn't had time to dry. I could still see the faces of my parents, mama's face distorted by her illness, certain I would never see her alive again. My thoughts pulled me back, not allowing myself to weaken, not even for a moment. At some point I realized that this was the very first time I had ever crossed the border of the Soviet Union—at last, albeit a border in the air, I was now beyond that border. My whole life had been spent as a "resident," with no right to go abroad, thanks to my past. They hadn't even let me visit one of the socialist countries as a tourist. Nor had I attempted it—I knew they would never let me.

The aircraft landed and we came out into the airport awash with sunshine. We were struck by the contrast—two hours before a dreary, rainy Moscow had bade us farewell without a smile, the scent of spring could barely be caught in the damp air. Here the sun was shining and it smelled of spring. Perhaps it was the smell of freedom that overcame us! The airport hummed with activity: small vehicles dashed about in all directions, taking their cargo here and there. They were painted in bright colours, as were the overalls of the workers—I had never seen anything like it in all my life. In this feast of light and colour my sorrowful soul was consumed by an overwhelming joy. The Rubicon had been passed, the worst was behind us!

We were met in the airport building by representatives of three organizations offering assistance to emigrating Soviet Jews —Sokhnut (The Jewish Agency for Israel), Joint, and Hias (Hebrew Sheltering and Immigrant Aid Society). Everything was remarkably well organized from the very first minute. The group of arriving former Soviet citizens was immediately divided into two sections— one section for those who had declared their intention to continue to Israel and were in the care of Sokhnut, and the other, to which we belonged, for those who had indicated they wanted to take advantage of other possibilities (we had a choice!), under the care of Hias and Joint. It was very strange to see the soldiers protecting us with automatic rifles: there was a fear of terrorist acts. The group of

"Israelites" was sent off in a special bus to the Schönau castle, where they would await their transport to Israel, again under the protection of the Austrian police. The rest of us were divided among several Viennese hotels. That week that we spent in Vienna was such a gift!

But here we are again on the road. This time by train to Italy, to the Eternal City. We couldn't be torn from the windows of the train: the Alps with their snowy peaks, the verdant valleys with the occasional castle on a mountain, right out of a fairy-tale. The sights would appear and then just as suddenly disappear as we entered the mouth of a long tunnel. I couldn't close my eyes at night, so great was my feeling of joy. In the morning we arrived in Rome. Spring was in full, luxuriant bloom with trees covered in a pink froth and an extraordinarily blue sky above our heads. The first unforgettable impression—Easter Sunday on St. Peter's Square, the grandeur of the basilica, but most of all the crowd of people openly celebrating Easter. There were no hostile policemen, no spies telling their tales to their masters. Happy faces surrounded us—young, old, little children—some who had come as we had, out of curiosity, and others who came from a spiritual necessity; each was free to think and act as he wished. We were blessed by the Pope and it was a symbolic moment for us. His voice carried across the square over the loudspeakers, its strength incommensurate with that small figure standing in the window high above the crowd. It was as though the heavens were blessing us in all the languages the Pope spoke.

I will not recount all the details of those unforgettable four months we spent in Italy waiting for our entrance visas to Canada. We called that happy time our "Roman Holiday" and always remain grateful to Italy for giving us asylum. Not long before our departure we were invited to the Canadian embassy: the Canadian consul wished to meet us. Sasha could express himself a bit in English and sometimes the translator would step in to help. The consul asked us about the reasons for our leaving the Soviet Union, about our education, our professions. Then the conversation turned by chance to my past, and he began to question me about what I had gone through during my arrest. He was interested in the details of conditions in the prison and in the camps. I knew no English and the conversation was carried on through the translator. I was sometimes surprised by his questions—Solzhenitsyn's *Gulag Archipelago* had already been published, surely he should have read it? It all became clear, however, when at the end of the visit the consul unexpectedly said: "So, then, everything that Solzhenitsyn writes is true?" These were the doubts that had troubled this nice man; doubts that most likely troubled many others like him.

The "Roman Holiday," like any other holiday, flew by much too quickly. On July 30 our flight was scheduled to leave for Canada. We were flying to Toronto—that was our choice. Already in Moscow we had known the name of this city, as we had known that of Montreal. We selected the anglophone part of Canada basically because Sasha had some knowledge of English. It was all the same to me since in school and the institute I had learned only German. The nine-hour flight across the ocean was uneventful. It was only our Lada that suffered, spending all those hours in her carrier in the baggage compartment of the aircraft. Several other families of Russian emigrants were travelling with us. The 30th of July 1974 became another historic date for our family—we stepped onto Canadian soil!

Coming out of the cool, air-conditioned terminal, we were unexpectedly plunged into hot and unusually humid air, as though we had suddenly arrived at a resort in the Caucasus or on the Black Sea, where the air was just as humid. Later we discovered that Toronto had saved its famous heat wave for our arrival. Even Torontonians could hardly cope when the temperature was above thirty-five degrees Celsius. Almost melting from the heat, we dove into the air-conditioned bus waiting for our group and were taken to a downtown hotel. From Union Station, which was nearby, we began our first tour of the city. In 1974 it wasn't the most attractive area in Toronto: the littered streets and squalid little shop windows presented a striking contrast with what we had left only hours before in Rome. Since then the area has changed a great deal. We wandered the streets, staying close to the hotel for fear of getting lost, and felt quite uneasy—what if we had made a mistake and should have gone to New Zealand? We didn't share our doubts, so as not to upset each other, but joked that now we were nostalgic for Rome.

All these doubts, however, were swept away when our real lives in the city began. Canada astonished us at every step. Our first journey was to some storage facilities where we were given all the necessities for a new life—bed linens, dishes, pots and pans, and so forth. We had not expected how everyone in the official institutions to welcome us with kindness, and smiles, trying to help. Soon we were set up for a five-month course in English at George Brown College. That was where we experienced for the first time the multinational mosaic that is Canada: there were Poles, Finns, Chinese, Vietnamese, Hungarians, Russians—my class contained a whole mixture of people from around the world. We were all beginners, at the same level in our command of English, but it was our common means of communication and we used it, not grandly as they might in Parliament, but we could understand each other. Over the period of our studies we were given a stipend, just enough to rent an apartment and live quite adequately. The school year began for both us and Vladimir at the same time. In the evening, we would exchange our impressions.

Vladimir immediately noticed the difference in the relationship between teachers and students. In his Moscow school there was a clear-cut subordination: the teacher would command and the student would obey. Some teachers even required their students to stand in front of them at attention. There was constant shouting and punishments with an almost military environment. During breaks the children were expected to file down the halls (there were no recess times in Moscow schoolyards, and indeed no spacious schoolyards as are the rule in Canada). Here, our son told us, you felt that the teacher related to you with respect. He liked the classroom atmosphere very much. Everything would have been perfect if we hadn't noticed that his school work was rather unchallenging, not unlike kindergarten. No homework was assigned and the curriculum and expectations were quite low. In a Soviet school students had to work hard in order to get a good mark. "Take it easy, have fun," was the slogan by which our son's school operated. Later we found out that this was typical of most primary schools. In Moscow, Vladimir had attended a special French school and by grade six had a good command of the language. Here, from the very beginning it was clear that French was poorly taught. And this in a country that called itself bilingual! Everyone with whom we shared our concerns told us that most schools taught at a low level. A much better situation would be found in a private school. But how could we manage that? The Jewish community came to our help and paid Vladimir's fees for the first two years at the private, non-religious Bialik School.

The fact there were any Jewish schools at all was an unbelievable thing for us. In the Soviet Union, except maybe in the Jewish Autonomous Region of Birobidzhan in the Far East, there were no Jewish schools as all had been closed along with the Jewish theatres. And anyway, what parent would want to send his children to such a school? Russification on the one hand, and anti-Semitism on the other had achieved their goal—the national Jewish culture had disappeared. The Yiddish language was no longer spoken and the synagogues had been shut down. We were struck by the abundance of synagogues in Toronto. Here there were all sorts: orthodox, conservative, and reform. In Moscow, with its millions of people and its large Jewish population, there was only one (!) synagogue, and we avoided it. There were often skirmishes there and police and plainclothes men mingled with the crowd of visitors. What an irony of fate that the first time in my life I set foot in a synagogue was in Rome!

During the New Year High Holidays Sasha received an unexpected invitation to sing in one of the conservative synagogues. Wearing a magnificent light-blue robe and a blue *kipa*, embroidered with gold thread, he sang for the first time music which had been unknown to him until then, and in the foreign language of Hebrew. It is easy to imagine the surprise of our acquaintances in Moscow when they received the photographs of this newly fledged cantor. We walked to the synagogue with high emotions, but no one was interested in where we were going: here people didn't hide their nationalities or their convictions. Smartly dressed and glowing, they celebrated their own holidays. And although we had been brought up far from our Jewish traditions and religion, the festive spirit inspired us too: We were in a country where equality of nationality was not only written into the Constitution, as it was proclaimed in the Soviet Union, but actually followed in life.

When we shared our impressions with Canadians, they told us that not so long ago discrimination by race or national origin had been widespread in Canada. "Don't look at everything through rose-coloured glasses, tone down your enthusiasm," our new friends advised us."Yes," we would agree, "but your society has the capacity to improve! We have come from a country of permafrost—an oppressive regime cannot change. You and we have different ways of measuring things: anti-Semitism, racism, and other 'delights' on the personal level, is one thing, but when it comes from the government, from the authorities, you feel helpless, humiliated, and overwhelmed." We had many conversations and arguments on this theme. We became familiar with a rather large group of people who still looked on the great socialist power as an example to be emulated. Compassionate people, they remained naïve communists. There were others who had been in the country of "triumphant socialism" and couldn't understand anything they had seen, and had only seen what was routinely presented to foreigners: the painted facade that hid the real picture. When we attempted to explain something, they wouldn't listen to us and, to justify their opinions, raised the same "proofs" over and over again: the Soviet Union had free education and medicine, low housing costs, and public transport. After such "proofs" there was nothing that we could say. In general, people who had not experienced what we had, who had not lived through what we had lived through, could not be expected to imagine the scale of abuse committed by an undemocratic country. "You," they told us, "were put in prison though you were innocent. It happens here, too. There are many such cases. They write about it in the newspapers, and they've had television interviews with the victims of such actions." At this point we usually lost that calm required to continue such arguments: "Yes, yes, yes—that's just the point," we almost shouted. "Sooner or later you will hear about these cases of injustice and you can count the number of victims. In the Soviet Union we had millions who disappeared into the Gulag without a trial or investigation. Entire ethnic groups were forced out of their homelands and died in Siberian exile!" Our opponents would sympathetically nod their heads and, without fail, add: "But did you know how unjustly we treated the Japanese Canadians during the war?" Yes, we know that fact, it was widely spread by the Canadian press after the war. Dear, dear Canadians! Such kind and open people! People who are prepared to help, to stand up in defence of a single humiliated person, who feel their shame for the First Nations as though it was their own guilt. We were captivated by these Canadians. In private, however, we joked that Canada was a nation of innocents. Many, but not all here, know how fragile democracy is. Many, but not all, understand that it is necessary to defend it daily. They accept freedom like something inalienable, natural, while we could only dream of such freedom and in our youth tried to fight for it.

We prized every sign of this freedom which was so new to us. For example, the absence of residence permits—we could live in any city in Canada we chose, what a miracle! We were taught much by this new country. After all, everyone brings their own past baggage with them, and there were many Soviet ideas about how things should be that we brought with us, and now we were realizing that things could be quite different. In our past, books were always a tool of ideology. They were divided into "useful" and "harmful," and in fact many "useful" books after awhile turned out to be harmful and vice versa. It was not in vain that Mayakovsky wrote: "I want the pen to be as powerful as the sword!" And it did become as powerful. Forbidden books were hidden in secret storage places. How many times had we come up against the cold stare of a librarian as she took our request, saying only, "The book does not circulate." In the children's section they spoke more gently: "This author is not recommended." "We don't need anyone's recommendations," we thought to ourselves, but didn't argue. This must have meant that the author had fallen into disgrace and was awaiting arrest or had already been taken care of. History books were rewritten in accordance with the political situation of the moment and the needs of ideology. The names of historical figures no longer suitable were removed, their portraits cut out.

Once, after we had been in Canada many months and Sasha was already working in the University of Toronto's Russian Summer School, we went together to the university's Robarts Library. We hadn't been in a Canadian library before, and imagined the procedures only from our own past experience. Inside the beautiful building we went through to the catalogue room (this was before computers), wrote out on a slip of paper the names of several Russian books, and prepared to hand over our request to the librarian and then wait until they brought us the books. At the Lenin Library in Moscow the wait would sometimes take several hours. But here there was no place to hand in our requests. We asked where the Slavic section was and were told to go to one of the top floors. When we came out of the elevator, we expected to finally find the desk where a librarian would assist us. But in the open area by the elevator there was no one to be seen. There were three doors in front of us. Which one should we take? Russian fairy-tales often confront the hero with such a dilemma: three roads or three doors, and all of them leading to destruction, but the hero in the end always triumphs. Encouraged by such happy endings, we decided to follow the fairy-tale pattern and went through the middle door. Our first impression was that we had found our way into a storage area: there were rows and rows of stacks, and not a person in sight. And then we realized that we were in the library itself and there was no intermediary standing between us and the books, WE COULD CHOOSE ANY BOOK WE WISHED!! After several seconds of confusion we were overcome by an unrestrained happiness. We practically ran between the stacks, taking books off the shelves, leafing through them, putting them back on the shelves, going over to another stack to still more books. We must have looked like we were crazy. Eventually, having picked out several books (and of course these were books that would never have circulated at the Lenin Library or any Soviet library!) we took the elevator down and found ourselves in front of the long-anticipated librarian. The books were stamped and we went out to the street. It was a hot summer day and people scurried past us, paying no attention to our precious load. We walked on, smiling stupidly, as though we had just celebrated our birthday or some other happy holiday. Sasha expressed our joy in these words: "Today we have touched Freedom with our own hands!"

Gradually our life began to flow into a normal routine. After completing my English lessons, I soon found work in a Red Cross laboratory. The work wasn't easy and I had night shifts, but I was happy that I could give Sasha the opportunity to look for something in his field. He had already gone to many auditions and there had been offers, of which he took one—he joined a small troupe which was devoted to contemporary avant-garde opera. Later he was invited to teach at the university's Russian Summer School, for which he could thank his first specialization in Russian philology.

The most difficult two years of our adaptation had now passed. For children, the period was somehow easier and went faster. After only a couple of months the English language ceased to be a problem for Vladimir. Our son also took his first steps towards his first million dollars: he began delivering newspapers. We discarded our former, Soviet (or maybe Russian!) ways of thinking rather easily— that it was bad to give children money, and that a child should not work under any circumstance, that there are professions that are respected by all, and that there are some that are beneath an educated person. Such an attitude toward labour was part of our recent past. We liked the fact that in Canada children often know the value of money, that they begin earning some money at an early age, shovelling snow, babysitting, delivering flyers, and so forth. Students, as a rule, work during the summer in order to pay for their education. We observed how children, even in families that were well off, strove to be independent. Vladimir took this well-worn path all the way to university: he worked at McDonald's, then a Coles bookstore, at a cemetery, and so on. But his first "responsible" job was a not very profitable one and has been preserved in our memories quite clearly. After his first week of delivering papers, Vladimir, who had already begun to count the great profits that would soon be filling his pockets, set out to collect from his customers. It was Sunday and many of them were not at home, but the ones who were gladly paid. Vladimir was in ecstasy. He returned home and immediately set aside the portion of the money that was his as delivery boy. Toward evening he went out again to finish his collection. All would have been fine if this future millionaire had in the morning jotted down the names of the customers who had already paid. But he hadn't done so and now, forgetting who had paid and who had not, he appeared at some customers' doors for the second time that day, asking for money. Their reaction is not hard to imagine, and our businessman was completely flustered. He returned home in tears and had less money than there should have been. We made up the difference. Thus, ingloriously, concluded the first work experience of this budding capitalist. We can well remember the reactions of our Moscow relatives and friends: You sent a child out into the streets to make money? What a horror! "It's obvious that the parents can't make ends meet!" is what these Muscovites were thinking, as they recalled the axiom we had all learned in our childhood: child labour is always exploited under capitalism. "Work will always leave its heavy mark on a child's fate," they wrote us. And it did leave its mark: after successfully graduating with a bachelor's degree in French language and literature, our son took his master's degree in Russian-French-English translation and soon defended his doctoral dissertation in comparative literature. Today he works as a professor in the Department of Modern Languages and Literatures at the University of Western Ontario.

Our life had changed radically and, unbeknowst to us, we had changed as well. We often caught ourselves with the thought that we would have behaved or thought differently *before*. Once, after work, I came to meet Sasha at the university (by this time he had a permanent position in the Slavic department). After the last of the day's lectures we met in the entrance of the large Sidney Smith Hall. It was Friday and in the spacious foyer they were selling books, as they always did before the weekend. On the tables books were spread out for every taste: medicine, politics, Buddhism, health foods, and so forth. Suddenly we stopped, dumbfounded: before us on one of the tables were books on Marxism and editions of Soviet propaganda. On another table lay *Mein Kampf* and other books bearing black swastikas. Like other people who had grown up in a totalitiarian regime, we were terribly upset by this freedom to spread harmful ideas—and we had scores to settle with both the communist and the fascist ideologies! My husband and I were united in our indignation, and all the way home discussed how to punish people who spread ideas that would eat away at the foundations of Canadian life. But we came off the boil soon. Not even home, we began to understand that it had been the "real Soviet person" speaking in us. Who is not with us, is against us—that was the formula that had been beaten into our heads from childhood. At that time, according to Soviet propaganda, those "against us" had been the anti-communists. Now everything was reversed—the communists had become the enemy. So, those who were "against us" were the dissenters! But to forbid dissent would be to turn Canada into another Soviet Union! Tolerance, respect for your opponent, striving to understand another point of view—this is what we had to teach ourselves. In the Soviet Union I had been sentenced to twenty-five years in the camps for "harmful" ideas, and one of my "crimes" had been to transcribe some forbidden verses. Reading a book about a hostile ideology might lead to a person's destruction, and the slogan "If the enemy doesn't surrender, then he must be destroyed," was a formula for a war against ideas. Could I possibly want something like this in Canada? Our new life had presented us with an excellent lesson.

One other important aspect of the psychology of people in the west drew my attention: the attitude of democratic society to compromise. Here, compromise is seen as a means of achieving peace, co-existence, and resolving conflict. The contemporary Russian language and the Russian mentality itself colours the word "compromise" with an entirely different shade of meaning. We were taught that to compromise was shameful, that it was a betrayal of our convictions, a surrender. I was struck by the observation by the emigré writer, Nina Berberova, who had left Russia during the time of the Revolution. Her words related not only to the post-revolutionary, Soviet psychology. This is what I read in her book, *The Italics are Mine*: "Russians are not often capable of compromise, and this very word, full of creativity and peace-making significance in the west, in Russian carries on it the seal of 'shallow baseness'." So, this is where such things have come from—something not at all introduced by the communists. There are many, many things that Communist Russia had inherited from the past.

Our time as immigrants was also a time of great literary discovery: we had finally fallen upon the literature that had previously been inaccessible, and about which it was foolish to even dream. We avidly read the writers of the "first wave," those who had emigrated during and just after the Revolution, which had thrown out a whole section of the Russian intelligentsia. Now we could read all the Russian-language works of Vladimir Nabokov and become acquainted with the literary life of the Russian emigrés in Berlin and Paris between the wars. All of the *samizdat* and *tamizdat* works were now available to us. We could read the translations of western authors who had never been translated in the Soviet Union. And what *was* translated? The selection of authors who were translated on the pages of *Foreign Literature* and other thick journals was always determined by ideological considerations and was strictly censored. Although I knew I should be reading books in English, in order to improve my command of the language, I devoured books in Russian one after another. How much we had not known, what terrible secrets were now exposed to us!

It was at this time that I decided to write a book about our youth organization. There was no chance of publication in Russia, but there might be a place for it in an emigré journal. I had already read Maya Ulanovskaya's memoir in the journal *Time and We.* She wrote about the prison, about the camps, about all that we had lived through. But each of us had our own prison, our own camps—our own experience. I had to drag out of my memory everything to the smallest detail and transfer it to paper. When now I reread the introduction to my book, written in 1975–1976, I am again reminded of how unexpected the events that transpired in the Soviet Union in 1991 were to us. The foundations of the system seemed unshakeable, the secrets in the KGB archives unattainable, and the empire indissoluble. But the colossus turned out to have feet of clay. It is a genuine miracle that my book was actually published in Moscow, that I found Russian readers. I am immensely grateful to my brother, Igor Reyf, who took advantage of that short period when the KGB opened part of its archives and devoted many hours to the study of our files. He succeeded in copying a number of documents that later were reproduced in the Russian version of my memoirs. Now, twenty-five years after our arrival in Canada, I hope that my book may be useful to an English-speaking readership: you can't take democracy for granted, as if it was some eternal given, for it is fragile and is always in need of defence and strengthening. And so it is important to know what the Soviet Union was like. For the Canadian reader, mine will be not only a voice out of the past but also a warning appropriate to the present and the future.

In 1980 my eighty-year-old father joined us, forever. They had kept him from leaving for seven years, referring to state secrets he might have known, although he had been retired for ten years. Father joked that having worked in the planning division of one of the ministries, he knew the one big secret: all the Soviet five-year plans had been a lie. He lived with us for seventeen years and all those years, apart from the last four, when he was ill, were happy and he thanked us and Canada for giving him shelter.

We have lived a full and interesting life. Sasha taught vocal ensemble and early opera at York University and Seneca College.

He had students of voice, solo recitals, recordings, and radio broadcasts. But as our life became more and more settled, it became clear that he would need another ten years to establish a career as a singer. He didn't have those ten years.

We spent eight wonderful years in Toronto! We liked the city and knew it inside and out. We established a circle of friends and acquaintances. It seemed that we had settled down once and for all and couldn't imagine moving, just as once we couldn't have imagined moving from Moscow. Sasha began graduate work at OISE, the educational institute at the University of Toronto. And then, in the midst of his work in the university's Slavic department and studies at OISE, he was advised to apply for a position at the University of Alberta in Edmonton. An appointment in Edmonton was more attractive than one in Toronto, and so Sasha decided to apply.

It was difficult to part from Toronto. It felt almost like a new emigration for us. We hadn't yet acquired the Canadian psychology that any place is good if you have work there. Here, people move easily, and we still had to learn that lesson. All our friends congratulated us, saying that we would be living in one of Canada's richest provinces, that although we were going to the "Wild West" we would see more cheerfulness and smiling than in Ontario. And so it was, but we noticed no particular wildness, although we were struck by the wild beauty and grandeur of the Rocky Mountains. We have lived in Edmonton now for seventeen years and it has become our home. Sasha later defended his dissertation and received the title of full professor. I worked for a while in a research laboratory. Now we are both retired. Three and a half years ago my memoirs were published by the Moscow publisher, Progress, and the book received many warm responses. Now, translated into English, I hope that it will begin a new journey through the English-speaking world.

Living in a new country and a new home, our lives have acquired new holidays. Without regret, we long ago discarded the old, Soviet ones. Then we celebrated only the New Year. Now we celebrate two New Years with our friends—the calendar one and the Jewish one. Thanksgiving Day is particularly full of significance for us. We sit at the holiday table with the requisite turkey and raise a toast to Canada, which took us in and so richly rewarded us, as it does all Canadians, with equal rights. It is no doubt because of our previous life in a totalitarian society that we deeply value all that we have. After twenty years we have not forgotten Russia, which has undergone such terrible times. We feel for her sorrows, although it is easier to sympathize from a distance. We try to keep alive our hope that life there will soon change for the better.

Today, our family is celebrating a great event—a quarter of a century of life in Canada. All day the phone rings: our Russian and Canadian friends call to congratulate us and there are phone calls from the US, from Israel, from Europe. Fate has tossed us all about in such a rich confusion! And now a call from London, Ontario. Vladimir's family, of course, is marking the anniversary too. We hear the voices of our children and grandchildren. Our son's wife Larissa, a native-born Canadian who didn't know a word of Russian before she met Vladimir, now speaks the language well. "Thank you," she says, "for bringing me Vladimir." She adds in jest, "What would we have done with Alec and Vanessa if you hadn't?" Six-year-old Alec and his two-year-old sister Vanessa both tell us what they've been doing. My friend from so long ago and far away in the camps, the fortune-teller Inga, would have been happy to see us now. Our guests depart, we are left alone, and each of us is immersed in thought. The moon and the sparkling stars look down at us through the window. Another day has passed. How good it is that we are all home.

Notes

1   **MGB**: The initials for the Russian term "Ministerstvo Gosudarstvennoi Bezopasnosti," Ministry of State Security. It was one in a long line of security police during the Soviet era, and was succeeded by the KGB, or Committee for State Security.

2   **Pioneers** are members of the All Union V. I. Lenin Pioneer Organization (ages ten to fourteen); the Komsomol is the organization for older young people (ages fifteen to twenty-seven), its name being the abbreviation of Communist Union of Youth.

3   **Pavlik Morozov** (1918-1932) was a young opponent of the kulaks in the period of collectivization, informing on his father for hoarding grain. He was supposedly killed by his grandfather, and presented to the Soviet public as a great martyr. In recent years the entire mythology around him has been dismantled.

4   Department of the MGB of the Moscow Region.

5   The relationship between Stalin and his son was notoriously strained. He was the son of Stalin's first marriage. At the beginning of the fighting between the Soviets and the Nazis, he served as a fighter pilot. When he was shot down and captured, his father refused all offers of an exchange and he was then shot by the Nazis.

6   **Mikhail Kalinin** (1875-1946), an early Bolshevik and participant in the 1917 Revolution, was Chairman of the Supreme Soviet from 1938, the equivalent of president, but effectively only the titular leader of the Soviet Union. Official propaganda presented him as a congenial "Grandpa," a peasant who had joined the Revolution.

7   **Vyacheslav Molotov** (born in 1890) held many important positions in the Soviet government; from 1939-1949 and from 1953-1956 he was Minister of Foreign Affairs.

8   **Anatoly Serov** (1910-1939) shot down eight planes in Spain, and was killed in an air accident; **Konstantin M. Simonov** (1915-1979) was a prize-winning poet and novelist, publicist and critic, as well as a war correspondent.

9   A *kolkhoznik* was a member of the collective farm, *kolkhoz* (from the Russian words for collective economy).

10 **Vladimir Illich Lenin** was sometimes known by his patronymic, a colloquial "peasant" mode of address.

11 **Nikolai Yezhov** (1895-1936) was leader of the NKVD (a predecessor of the MGB) from 1936 to 1938, and active in the first waves of purges in the late 1930s. He was removed from his post in December 1938, and was himself liquidated, either in January or February 1939.

12 The phrase "with an iron rod" is a pun on Yezhov's name in Russian, where the term is "*v yezhovikh rukavitsakh.*"

13 The "Thaw" (1956-1965) was a period of relative artistic freedom, marked by a liberal and optimistic climate in the arts.

14 The Cathedral of Christ the Saviour, built during the nineteenth century as a monument to the Russian soldiers who fought against Napoleon, was blown up in the 1930s to make way for a monumental government building that was never begun, and eventually the site was turned into an open-air swimming pool. In the mid-1990s the Cathedral was rebuilt on the site as part of the 850th anniversary celebrations of the city of Moscow.

15 The term "*kulak*" (also the Russian word for fist) was used to describe the rich farmers, but in practice was extended to any productive farmer who was, therefore, a threat to the unproductive ones. The simple declaration that someone was a *kulak* was often a way of settling personal accounts among the peasants.

16 The period of Russian history at the end of the 16th and beginning of the 17th centuries is known as the "Time of Troubles." During this period Russia suffered a confusing succession of rulers, political disintegration, and military invasions from Poland and Sweden.

17 *The Tale of Prince Igor's Campaign* is an epic poem from the end of the 12th century, describing the invasion of the Polovtsians and the defeat of the armies sent to repel them.

18 **Maxim Gorky** (1868-1936) was one of the great Soviet writers whose career began before the Revolution. His writing inspired the official style of Socialist Realism. **Vladimir V. Mayakovsky** (1893-1930) was a powerful poet, originally a Futurist who came to support the Revolution and was a favourite of Stalin's. He died by his own hand. **Dzhambul Dzhabayev** (1846-1945) was a national poet of the Kazakhs; **Suleyman Stalsky** (1869-1937) was a national poet of the Lezgins in Daghestan (Caucasus region); **Alexander Serafimovich** (1863-1949) was a Soviet author whose *Iron Flood*, about the Russian Civil War, was one of the first successful exemplars of the principles of Socialist Realism.

19 **Konstantin Balmont** (1867-1942) was a Symbolist poet who emigrated in 1920; **Igor Severyanin** (1887-1941) was a poet at the turn of the century who described himself as an Ego-Futurist); **Valery Briussov** (1873-1924) was a Symbolist poet who accepted the Revolution; **Semyon Nadson** (1862-1887) was a popular salon poet. **Anna Akhmatova** (1889-1966), **Nikolai Gumilev** (1886-1921; shot by the Bolsheviks for supposed treason), and **Osip Mandelshtam** (1891-1938; died in the camps) were three of the

greatest poets of the 20th century, all uniquely gifted yet joining in what
was known as the Acmeist group in the first decades of the century. **Marina
Tsvetaeva** (1892-1941) was the fourth of the great 20th-century poets.

20 The Decembrists were a group of ardent Russian nobles who used the
occasion of the death of Tsar Alexander I in December 1825 to attempt to
raise rebellion against the new tsar, Nicholas I, in order to bring in a more
Western-style constitution, abolish serfdom, and establish certain civil
freedoms in Russia. Their failure ushered in three bleak decades of repression
in Russia.

21 The campaign had the goal of uniting the Soviet people under the flag of
patriotism and appealed to xenophobic fears. The "rootless cosmopolitans"
were accused of worshipping the West. The campaign also had the goal of
eliminating the intelligentsia and dissidents and, as it was targeted primarily
at Jews, it was a thoroughly anti-Semitic operation, in which Jews were
blamed for all the troubles the country was suffering.

22 The Jewish Anti-Fascist Committee was formed by the Soviet government
in April 1942 to mobilize Jewish support abroad for the war effort. The
president was Solomon Mikhoels, and the organization included such
renowned cultural figures as David Oistrakh and Ilya Ehrenburg. Mikhoels
undertook missions abroad in 1943. The Committee was dissolved in
November 1948 (Mikhoels having been murdered "in a car accident" in
January of that year). Many of the members of the Committee were involved
in the persecution connected with the so-called "Doctors' Plot" of 1953 (see
note 43). **Solomon Mikhoels** (1890-1948) was an actor, director, and
pedagogue. He worked in the Moscow State Jewish Theatre from 1919 and
was the artistic director from 1929. **Peretz Markish** (1895-1952) was a
novelist, satirist, and poet; **Lev Kvitko** (1890-1952) was a lyric poet.

23 **Margarita Aliger** (1915-1992) was a Russian poet, born in Odessa, who
wrote extensively about her experiences during World War II. **Ilya Ehrenburg**
(1891-1967) was a journalist, prose writer, memoirist, poet, and translator.
He was a public figure, representing the Soviet Union abroad, and the most
"Western" Soviet writer of his generation. He passed through the Stalinist
period unscathed, and his works served as a weather vane for the political
climate of his time.

24 **Fanny Kaplan** (Feiga Roidman), an anarchist before the revolution, tried to
assassinate Lenin in August 1918. She was not shot for the attempt, but was
kept in captivity long after the event.

25 A "wall newspaper" is a typewritten series of sheets on various topics or
political matters, sometimes full of propaganda but often humorous, pinned
to the wall of offices, student dormitories, and other "collectives."

26 **Viktor Abakumov** (1894–1954), a member of the Cheka from 1917,
directed Moscow's security agency in the 1920s and 1930s. From 1942
he was head of *Smersh*, the Soviet wartime counter-espionage organization.

He became Minister of State Security in 1949 and was notorious for being a vicious interrogator. He was implicated in the Doctors' Plot of 1953 (see note 43), possibly as part of a move by Stalin against Beria (see following note). He was tried and shot on 24 December 1954.

27   **Lavrentii Beria** (1899-1953) headed the Cheka and the local Communist Party apparatus in Georgia from the early 1920s. He led the purges in the Transcaucasus in 1936-1938, and became deputy head to Nikolai Yezhov of the the Secret Police in July 1938, succeeding at Yezhov's fall in December of that year. He was a full member of the Council of Ministers from 1946, and head of the atomic energy program. Considered one of Stalin's heirs, he began to fall from favour in 1951. He was replaced as head of State Security by V. S. Abakumov in 1949, and seemed to be saved from his implication in the Doctors' Plot by Stalin's death in 1953. But he was arrested in June of that year, and apparently tried and executed with other police officials on 23 December 1953.

28   **Mikhail Bulgakov** (1891-1940) was a Soviet writer and playwright. His novel, *The Master and Margarita* (written in the years just before his death and published in the Soviet Union in the 1960s), satirically describes the visit of the Master (Satan) to Moscow in the 1930s alongside a retelling of the final days of Christ.

29   In the Soviet justice system, every judicial sitting was obliged to have two jurors who, as a rule, rubber-stamped any decision taken by the judge. They did not deliberate independently, but "discussed" the case with the judge. The non-cooperation of the jury in this case was unprecedented.

30   Alexander Fadeev's 1945 novel about an underground youth organization during World War II has as a central plot development the betrayal by one member of others in the group. The novel was loosely based on fact. It was later determined that such a betrayal had never occurred.

31   A "Palace of Pioneers" was the building in which the Pioneers (see note 2) held their activities and meetings, and often included a gymnasium, classrooms, workrooms, and an auditorium. Among their activities were art classes, choirs, literary circles, and so forth.

32   A Soviet internal passport would include such information as "nationality" in point #5: in this case it indicates he is Jewish.

33   The Soviets use the term "Great Fatherland War" for the period of World War II fought between USSR and Nazi Germany.

34   According to Marxist theory (to which, in this case, Trotsky adhered), after the success of the revolution in one country, a "permanent revolution" would break out, eventually spreading through the entire world. This did not happen after 1917. Therefore, in order to reconcile theory with practice, Stalin put forth the idea of the establishment of socialism in a single country which, in essence, contradicted Marxism.

35 The Treaty of Brest ended the phase of World War I on the Eastern Front, to the immediate advantage of the Central Powers; **John Reed** (1887-1920), American writer, journalist, and communist, took part in the October Revolution which he described in his book, *Ten Days that Shook the World*. Reed's book was prohibited in the USSR until perestroika in 1985.

36 The Fourteenth Congress of the Bolshevik Party took place from 18-31 December 1925 in Moscow and had as its prime result the affirmation of the need to quickly industrialize the country. In addition, it condemned the "New Opposition" of Zinoviev and Kamenev.

37 Vorkuta is the administrative and mining centre of the Komi region, spanning the Arctic Circle. It became important for the Soviet coal industry in the 1930s, when camp labour was used to exploit the surrounding Pechora coal fields.

38 **Anton Makarenko** (1888-1939) was a Soviet pedagogue and writer who devoted his life to the mass re-education of young offenders in work "colonies" or "camps." He developed a theory and method of collective communist education, group instruction, and vocational education.

39 The "hero" of Alexander Solzhenitsyn's famous story of 1962, *One Day in the Life of Ivan Denisovich*, lives out the principle of completing even slave work well.

40 The **Rabfak** (abbreviation for *Rabochii fakultet* or "Workers' Faculty") existed between 1919 and 1940 to prepare young people without a secondary education for their higher education. It was located alongside the institutions of higher education, providing both daytime and evening classes.

41 **Grigory Kozintsev** (1905-1973) was a film director, directing films based on Gogol's *The Overcoat* (1926), and Shakespeare's plays (*Hamlet*, 1964, and *King Lear*, 1971), among others.

42 **Kliment Voroshilov** (1881-1969) was a leading military and political figure in the Soviet Union, with important administrative positions in the government and party. His career spanned the Revolutions, Civil War, World War II, and the post-war period.

43 The "Doctors' Plot" was a supposed conspiracy (publicized in February 1953) by Soviet medical men to assassinate prominent military and Party officials, and was allegedly in the service of American intelligence. The death of Stalin (March 1953) brought the affair to an end.

44 The Twentieth Party Congress took place between 14-25 February 1956. It was especially remembered for Khrushchev's "secret speech" to delegates which denounced Stalin's cult of personality and its consequences for the Party.

45 On the Jewish Anti-Fascist Committee and Mikhoels, Kvitko, and Markish see note 22. **Veniamin Zuskin** (1899-1952) was an actor with the Moscow State Jewish Theatre.